# TRUE CRIMES

D0531443

# SERIAL
# KILLERS
# &MASS MURDERERS

# TRUE CRIMES

# SERIAL
# KILLERS
# &MASS MURDERERS

JOYCE ROBINS & PETER ARNOLD

**Bounty**
Books

ACKNOWLEDGEMENTS

The publishers wish to thank the following organizations for their kind
permission to reproduce the pictures in this book:

The Hulton-Deutsch Collection Ltd: 7, 14, 41, 103, 123, 135, 184, 357, 372

Topham Picture Library Source: 27, 33, 57, 68, 82, 91, 96, 117, 145, 148, 190,
197, 207, 287, 313, 322, 352

Popperfoto: 139, 151, 161, 164, 170, 210, 228, 250, 260, 266, 295, 303, 327, 342

First published in Great Britain in 1993 by
Chancellor Press (Bounty Books), a division of Octopus Publishing Group Ltd

This edition published in 2009 by Bounty Books,
a division of Octopus Publishing Group Ltd
2–4 Heron Quays, London E14 4JP
www.octopusbooks.co.uk

An Hachette Livre UK Company
www.hachettelivre.co.uk

ISBN: 978-0-753717-45-5

A CIP catalogue record for this book is available from the British Library

Printed and bound in the UK by CPI Mackays, Chatham ME5 8TD

# Contents

# Introduction

THIS book is not a treatise on the psychology of the serial killer, nor an attempt to describe the latest work being done by such bodies as the FBI's Behavioral Sciences Unit or the National Center for the Analysis of Violent Crime. It does not discuss how to build up a profile of a killer to fit a particular crime.

It is, instead, a recognition that murder is a fascinating subject for the armchair student; how else to explain the world's continuing fascination with the story of Dracula, or the large sales of the Sunday newspaper scandal sheets, or the prominence given to sensational cases of murder on the television? Collected here are the stories of some of the most prolific and shocking murderers to have made the world's headlines over the years.

We hope you enjoy reading them.

# Chapter One

# CASES FROM HISTORY

# Introduction

IN THE current era of mass slaughter by guns and particularly horrific strings of sex murders it is easy to think that these are 'signs of the times' and that evil, like everything else, is now more advanced than it ever was. The crimes in this section, from the 15th to the 19th centuries, prove otherwise, for these are horror stories to match anything of today.

Take, for example, Vlad the Impaler, the original Dracula, who liked to have his skewered victims dripping blood while he ate his dinner; Countess Bathory, who literally enjoyed a blood bath and kept young girls to provide the blood; Cesare Borgia, who poisoned anybody in sight; and Marie de Brinvilliers, who practised her poisons on the inmates of a local hospital to make sure they would work when used on her chosen victims.

Poison was a favourite method of mass killing in the 19th century. William Palmer is the classic case of the deadly doctor, Hélène Jegado the ultimate 'below-stairs' poisoner who removed her employers, Dr Thomas Neill Cream the poisoner with a hatred of prostitutes. Jean-Baptiste Troppmann was willing to murder a whole family, one by one, including six children, to further his plans, while Mary Ann Cotton went from husband to husband, improving herself as each was disposed of. Amelia Dyer practised the peculiar 19th-century profession of 'baby farming' – the 'adoption' of children unwanted by respectable ladies who had secretly strayed from the straight and narrow paths of virtue. Since these ladies were usually not interested in the fates of their offspring after handing them over together with a considerable sum of money, Amelia Dyer showed as little interest and disposed of many in the Thames. Frederick Deeming was an English rogue who preyed on women all over the world, while H.H. Holmes and Johann Hoch confined themselves to America. Both Holmes and Hoch killed a succession of women for their wealth, Holmes preferring to have them come to him in his 'murder castle' while Hoch travelled the land finding a victim in every town.

Joseph Vacher was a stereotype monster – intensely ugly and vicious. He was called the 'Jack the Ripper of France'. The most famous serial murderer of all, of course, was the original Jack the Ripper himself. Since he was never found, his story is reserved for the last section – that of the unsolved cases.

# Cesare Borgia

RODERIGO LANZOL BORGIA was an Italian cardinal who was to become Pope Alexander VI. Meanwhile he kept a mistress, the courtesan Vannozza Cattanei, who shared a luxurious palace with him and gave him five illegitimate children. Among these were Cesare Borgia, born in 1476, and the youngest of all, Lucrezia Borgia, born in 1480.

Cesare became a cardinal, a military leader and politician. Pampered as a child, he never came to terms with the fact that sometimes in life it is not possible to have everything one wants. Cesare was handsome, his mother and sister adored him, and his father indulged him. This wasn't enough for Cesare, who wanted the whole world to love and obey him, particularly the latter. He wanted to have every woman to whom he took a fancy: his sister was probably one of the first of his sexual conquests, while his brother's wife would later become another. When he was a soldier the virgins of captured towns would be rounded up for his pleasure.

If by chance Cesare could not get his way he would throw a tantrum and, if so moved, would resort to murder to remove obstacles from his path. If he could not dispose of his enemies openly – for example, torturing soldiers who had looted his mother's house – he would kill quietly. For this purpose, he became an expert on poisons. Cesare knew how to kill quickly with a poison which caused death like a heart attack, and also how to kill slowly, so that he could enjoy watching his victim's gradual disintegration. His easy-going father preferred his brother Juan, so Cesare had Juan murdered. When Lucrezia was married off by her father to Alfonso of Aragon, Cesare was so jealous at losing the singular devotion of his young sister that he engineered the death of Alfonso, too. He later resumed his close

*Cesare Borgia*

relationship with Lucrezia and her first child was almost certainly his son.

Cesare was not only handsome, he was energetic and intelligent. He was a great patron of the arts and promoted the work of Leonardo and the young Raphael. His ultimate ambition was to rule Italy, dispensing favours to those he liked and removing those he didn't. His ruthlessness was such that after his return from a period at the French court where he fancied he had not been treated in the manner appropriate to his view of himself, he executed many of the servants who had accompanied him so they could not relate to others at home the stories of the various slights he had endured. Thus were removed not only political opponents but even those who were just embarrassments.

Cesare Borgia, whose dozens of victims included many who were poisoned, was himself poisoned and, although he was not to die, the event marked the beginning of his downfall. He and his father were taken ill after they had dined with Cardinal Adriano de Corneto, who himself fell sick – although it is not known if the cardinal's illness was a cover-up. While Cesare recovered, his father, the Pope, did die. Cesare was imprisoned by the new Pope, and his supporters, his army and his influence were lost. On his release he went to Spain but was imprisoned again, for the murder of his brother. He escaped and, with Lucrezia's help, joined forces with his brother-in-law, but he was badly injured in a battle and left to die. He was only 32.

Lucrezia lived for another ten years, married again and was renowned for her kindness. However, because of the lifelong support she gave Cesare throughout his career, she has acquired the reputation of being an accomplice in his murders and is regarded as a poisoner herself, although there is no evidence she ever killed anybody. There is no doubt, though, that Cesare Borgia was a classic case of a serial killer.

# Vlad the Impaler
# and Elizabeth Bathory

BRAM STOKER could not have known how widespread were the deep
fears and fantasies that his classic horror story *Dracula* would stir.
The idea that a human could be literally thirsty for blood caused such
a frisson as to provoke endless variations on the vampire theme in
books and films. Yet a real man and woman from the 15th and 16th
centuries were Dracula figures whose atrocities can hardly be
imagined.

The original Dracula was Vlad Tepes, ruler of Wallachia, which is
separated by the Carpathian Mountains from Transylvania in what
is now part of Romania. His father had been given the name Dracul,
which means 'Devil' or 'Terrible One'. When Tepes came to the throne
in 1456 he inherited a country where the nobles were at war with each
other, his own father and brother having been slain in these conflicts.
He began his reign by exterminating his enemies and his enemies'
families in the most barbaric way – torturing and burning. He solved
the problem of the local poor and sick by inviting them to dine, and
then locking up the palace and setting it on fire. However, his favourite form of execution was impaling his victims on long upright spikes.
As they struggled, or even moved at all, so their weight would fix them
more securely on the spike, and they would gradually work their way
down the spikes until they died. This perversion earned him the
nickname of Vlad the Impaler. There is no doubt he achieved sexual
satisfaction from this torture, and he liked to take his meals in the
presence of these poor victims and listen to their cries of agony. He
would vary the positions in which the doomed were placed on the

spikes, and – the Dracula hallmark – he would drink his victims' blood.

Vlad the Impaler was himself murdered in 1476, but his grave in the monastery at Snagov was never found.

About 100 years after Vlad's reign of terror, Elizabeth Bathory was born in Hungary to rich aristocrats and was brought up in the Carpathians, just to the west of Vlad's empire. When she was 15, in 1575, she married General Count Nadasdy, the 'Black Hero' of Hungary. They lived in a castle at Csejthe but the General was often at the wars, leaving the Countess to her own devices, which included satisfying a well-developed sexual appetite and establishing a large colony of cats, which she believed were endowed with supernatural powers.

The Countess acquired a taste for blood accidentally when she wounded a maid who had upset her. Some of the blood splashed upon the Countess's skin and, when it was washed away, she fancied that her skin glowed. When her husband died young in 1600, the Countess developed her new taste for blood. Except for a 'witch-nurse', some carefully chosen servants and a collection of 'enchanted' cats, she lived in seclusion. Local peasant girls began to vanish and soon rumours circulated of girls kept to provide blood for the Countess's baths, which she took to keep her skin young.

On New Year's Eve 1610, Count Thurso, the Countess's cousin and Hungary's prime minister, visited Castle Csejthe with soldiers and police to investigate the rumours. The discovery he made was horrifying.

Girls were chained up everywhere. Many were dead and the corpses stank; many were on the point of death, with the blood drained from them. Many more were well-fed, clearly being prepared for their task of providing blood in the future. Some of these were already 'in production', punctured with small holes at the neck, chest or stomach, from where the blood was drawn off. There were also many instruments of torture, such as scissors, chains, handcuffs and a gruesome 'iron maiden' – a device like a mummy case with many spikes pointing inwards, so that when a victim was placed inside and the case was closed, she would be punctured in several places at once. And around all the girls, alive, bleeding, or dead, the cats picked their way.

It was estimated that some 300 women had been put to death by the Countess. While alive they had been fed on their own flesh, grilled. 'We have the right to do what we wish to those beneath us,' she said. 'We are of royal blood.'

The Countess was 50, but her skin was that of a much younger woman. She was walled up in her room for the rest of her life and fed through slits in the wall. Without her blood baths she lived only three more years.

# Marie de Brinvilliers

IN THE 17th century, the 'Age of Arsenic', the notorious Marquise de Brinvilliers was able to poison several dozen people before a chance discovery led to her arrest. Her lessons in the art of poisoning came from her lover, the Chevalier Jean Baptiste de Sainte-Croix, who had shared a prison cell with a master-poisoner and had learned some of the secrets of his craft.

Marie de Brinvilliers, the eldest of five children in the aristocratic French family d'Aubray, had married at 21, but her husband the Marquis was a gambler and womanizer who paid little attention to her. When she took Sainte-Croix as a lover her husband scarcely noticed, but her father was outraged and had the young man thrown into the Bastille – thereby ensuring for himself an early death.

When Sainte-Croix emerged from prison, having made good use of his time behind bars, the Marquise began to plot with him to dispose of her father and inherit her share of his fortune. In 1666 Marie and her family were staying with the Viscount d'Aubray on his estate when he began suffering severe stomach pains. The doctor diagnosed indigestion and the Marquise nursed him devotedly, but no medicines seemed to help and after a long and painful illness he died.

Marie's share of her father's estate did not last the extravagant young woman long and she began to covet the inheritance of her two brothers. However, she was well aware that several similar deaths in the same family might arouse suspicion, so she set about practising with various poisonous concoctions in differing strengths. The Sisters of Mercy at the public hospital were delighted when the gracious noblewoman made frequent visits, bringing soups and gifts of fruit. Many of the inmates developed a strange illness which left them lethargic, their limbs numb, and resulted in a gradual wasting away. No one was more solicitous than the Marquise, who never failed to follow the progress of the unfortunate patients. As many as 50 people may have died in furthering Marie's lethal experiments, though some historians claim that this is a wild over-estimate.

When she was certain that she knew the exact dosage to bring about death without leaving detectable traces she hired a valet who could be bribed to administer the right brew in small amounts over several months. Her elder brother died in June, 1670, her younger brother in September. Later it was the turn of her sister Thérèse, a nun, and her sister-in-law Marie Thérèse Mangot, leaving her in full possession of the family fortune.

It seemed that once the Marquise found herself established as a successful poisoner she found it hard to stop, and several other people – discarded lovers, anyone who slighted or annoyed her – died at her hand. At one time she decided to poison her husband so that she could marry Sainte-Croix but the latter, who already had a wife, was quite happy for the penniless Marquis to remain alive. Consequently, he would supply her first with poison, then with the antidote, so that her husband suffered bewildering extremes of health but managed to survive.

Sainte-Croix was accustomed to spending many hours hunched over his laboratory bench experimenting with poisons but one day in July 1672 his face-mask slipped and he inhaled deadly fumes and collapsed, dying soon afterwards. He had left instructions that a small box from his laboratory should be conveyed to Marie de Brinvilliers but his estranged wife, arriving to take charge of his papers, insisted that it should be opened in the presence of officials. Inside were various incriminating documents and a whole array of vials of poison.

Marie fled the country, staying first in England and then Germany before finding refuge in a convent in Liège. She was only captured by trickery, when a law officer posed as an abbé and asked her to join him on a drive. Once outside the convent, she was arrested and taken

*Marie de Brinvilliers en route to execution*

back to Paris. Her trial lasted for nearly three months in the summer of 1676 and one of the chief witnesses against her was one of her ex-lovers, Briancourt, who had tried to stop her endless string of poisonings and had narrowly escaped an attempt on his own life. She was found guilty and sentenced to be beheaded, then her body would be burned and the ashes thrown into the air. Before her execution she was tortured to force her to name her accomplices but she bore the torture with great courage and refused to involve others in the blame for her crimes.

She was taken through the streets to the scaffold in a cart, with a rope round her neck. The executioner spent 15 minutes preparing her, which caused members of the crowd to complain of unnecessary cruelty, but when the final moment came he severed her head with a single blow of his sword. He then tossed both the head and the body on to a fire built behind the scaffold.

A letter from Madame de Sévigné to her daughter described the scene:

'It is all over, Brinvilliers is reduced to ashes, her poor little body after her execution was thrown into a very great fire, and her ashes into the air; so that we shall draw them in with our breath and by the communication of small particles we shall be seized with an inclination to poisoning, which will do a great deal of mischief.'

# Burke and Hare

TO 'BURKE', according to the dictionary, is to murder by suffocation so as to leave no mark. The word comes from William Burke, famous with his partner William Hare for selling bodies to the medical profession for dissection. Yet Burke and Hare were not the bodysnatchers or grave-robbers of legend; they acquired their bodies by murder. Only Burke was punished, as Hare, the main instigator of the trade, turned King's evidence.

Burke and Hare were Irishmen who, like many others, came to Scotland to work on the Union Canal between Glasgow and Edinburgh. They met in 1826 when both were living in squalor in neighbouring lodging houses in Edinburgh's West Port. The activities which earned them notoriety began by chance on 29 November 1827 when a fellow lodger of Burke, an army pensioner named Donald, died while owing Hare £4, a large sum in those days. Desperate to regain the money in some way, Hare decided to sell Donald's body to Dr Knox of the Anatomy School. The grave-robbing trade was already well established, but it was a skilled and arduous practice, carried out by men who were called 'Resurrectionists'. Hare's idea was to cut out the 'middleman' of the parish undertaker so, while the body was in its coffin in the house, awaiting collection, he removed it with the help of friend Burke and substituted tree bark. The two men trundled the body round to Dr Knox at 10 Surgeons' Square and were delighted to get £7.10s for it, with the hint that more of the same would be gratefully accepted; Dr Knox had a great number of students, and bodies for dissection were not easy to obtain.

Burke and Hare discovered that the latter held true for them, too. They could hardly sit around waiting for fellow lodgers to die, so when

16

one of them, a miller, was taken ill with a fever they smothered him. Dr Knox paid £10, which became the standard fee. Hare's common-law wife Maggie and Burke's mistress, Helen McDougal, joined the 'business', but after another lodger had been released from the suffering of jaundice, the quartet ran out of sick acquaintances.

The problem was solved by luring poor people off the streets for a party, rendering them insensible with whisky (usually while Burke, who had a fine voice, sang) and despatching them to the next world before trundling them along to 10 Surgeon's Square, the premises of Dr Knox. This was done by Hare placing his hands over the victim's nose and mouth from behind and pulling the victim to the floor, when Burke would sit on the victim's chest as he or she suffocated. The £10 revenue per transaction more than paid for the expenses of whisky, and soon the four of them were living in relative style.

There were upsets and misunderstandings. Helen McDougal, discovering Burke apparently enjoying himself with two buxom 18-year-old prostitutes, needed a lot of persuading that Burke was merely about his business and was only subdued by a clip round the ear with a wine glass. As Burke and Hare wheeled a tea chest carrying the body of one of the girls to Dr Knox they were followed by some scruffy street-boys, who shouted out that they had a body in the box. Dr Knox was so impressed by the young and voluptuous body that he preserved it in whisky for a special occasion, and a student invited an artist to sketch it.

On another occasion, after Hare had acquired a diseased and decrepit old horse to help take the bodies of a woman and her 12-year-old son to Dr Knox, the horse collapsed, and Burke and Hare had to hire a porter to help them complete the journey. At £16 the pair of corpses, they could afford it. The visit of Ann McDougal, a distant relative of Burke's, provided more income, as did Burke's washer-woman. Another 'double' was scored when the daughter of an old prostitute, already in the tea chest, came searching for her, and was reunited with her mother for ever.

The criminals took dreadful risks. An 18-year-old called Daft Jamie, well-known in the area as what used to be called the 'village idiot', was a victim. His body was, of course, immediately recognized by Dr Knox and his students. Daft Jamie put up a great struggle because he did not drink whisky, so Burke and Hare devised a wax mask to hold over their victims' faces to make suffocation easier.

The game was up when two new lodgers in Burke's house, Mr and Mrs Gray, discovered the body of a woman who had been brought to the house the previous day. Helen McDougal was asked about it, and tried to bribe them to keep quiet with a few shillings and a hint of £10 a week for them if they wanted. But the Grays went to the police.

The trial of Burke and Helen McDougal was held on Christmas Eve and continued until 9.25 am on Christmas morning, when the jury brought in their verdicts. The conviction of Burke was a formality after both the Hares had turned King's evidence. Helen McDougal escaped the gallows through the peculiar Scottish verdict of 'Not Proven'.

A crowd of 25,000 spectators cheered when Burke was hanged in a downpour on 28 January 1829. His body was dissected for the education of the students of Dr Monro, Dr Knox's rival, then publicly displayed. His skeleton is still at the University of Edinburgh. His three collaborators narrowly escaped lynching. The two women were smuggled out of the country – McDougal to Australia and Mrs Hare to Ireland. Hare fled to London, where workmates discovered who he was and threw him into a lime pit. He was last seen as a blind matchseller.

A year after Burke's execution the law that required every corpse to have a Christian burial was repealed. Two years later an act was passed enabling bodies, under certain circumstances, to be sent to medical schools for dissection – so the trade that Burke and Hare made famous ceased.

# Hélène Jegado

HÉLÈNE JEGADO was an illiterate French peasant girl who murdered anyone who displeased her and a few more besides by mixing arsenic in their food. She was eventually tried for three murders and three attempted murders but she was implicated in no less than 23 deaths, one of them that of her own sister.

As a young girl she was sent into service, a dismal life of hard work and few pleasures which she tried to brighten by stealing from her employers. She was dismissed from several jobs but always managed to find new employment because she appeared so submissive and pious. At one time she joined a convent as a novice but before long small items began to go missing and were traced to the newcomer, so she was sent away.

Her murderous impulses began to emerge when she was in her 30s. She worked as a maid for one clergyman after another and in each household, illness and death spread like a virus. 'Wherever I go, people die!' she lamented, putting on a convincing show of grief as yet another body was carried out. There was no reason why she should be suspected; after all, she had nothing to gain from the deaths. She was just as likely to poison her fellow servants as the families of her employers, so the deaths assumed a random pattern and were always written off as due to one of the many diseases prevalent in the mid-19th century.

In 1849 she was working for the Rabot family in Rennes, but was given notice when she was caught pilfering. Next day the three members of the household suffered violent stomach cramps and vomiting. For once, Hélène's skill as a poisoner had deserted her and her victims lived to give evidence against her later.

She moved to take another job in the same city, this time with Professor Théodore Bidard. Shortly after her arrival a younger maid fell ill and, with Hélène as her nurse, she was soon dead. Hélène told M. Bidard that sooner than have a stranger filling her friend's place, she would do the work of both girls and he was touched by her devotion. The following year another servant, Rosalie Sarrazin, was taken on and the two girls became close friends but things changed when Rosalie took on the household accounts, sitting studiously over her books at the table while the illiterate Hélène watched enviously. In the summer of 1851 Rosalie was taken ill with the familiar gastric symptoms and she died in July.

This time the doctor had his doubts about the cause of death but Hélène might still have escaped detection save for an unguarded exclamation when the magistrates, accompanied by police, arrived to investigate. Her first words were, 'I am innocent!' The magistrates pointed out that no one had accused her of anything yet, but soon afterwards she was arrested.

There was surprisingly little hard evidence against Hélène Jegado. It was never proved that she had ever obtained arsenic and no convincing motive was established, but the circumstantial evidence was overwhelming and she was sent to the guillotine in December 1851.

# Dr William Palmer

THE CLASSIC British case of systematic poisoning is that of Dr William Palmer who, when he was born in 1824, was the only legitimate child of the several in the family. When his father died, each child inherited £7,000 of ill-gotten gains, although they could not claim their money until they were 21. William was a happy if self-willed lad who at 17, when apprenticed to a chemist, stole from his employers to pay for his girlfriend's abortion. His mother made good the sum, saving his honour if not his job, but when, soon afterwards, a man whose wife William fancied died after drinking some brandy in his company, he decided to leave his village of Rugeley in Staffordshire and go to London. He qualified as a surgeon at Bart's Hospital, and returned to Rugeley to practise medicine from his rooms opposite the Talbot Arms.

Palmer had developed an expensive taste for horse-racing and gambling and soon found his inheritance disappearing, so he married Annie Brooks, who had an inheritance of her own. Her father, Colonel Brooks, was one of five brothers who all committed suicide separately, in the Colonel's case leaving his wife and daughter well off. Mrs Brooks was a drunkard with whom Annie had broken relations but after a while there was a reconciliation and she was persuaded to come and live with her daughter and Palmer. Within two weeks she had died, and Palmer gained access to her wealth: seven houses and more capital for his horse-racing. By now, he owned his own stables.

Palmer seemed to become surrounded by sudden death. An uncle died the day after Palmer visited him (as far as it is known, Palmer didn't benefit): two of Palmer's illegitimate children died: and an acquaintance who came to stay with Palmer for the races (and to collect a debt) passed away also. Even his wife Annie, extremely happy at first, began to remark upon the coincidence. Four of her own children died young. When a friend called Bly, who was owed £800 by Palmer, died, so allowing Palmer to deny the debt, Annie asked 'What will people say?' Soon Annie herself died, and Palmer collected £13,000 from an insurance policy he had lately taken out.

Gossip about Palmer was widespread in Rugeley, of course, where people had not failed to notice these happenings, and it was not abated when the housemaid gave birth nine months after Annie's death, nor when the baby shortly died.

Palmer's gambling meant he always needed money, and now he struck a deal with his brother Walter, who had also married into money but was spending it rapidly on gin, which threatened to end his life early. Palmer suggested to his brother that he insure his life for a small sum on the understanding that he, Palmer, would keep him well stocked with gin, to be repaid in full when Walter died and the policy could be cashed. Walter agreed and even went on the wagon temporarily to convince the insurers he was a good risk. He soon died, whether from the copious gin he was given or from something else nobody knew. The policy, however, far from being a small one, proved to be another for £13,000, the company having declined Palmer's wish to make it £82,000. The insurance company disputed the claim, together with another on a friend of Palmer's for £25,000, and Palmer's cash flow became even more of a problem.

One day Palmer went to Shrewsbury races with his friend John Cook, whose mare, Polestar, won. Cook returned to Rugeley with Palmer to celebrate, but became ill after drinking a brandy. Palmer installed him in the Talbot Arms under his own care, then went to London to collect from a bookmakers the money owed to Cook. On the morning after his return, Cook took pills Palmer had prescribed, went into a convulsion and died. Palmer soon produced a money order for £4,000 in his favour signed by Cook. However, Cook's stepfather was suspicious, claimed it was a forgery, and demanded an autopsy.

Although only a little antimony rather than the suspected strychnine which Palmer was alleged by witnesses to have bought was found in the body, the circumstantial evidence at the inquest led to a verdict of 'wilful murder' and Palmer was arrested. The bodies of his wife and brother were exhumed and plenty of antimony was found in the former's body, although there was none in that of Walter.

Palmer was tried for the murder of Cook at the Old Bailey, and although the medical evidence was poor – seven medical men declared there was strychnine in the body, 11 that they could find nothing – Palmer was found guilty. There was a crowd of 50,000 at Stafford Gaol on 14 June 1856 to see him hanged. The citizens of Rugeley petitioned for the name of their now infamous village to be changed, but it is still there.

# Jean-Baptiste Troppmann

JEAN-BAPTISTE TROPPMANN came from Alsace, a much-disputed part of the world which, a year after Troppmann committed his horrific crimes, switched from France to Germany. Troppmann was a sensitive, intelligent and secretive homosexual youth who had been tormented at school and work and whose aim was to get some quick money and seek his fortune in the United States.

The opportunity came in 1869 when the long-haired 19-year-old was sent by his father, who made textile machines, to Roubaix, in north-east France to supervise the erection of such a machine there. In Roubaix Troppmann met Jean Kinck, a man who also came from Alsace but who had lived in Roubaix for 30 years and was very homesick. Kinck was delighted to meet the young man from his region and made him welcome in his home, which contained his wife and six children, ranging from Gustave, 16, down to Marie, the baby. Troppmann was a good talker and soon interested Kinck in one of his schemes, a plan to make counterfeit money. Saying he could get hold of the machinery from friends, Troppmann invited Kinck to meet him on the way to Cernay in Alsace, where the ruined castle of Herrenfluch would make the ideal headquarters for the operation. He counselled secrecy and the two travelled separately, but on arrival Kinck was despatched by means of prussic acid.

Troppmann then wrote to Madame Kinck in the name of her husband (who, he said, had 'hurt his hand'), enclosing a cheque for 5,500 francs on which he had forged Kinck's signature and asking her to cash it and forward the money to the Guebwiller post office. Madame Kinck complied but, because the package was addressed to Jean Kinck, the postmaster would not hand it over to Troppmann, even though the latter claimed to be Kinck's son. Indeed, Troppmann was nearly caught when a real relative of Kinck entered the post office.

Troppmann then went to Paris and booked into a hotel at the Gare du Nord in the name of Jean Kinck. He forged a letter to Madame Kinck which purported to come from her husband, telling her to send her eldest son Gustave to collect the money from the Guebwiller post office, and then to bring herself, the children and everything else to him in Paris. He enclosed the document which, duly authorized, would enable Gustave to collect the package. However, Madame Kinck took too long to get the document properly signed and Gustave left without it, so was also refused the package. Gustave wrote to his 'father' from his aunt's house in Guebwiller, confessing he had failed to get the money whereupon Troppmann cancelled his instruction to Madame Kinck to bring the family to Paris.

Gustave then went straight to Paris to ask his father what they must do next. Instead, he encountered Troppmann who, reverting to his earlier plan, told him to send a telegram to his mother, telling her to bring the children and all the family papers to Paris. He then took Gustave outside Paris on the road to Pantin, overpowered him with several blows from a pickaxe, stabbed him in the neck and heart with a kitchen knife, and buried him in a shallow grave.

In the meantime Madame Kinck dressed her children in their best clothes, collected together the valuables and papers, and began the long train journey to Paris. She arrived in the evening and went to 'her husband's' hotel, where she was told he was out (he was actually buying a new pick and spade, with reinforced handles). Consequently, she returned to the railway station, thinking her husband might be awaiting the next train.

At 10.45 pm Troppmann arrived at the station and told Madame Kinck that her husband was waiting for her at a property he had bought in Pantin: they must take a cab and go there at once. At the gate out of Paris to Pantin the cab driver raised objections to leaving the city so late at night, but Troppmann insisted, only to stop him a

25

little further on by a field. He asked Madame Kinck, who was carrying the baby girl, and the youngest boy to come with him, telling the three older boys to wait in the cab for a while until he returned for them with their father. Madame Kinck and the youngsters were quickly murdered; the mother was stabbed several times, while the children were brutally despatched with the pick.

After 25 minutes Troppmann returned to the cab and told the driver that the family were staying the night. The last the cab driver saw of the three boys they were walking off into the night with the murderer.

Next morning, on 20 September 1869, a workman noticed the freshly dug earth and a pool of blood. He disturbed the ground with his pick and uncovered a face. Soon the whole of France was horror-struck at the news of this wholesale slaughter of the young and inno-cent. Around the children in the narrow grave were the toys they had brought with them from their old home to the new; the bodies showed signs of an attack, and the two-year-old was even disembowelled.

The proprietor of the hotel soon identified the woman and five children who had come asking for M. Kinck, and it was realized that the pale, weedy youth who had stayed at the hotel could hardly be the father of this family. Troppmann, meanwhile, had gone with the fami-ly's papers to Le Havre, where he was going to cash his ill-gotten gains and begin his journey to the New World. He was in a café on the harbour front asking a new acquaintance about obtaining papers when a passing policeman decided to ask the stranger his name. Troppmann panicked, ran for it and jumped into the harbour; he even fought the man who plunged in to rescue him. He was found to have some belongings of Jean Kinck in his possession and was taken into cus-tody. Soon he confessed his real name and told the first of a series of stories designed to deliver him from a charge of murder. This was that Jean Kinck and the eldest son Gustave had killed the rest of the family while he, Troppmann, had been powerless to interfere. This explanation had many believers, for it was thought that the crime was too horrendous for one person to perform alone. Two days later,

*The bodies of the Kinck family are discovered in a field outside Paris*

however, the body of Gustave was found close to where the other six had been.

On 26 November, the body of Jean Kinck was discovered by the castle of Herrenfluch in Alsace. Troppmann had no chance at his trial. Seldom had a criminal been so loathed and there was great satisfaction when he faced the guillotine.

# Mary Ann Cotton

WHEN Thomas Riley, a public relief officer in County Durham, England, reported his suspicions over the death of young Charlie Cotton in the village of West Auckland, he had no idea that he was taking a step towards unmasking a mass poisoner. The exact number of murders committed by Mary Ann Cotton will never be known but it was likely that by the age of 40 she had killed at least 21 people, including 3 husbands, 10 children, 5 stepchildren and a lover.

In July 1872, Mary Ann had approached Thomas Riley to ask him to find a place for her seven-year-old stepson Charlie in the workhouse. 'It's hard on me to keep him when he's not my own and he is stopping me from taking in a respectable lodger,' she explained. Riley thought he knew who she had in mind; according to local gossips she was planning to marry the excise officer Mr Quick-Manning. 'It might be so,' Mary Ann told him, 'but the boy is in my way.'

Only six days later Riley passed her cottage on his way to work and saw her standing in the doorway, looking upset. When he asked her what was wrong, she said: 'My boy's dead.'

Riley, who had seen Charlie the previous week, when he seemed perfectly fit, was astonished. So was Dr Kilburn, who knew that Charlie had been suffering from gastro-enteritis and had visited him only the day before, but had expected him to make a full recovery. The doctor decided on a postmortem and the inquest was held at the Rose and Crown public house. The postmortem was a hasty affair carried out on Mary Ann's kitchen table and the doctor found no evidence of poison, so the inquest returned a verdict of death by natural causes. Dr Kilburn, still not satisfied, took away some of the contents of the stomach for further examination and when evidence of arsenic was found, Mary Ann was arrested and charged with murder.

This was only the beginning of the investigation, for the authorities now began to wonder about several other deaths among those close to Mary Ann since she had arrived in West Auckland two years before. What they found led them to the horrifying truth about the apparently good-natured and devout Methodist matron who spread death wherever she went.

Mary Ann Cotton was a miner's daughter from a Durham pit village who was married for the first time in 1852 to William Mowbray. The couple had eight children but six died of 'gastric fever' and a seventh of 'convulsions'. Eventually their father, too, succumbed to gastric fever. The only surviving child was Isabella, who had been sent to live with her grandmother. Mary Ann took a job looking after George Ward, a 32-year-old engineer, and they were soon married. Shortly after losing his job George Ward died; he had been married for only 14 months.

Mary Ann moved on to become housekeeper to James Robinson, a Sunderland widower with five children. Just at the time he asked her to marry him Mary Ann's mother fell ill and she had to go and look after her, but she was eager to hurry back in case Robinson found someone to replace her. Conveniently, her mother was dead within nine days. Mary Ann took her daughter Isabella back to Sunderland with her, so signing the girl's death warrant; within a period of two months, in 1867, Isabella and three of the Robinson children died.

Robinson was to be the only one of Mary Ann's husbands to survive, for after several rows over money and the way Mary Ann kept spending it, he took his remaining children and moved in with his sister. Mary Ann soon found another man, a miner called Frederick Cotton, and the fact that she was still married to Robinson did not prevent her from contracting another marriage. She settled into the cottage in West Auckland with Cotton and his two children by a previous marriage and gave birth to another baby. The couple had only been together for a year when Cotton died, yet another victim of 'gastric fever'.

29

By then Mary Ann had met up with an old lover, Joseph Nattrass, who moved in with her – but his fate was sealed when she saw a better matrimonial prospect in the excise officer, Quick-Manning. Both Nattrass and the children were now seen as an impediment to a more comfortable lifestyle. Ten-year-old Frederick Cotton died first, then Mary Ann's 14-month-old son, followed by Joseph Nattrass. Next it was Charlie's turn. After the discovery of arsenic in Charlie's body, Nattrass was exhumed and there was no question about the cause of death; there was a large quantity of arsenic in the stomach and bowels, with four or five grains still undissolved.

Orders were made to exhume the remainder of the Cotton family but here there was a problem, for paupers were buried in unmarked graves, crowded together in one corner of the graveyard. After many graves had been opened, the bodies of young Frederick Cotton and baby Robert were discovered but their father's corpse was never located. Both children were found to have died from arsenical poisoning.

Mary Ann Cotton went on trial for the murder of Charles Edward Cotton at Durham Assizes on 5 March 1873, after she had given birth to Quick-Manning's baby. The prosecutor, Sir Charles Russell, argued that she had disposed of Charlie because she would benefit from a small life insurance policy and would be unencumbered for her planned marriage. 'She was badly off and Charles Edward was a tie and burden to her,' he said.

Thomas Riley gave his evidence and Mary Ann Dodds, one of Mary Ann's neighbours, explained that some weeks before Charlie's death she had bought for the defendant a mixture of arsenic and soft soap to deal with bed bugs in the latter's home. The chemist from whom she had obtained it gave evidence that the mixture would have contained about half an ounce of arsenic, some 480 grains, while three grains was sufficient to kill an adult. When the prosecutor wanted to introduce evidence about the other deaths in the family, the defence lawyer, Thomas Campbell, protested – but the judge ruled against him. After that there was little doubt about the verdict, though Campbell tried to argue that the boy might have taken poison by accident on the grounds that the peeling flock wallpaper in the bedroom had arsenic in its green colouring.

The jury took only an hour to reach a verdict and the judge, donning the back cap to pass the death sentence, said: 'You seem to have given way to that most awful of all delusions, which sometimes takes possession of persons wanting in proper moral and religious sense, that you could carry out your wicked designs without detection. But while murder by poison is the most detestable of all crimes, and one at which human nature shudders, it is one the nature of which, in the order of God's providence, always leaves behind it complete and incontestable traces of guilt. Poisoning, as it were, in the very act of crime writes an indelible record of guilt.'

Mary Ann seems to have poisoned for the most trivial of reasons – for trifling amounts of insurance money, or to dispose of children or men who were inconvenient at a particular stage in her life. The *Newcastle Journal* described her as 'a monster in human shape' but went on to say:

'Perhaps the most astounding thought of all is that a woman could act thus without becoming horrible and repulsive. Mary Ann Cotton, on the contrary, seems to have possessed the faculty of getting a new husband whenever she wanted one. To her other children and her lodger, even when she was deliberately poisoning them, she is said to have maintained a rather kindly manner . . . pity cannot be withheld, though it must be mingled with horror.'

Mary Ann spent her last days on earth trying to organize a petition for a reprieve and choosing a new family for her baby, Margaret, who had to be dragged forcibly from her arms five days before the hanging. She went to the scaffold at Durham on 24 March 1873, maintaining her innocence to the last. Within days of the execution theatres were putting on a stage play called *The Life and Death of Mary Ann Cotton*, billed as 'a great moral drama'.

# Dr Thomas Neill Cream

THOMAS NEILL CREAM was the oldest of eight children. He was born in Glasgow in 1850 but, when he was four, the family moved to Canada. There he graduated in medicine, performed an abortion on his girl-friend (who nearly died), was forced to marry her and fled next day to Britain, where he gained excellent medical qualifications. Returning to Canada, Dr Cream made the provision of abortions his business. Following the death of a client he moved to Chicago, where he was subsequently charged with the death of another client, but escaped justice.

Cream went on to form an adulterous alliance with the attractive wife of a patient, Daniel Stott, who died in agony. Stott's death was attributed to epilepsy, but Cream inexplicably wrote to the coroner stating that the death was a mistake of the pharmacist. The district attorney, as a matter of form, exhumed the body and strychnine was found, with the result that Cream, not the pharmacist, was sentenced to 20 years' penal servitude in the Illinois State Penitentiary. He served less than ten, and was released as his father died and left him £16,000. Cream returned to England and, in October 1891, settled in Lambeth Palace Road, in one of the seedier districts of South London.

Cream immediately bought from a chemist a quantity of *nux vomica*, which contains strychnine, and some gelatine capsules. He made the acquaintance of a prostitute, Mathilda Clover, who shortly died, after suffering terrible convulsions. Her death was attributed to alcoholism. At about the same time another prostitute, Ellen Don-worth, collapsed in the street, and told a man who went to her assistance that 'a tall gentleman with cross eyes, a silk hat and bushy whiskers' had given her a drink of some white liquid. Before she got

*Dr Thomas Neill Cream*

to hospital she died of what turned out to be strychnine poisoning. The verdict was murder by person or persons unknown, but at the end of the inquest the coroner received a letter signed by a detective named O'Brien which offered to name the murderer for £300,000.

Dr Cream now became engaged to a respectable young woman named Laura Sabbatini, and paid a visit to his old home in Canada. Days after his return, two more prostitutes died in a house in Stamford Street, near Waterloo station. A policeman, George Cumley, had seen a man being shown out of No. 118, where the girls were staying, and realized the significance when, two hours later, the two girls were discovered dying of strychnine poisoning.

As the two notes to coroners indicate, Cream was not a man who could keep his deeds a secret – in fact, he wanted to draw everybody's attention to them. He lost no opportunity to bring up the subject of the murders in conversation with his landlady, and he wrote (under a pseudonym) to an eminent medical man, claiming the man's son was the murderer and demanding money for silence. Becoming even more reckless, he told an acquaintance that a medical student living in the same lodgings as himself was a murderer. He mentioned a girl called Loo Harvey who, he said, had been given pills by the student and collapsed in the street. This acquaintance decided to mention the matter to Scotland Yard and was interviewed by an Inspector McIntyre, but, as nobody called Loo Harvey was missing, nothing transpired. The inspector, however, made a mental note of the name of the accuser – Neill Cream.

Cream, as if impelled by some instinct of self-destruction, then went to Scotland Yard himself to complain of being followed. By chance he too saw McIntyre, who remembered the name and deliberately befriended Cream. On one of their walks McIntyre arranged for them to pass PC Cumley, the policeman who had seen the man leaving 118 Stamford Street just before the double murder. He could not be sure, but he thought that Cream could be the same man.

McIntyre obtained a specimen of Cream's writing, and it proved similar to that on some of the letters the police had been sent about the case. A drawback was that the blackmailing letter to the medical man was in a quite different hand.

Eventually Cream, having at first been excited by his acquaintanceship with Inspector McIntyre, began to have suspicions about the policeman's interest in him. He mentioned he was going away, and asked McIntyre if he were likely to be arrested. McIntyre had no evidence, but had Cream watched very carefully, and, when it was clear that the latter was about to flee, decided to close in on him.

The body of Mathilda Clover was exhumed, and strychnine found. McIntyre then searched for, and found, witnesses to state that Cream had been seen with Mathilda Clover. Cream was charged with murder. What sealed his fate was an incident at the committal proceedings at Bow Street: the accusation concerning the mysterious Loo Harvey was mentioned, whereupon a woman stood up and identified herself as Miss Harvey. She related how Cream had given her two pills when she was unwell, just as Cream had described the event, except that it was he, not the medical student, who had been the intended murderer. She described how she had been suspicious and had thrown the pills from Waterloo Bridge when Cream was distracted. Cream, no doubt, had imagined Miss Harvey taking the pills and becoming an unidentified corpse a couple of hours after he left her, and he must have been annoyed that this supposed murder had escaped the publicity of the others.

Loo Harvey was the star witness of the trial, and Cream had no chance. The blackmailing letter to the medical man was shown to have come from Cream's fiancée. Cream was sentenced to death, and executed on 15 November 1892.

# Amelia Dyer

IN VICTORIAN times strict nannies would threaten the children in their charge: 'If you don't do as you're told, Amelia Dyer will come and get you.' Everyone knew that if Amelia Dyer once got her hands on you, you would never be seen again. Many mothers left their children in her charge over the years – unmarried mothers, most of them, or wives whose babies were not fathered by their husbands – and all the children disappeared very quickly, most of them ending up in the river.

Her 'baby-farming' business began in 1875, when she had to support herself and her daughter Polly after her marriage broke up. She had been working as a midwife in a village near Bristol, England, but she soon found that it was more lucrative 'farming' babies, charging mothers a fee for taking their unwanted offspring off their hands. Most of these desperate women never enquired what happened to the babies afterwards and some baby farmers succumbed to the temptation to dispose of their charges as quickly as possible to make room for more.

The authorities tried to stamp on the practice and eventually Amelia's flourishing business was discovered and she was gaoled for six weeks. After that she became better at evading detection, moving house often and usually managing to keep ahead of both police and creditors, though in the 1890s she fell on hard times and spent some years in a workhouse. When she came out she went to live with her daughter Polly, who was now married to an out-of-work labourer. While they were living in Piggott's Road, Caversham, Amelia went back to her old trade, advertising in the local paper: 'Couple having no child would like the care of one or would adopt. Terms £10.'

On 30 March 1896, a bargeman working on the River Thames near Reading caught his hook on a soggy parcel and when he pulled it in was horrified to see a baby's foot protruding from the torn paper. The child had been strangled with a bootlace, then weighted down with a brick. On one of the sheets of wet paper was an address that was to lead the police to the murderess: Mrs Harding, Piggott's Road, Caversham. By the time they arrived to interview Mrs Harding, a carpet bag containing two more tiny bodies, both with bootlaces round their necks, had been found in the same section of the river.

Enquiries revealed that Mrs Harding had been living in Piggott's Road with her daughter's family, where she had fostered several children; she had now moved to Reading, while her daughter and son-in-law had gone to London. The police decided to set a trap for 'Mrs Harding' and engaged a young woman who would pose as an unmarried mother wanting to have her baby adopted. She met a short, squat woman with a well-scrubbed look and her hair neatly pulled back in a bun, who offered to take the child for £100 with no further questions asked. The exchange of child for money was to take place the following evening, after dark, but at the appointed time it was not a mother with a baby in her arms who arrived on the doorstep, but a police inspector and his sergeant. They soon discovered that Mrs Harding was in reality Amelia Dyer and proceeded to search the house where, the inspector said later: 'In a cupboard under the stairs we found a quantity of baby clothing, and noticed a most unpleasant odour, as though some decomposing substance had been kept there. Doubtless, as subsequent events showed, the body of a little child had been concealed in this cupboard for some days before being taken out and disposed of.'

Amelia was arrested and charged with murder. One of the babies in the carpet bag had been identified as Doris Marmon, whose mother Evelina had answered an advertisement offering adoption and had given her baby to Amelia, posing as Mrs Harding and offering 'a good home and a mother's loving care' in return for £10. The other was

Harry Simmons, left with Amelia by a lady whose maid had given birth and then disappeared. Police were still dragging the river and had recovered the remains of several other infants.

At first Amelia's son-in-law Arthur Palmer was charged with her but she made a statement exonerating both Arthur and Polly, saying: 'I do most solemnly swear that neither of them had anything to do with it. They never knew I contemplated doing such a wicked thing until too late.' While she was in prison Amelia made two suicide attempts, once with scissors and once with bootlaces, but each time she was found and revived.

Polly became the chief witness against her, for she told how her mother had arrived at their home in London with the baby Doris Marmon and a carpet bag. Polly had settled her mother by the fire and gone to make some tea; when she returned there was no sign of the baby and her mother was stowing the carpet bag away under the settee. By the next morning the baby Polly had been minding for her mother, Harry Simmons, had also vanished and though she had been worried, she did not know what to do about it. That afternoon the Palmers had taken Amelia to Paddington Station to catch the train back to Reading and Arthur had carried her carpet bag part of the time, remarking on how heavy it was. It was the bag that was later fished out of the Thames with two little bodies inside.

There was no doubt that Mrs Dyer was guilty but the defence argued that she was insane. Dr Logan of Gloucester Asylum and Dr Forbes Winslow both testified that she was suffering from melancholia and delusions, one of which was that the birds were talking to her. However, the medical officer of Holloway Prison, who had been observing her every day, decided that her delusions were feigned.

Amelia Dyer was judged sane and was hanged on 10 June 1896, leaving behind a letter regretting the trouble she had brought on her family and saying, 'What was done I did do myself.' She never admitted how many children she had killed but said, without emotion: 'You'll recognize mine by the tape around their necks.'

# Frederick Deeming

FREDERICK DEEMING was born in the 1840s, the youngest of seven children. His father gradually went mad, and Deeming himself was odd enough to be known as 'Mad Fred' as a boy. The balance of his mind, like his father's before him, deteriorated until, in his last years, he committed some callous crimes.

Deeming became a ship's steward at 18, and never lost his inclination to travel round the world. Unfortunately, in most places he visited he lived as a confidence-trickster, assuming numerous aliases and posing as rich men, usually with a title. He cheated jewellers by masquerading as a diamond mine owner, an idea he probably got when working in South African goldfields. The death of his mother in 1875 affected him deeply, and he began to see visions of her. He went back to sea, and suffered some mental illness in Calcutta.

Back in his native Liverpool, he married and then, with his wife, went to live in Australia. However, after fathering four children he abandoned the family in Sydney, leaving his wife to beg on the streets, and began to make his way back to England. In 1890 he was posing as Lord Dunn in Antwerp, trying to raise cash by cheating diamond merchants. He returned to Liverpool but did not stay long, going off to Rainhill, just outside the city. Here he found himself accommodation by posing as Albert O. Williams, an Inspector of Regiments searching for a house to rent for his employer Colonel Brooks. He rented a property called Dinham Villa from a Mrs Mather and stayed in the local hotel while pretending to await Colonel Brooks. In this short period he courted Mrs Mather's daughter Emily.

Deeming's surprise when his wife and four children turned up one day was considerable. Having bravely made her way to Liverpool,

Mrs Deeming had been directed to Rainhill by Deeming's brothers. However, Deeming persuaded Mrs Mather to allow his 'married sister' and her family to stay in Dinham Villa for a day or two before going abroad. He also gained permission to move into Dinham Villa himself to re-cement the floor in one room, as it was not level enough for Colonel Brooks' rich carpets. Soon the family disappeared and the room had an excellent new cement floor.

Deeming now speeded up his courtship of Emily, married her, announced his intention to take her to Australia, threw a farewell party and left, leaving Colonel Brooks, who, of course, was never to arrive, to pay the bills.

The scene now shifts to a house in Windsor, a suburb of Melbourne, later in the year. A Mr Druin, an Englishman with a Liverpool accent, had been renting it, but had left suddenly. The house was being shown to a prospective new tenant, who turned it down because of a nasty smell in one bedroom. The owner and agent later returned to investigate the smell, and found it came from beneath the hearthstone. As they began to raise it, the smell became so overpowering they called the police. Buried in the concrete were found the remains of a woman.

In the grate, police found a torn luggage ticket issued by a shipping line at Melbourne, covering the luggage of two people. It was issued to Albert Williams, and the police issued a warrant for Williams' arrest. In rubbish at the back of the house they also found a screwed-up invitation for a party at the Commercial Hotel in Rainhill – the very farewell party Deeming had thrown before leaving for Australia. The Australian police quickly compared notes with those at Rainhill. Dinham Villa was entered, and the new floor was discovered to be giving off a dreadful smell. Under the concrete were the bodies of a woman and four children. Deeming's brothers identified them as being Deeming's family, whom they had directed to Rainhill only a few months earlier.

Meanwhile, back in Australia, Deeming had gone to Adelaide and taken a ship to Sydney. On board he met 19-year-old Kate Rounsefell,

# EXECUTION
## Of DEEMING.
### Alleged Confession.

### Last Moment

*Contemporary poster of the execution of Frederick Deeming*

who was on her way to see her sister in Bathurst. Deeming, now 'Baron Swanston', swept her off her feet, stayed with her for 24 hours in Sydney, proposed, was taken to see the sister and was accepted. When Baron Swanston left, Miss Rounsefell agreed to meet him after her visit at his hotel in Melbourne.

When she arrived there, the fortunate Miss Rounsefell found a telegram from her sister urging her to go no further. The reason soon became clear: Baron Swanston's picture was in the newspapers. He was described as Albert Williams, wanted for questioning about the murder of his wife.

Deeming did not turn up, anyway. He had fled to a mining town called Southern Cross, over 1500 miles away in Western Australia. He was nevertheless recognized and arrested and brought back to Melbourne, a long journey by train and ship during which he was in constant danger from an incensed public.

Thousands jammed the docks at Melbourne, and Deeming had to be smuggled ashore after a decoy had been sent in the opposite direction. He was brilliantly defended by Alfred Deakin, who later became prime minister of Australia. The main defence was insanity, but judge and jury would not let him escape. He was hanged on 23 May 1892, to the cheers of thousands. It was alleged later that three houses in which he had lived in South Africa also harboured female bodies under the floor.

# H.H. Holmes

AMERICA'S classic serial killer is Hermann Mudgett, otherwise H.M.
Howard or, most famously, H.H. Holmes. He was a man who would
indulge in any sort of crime, but who graduated mainly through confidence trickery and fraud to well-planned murder in a purpose-built
'castle'.

Holmes began life in 1860 in New Hampshire, studied medicine in
Michigan and began to practise in New York. He was married at 18,
and perpetrated what was probably his first big swindle at medical
school by faking the death of a partner in crime with the use of a body
stolen from the school, the pair to share the insurance money.

In 1886 he moved to Chicago and assumed the name of Holmes in
order to escape his wife and child. He bigamously married the pretty
and well-off Myrta Belknap, but was soon discovered forging her
uncle's signature, which led to a separation. Holmes found another
route to quick riches by teaming up with the owner of a drugstore, a
Mrs Holden. Soon he became a partner, and then became the owner
when she disappeared.

Holmes profited vastly from the sale of patent medicines and with
the proceeds began to build his spectacular 'murder castle' opposite
the drugstore. It was ostensibly a massive hotel, built in anticipation
of housing visitors to the Columbian Exposition of 1893. The ground
floor was stores, while the second and third floors contained 100
rooms or so, some for Holmes' use as living accommodation and
offices, others for guests. In fact, by picking arguments with successive builders and replacing them during construction, Holmes was able
to erect a warren of secret rooms and passages.

Some of the rooms in Holmes' hotel were gas chambers, without windows and with strong doors. There were peepholes and Holmes could control the gas from outside. Some rooms had chambers built below false floors, while others had chutes to convey bodies to the basement. The basement was fitted with quicklime pits and vats of acid. The execution chambers were even fitted with alarms which warned Holmes in his own quarters of escape attempts.

The victims for Holmes' hotel were nearly all young women who met him socially and accepted his swift proposals of marriage or applied for jobs which he advertised in the press. Those who were found suitable (that is to say risk-free) were installed in one of his rooms while he set about realizing their assets. He would resort to torture on women not immediately forthcoming with their valuables. When Holmes had acquired a victim's goods, and had satisfied his sexual desires, she would be despatched to the basement.

A jeweller who took a corner of the drugstore to repair watches moved out when he discovered his wife, Julia, and her 18-year-old sister had both become Holmes' mistress. The sister disappeared soon after becoming pregnant. Soon Julia herself became jealous of Holmes' stunning new secretary, blonde Emily Cigrand. She was despatched with her eight-year-old daughter, and Miss Cigrand followed only three months later; her demise may have been hastened by the appearance of pretty Minnie Williams, an heiress worth $20,000. Minnie moved in with Holmes, and she too brought a sister to stay who later disappeared.

Holmes had been unable to get out of the debt incurred by his building works and after the Exposition was over he tried to recoup $60,000 from an insurance company for damage to the upper storeys. However, he was thwarted after an investigation and when details of his past began to come to light he fled from Chicago with Minnie, who had made her fortune over to him, and Benjamin F. Pitzel, a partner in many of Holmes's swindles. In Denver, Holmes married again, the bride being lovely Georgiana Yoke, and at about this time Minnie disappeared.

Holmes bought a drugstore in St Louis after raising loans on Minnie's property. He insured the stock, which Pitzel promptly removed by arrangement, but the insurance fraud was discovered and Holmes was gaoled (for the only time in his career of swindling). In gaol, Holmes met Marion Hedgepeth, a notorious gunfighter and train robber. Holmes asked Hedgepeth if he could recommend a crooked lawyer, and outlined his next insurance fraud to him. The latter recommended Jephta D. Howe, for which service he was promised $500.

On his release, Holmes (now calling himself Howard) moved with Pitzel to Philadelphia, and rented a house near the morgue. The plan was a repeat of Holmes' first fraud. Pitzel would set up in business as R.F. Perry, there would be an accident and the body of Perry would be found. Holmes would collect the insurance, and the two would split the money. No doubt Pitzel believed the body would be stolen from the morgue, but in the event it was his own that was found. Holmes identified the body, and the lawyer collected the cheque on behalf of the family. Holmes paid him off and kept for himself, of course, a double share.

Holmes now had to remove Pitzel's family to escape detection, for the latter's wife was in on the scheme, and there were five children. On the pretext of taking them to their father, Holmes took the three middle children to Indianapolis, where he disposed of the boy. He then took the two girls to Toronto, where they too were killed. Meanwhile, Hedgepeth had decided he was never going to get his $500, so he told the authorities of Holmes' plan in a bid to get his sentence reduced. The insurance company realized they had been swindled, and some smart detective work led them to find Holmes in Burlington, Vermont, where he was living with Georgiana. Mrs Pitzel and her two remaining children were living nearby, awaiting their chance, they thought, to join the rest of the family.

Holmes was taken to Philadelphia, while more detective work found the bodies of the three Pitzel children. A thorough search was now undertaken of Holmes' 'castle' in Chicago. Nobody knows how many bodies the bones and remnants found there belonged to. One newspaper estimated 200, a figure quoted by many accounts since. Holmes sold a 'confession' to a Chicago newspaper for $5000, but later disowned it. He claimed 27 victims but, as he named some people who were still alive, and ignored others who were known to be dead, this list is worthless.

Holmes was hanged on 7 May 1896 for the murder of Pitzel, Philadelphia declining to allow Chicago the pleasure of executing him for the more horrific crimes carried out in his 'castle'. Altogether, Holmes probably killed upwards of 40 people. Had he not foolishly boasted to Marion Hedgepeth, he could possibly have added many more to his list over the next few years.

# Johann Hoch

NOBODY knows exactly how many women Johann Hoch poisoned, but 15 to 20 is the most reasonable estimate. His reasons and methods were always the same. Changing his name from one wife to the next, he would make the acquaintance of his victim, marry her, if necessary poison her, and abscond with her wealth. He did not always kill: the number of his marriages is also unknown, but 55 in 15 years is not far off.

Hoch was born John Schmidt in 1862 in Horweiler, Germany, but was taken to the USA when young. Having deserted his first wife and three children, he embarked on his systematic way of life and death around 1890. His favourite means of attracting likely candidates for his plans was an advertisement in German-language newspapers – a good way to meet homesick countrywomen. The advertisement which attracted the last victim read:

> Widower, quiet and home-loving, with comfortable income
> and well-furnished house, wishes acquaintance of con-
> genial widow without children. Object: matrimony.

Hoch was an intelligent man who used arsenic to kill. He was careful and patient, so that the victims gradually got worse, and the doctors diagnosed the kidney disease nephritis, for which there was then no cure. Hoch made sure the corpses were heavily embalmed, because at that time all embalming fluids contained arsenic, and if by chance a suspicious authority exhumed a body for study the presence of arsenic would be explained.

In the middle of his rampage, Hoch was almost exposed. He was arrested in Chicago under the name of Martin Dotz for suspected bigamy and the swindling of a furniture dealer. His picture appeared in a newspaper and was recognized by a Reverend Haas of Wheeling, West Virginia. Haas knew the balding man with the moustache as Jacob Huff who, three years earlier, had arrived in Wheeling and quickly married Mrs Caroline Hoch, a well-off widow. The Revd. Haas had officiated at the ceremony. It wasn't long before the new Mrs Huff became ill, and in three months she was dead. The Revd. Haas had seen Huff give his wife a white powder, and was suspicious. After the death, Huff collected the insurance, withdrew his wife's money from the bank, sold the house and disappeared. According to the Revd. Haas, he faked a suicide by leaving a note and his clothes on the bank of the Ohio River.

All this was related to Inspector Shippy in Chicago, who put it to 'Dotz' that he was Huff. Hoch immediately agreed, but then thought better of it and said no more. Mrs Huff's body was exhumed but nothing could be proved. While 'Dotz' was serving a year's imprisonment for his swindle, the Chicago police tried to trace his life and activities between Wheeling and Chicago. Discovering a trail of marriages and early deaths, and convinced of the truth of the story of the Revd. Haas, they now felt sure they had a mass murderer in custody. However, no solid proof of murder could be unearthed and Hoch had to be released.

It was a narrow escape, and Hoch realized another mistake would be his last. For this reason, perhaps, he speeded up his operations, not wishing to remain too long in any one place. Ironically, it was in Chicago that he made his final mistake, and he was using the name Johann Hoch – Hoch being, of course, the name of the previous wife he had killed in Wheeling. It was a peculiarity of Hoch that he often used as his alias the name of one of his wives, a macabre and dangerous trait. It was not this that finished him, however.

A Mrs Marie Walcker answered a seemingly innocuous advertisement for a wife. In a few days she was married, and within a month was dying. Her sister Amelia came to visit her on what turned out to be her last day. Hoch embraced her, and told her his wife was dying and that he couldn't face being alone. He proposed marriage. Amelia was stunned, but, as Hoch said: 'The dead are for the dead.' They were married four days later. Hoch took her money and disappeared. That was his mistake. The trusting and sorrowful Amelia reported him missing to the police. Hoch's picture was published in various newspapers. Suddenly from everywhere there were claims from women that the missing man was their husband under another name, or from other sources that he was the short-term husband of a friend or relative who had died soon afterwards. Bodies were exhumed and arsenic found. A big police hunt was launched.

Hoch was found in New York. He was the new boarder, 'Henry Bartels', of a widowed landlady to whom he had proposed 20 minutes after their meeting. Incriminating articles were found in his room and many ex-wives came forward to testify against him. He was charged with the murder of Marie Walcker, whose embalmer, as it happened, had switched two weeks before to one of the new embalming fluids which did not contain arsenic. It was the clincher. 'It's all over with Johann,' said Hoch, as he was sentenced to be hanged. His last day was 23 February 1906, and 100 people witnessed his death.

In 1955 some bones were found in the wall of a cottage in which he had lived – a place searched without success by the police seeking evidence at the time.

# Joseph Vacher

VACHER was the classical killer of the horror movies, an unspeakably ugly tramp who was almost certainly mad and who performed outrageous atrocities on his victims, always working in a frenzy but in a deadly silence. In France he was called 'Jack l'eventreur du sud-est' – Jack the Ripper of the south-east.

He was born on 16 November 1869 at Beaufort, Isère, the fifteenth child of his family. He claimed after his capture that at eight years of age he was bitten by a mad dog, and that this, plus the fact that he took in one swig a bottle of medicine from the local quack, permanently upset his brain. It is likely there was an incident with a mad dog, but exactly what it was is unknown. He began work as a farmhand, but found himself in trouble for attempting to rape a youth. After he developed an inflammation of the scrotum, he underwent an operation which necessitated the removal of part of a testicle; his mutilation later of male victims echoed this experience. He joined the army and a liking for knives and an aggressive readiness to use them at first won him promotion to sergeant, but then landed him in hospital for observation.

On his release, Vacher courted a girl who finally preferred a rival. He shot her three times, and then turned the gun on himself. She recovered quickly and Vacher, who shot himself in the head, merely gave himself a hideous face. The bullet lodged behind his right eye, which thereafter was permanently bloodshot and raw, without a lower lid, and continuously weeping. A scar ran from below his lower lip to the right side of his upper lip, which was raised and twisted. Since his face was pale with yellow patches and part of it was paralysed, it presented a repulsive contorted appearance. This shooting, added to his previous history, meant that in July 1893 he was committed to Saint-Ylie asylum, where his behaviour was ferociously aggressive and his cunning enabled him to escape from time to time. However, after being transferred to an asylum at Saint-Robert, he was discharged as cured on 1 April 1894.

Vacher's first murder occurred about six weeks later and, for the next three years, he roamed the countryside as a tramp, carrying an accordion to which he sang, and a sackful of other odd objects including a cudgel, a pair of scissors, several knives and a cleaver.

On 20 May 1894, 21-year-old Eugénie Delhomme awaited her boyfriend in a quiet country road near Beaurepaire, south of Lyon. Instead, along came Vacher and Eugénie was later found behind a hedge, strangled, raped and disembowelled. Six months later, in August, the body of a 13-year-old girl, Louise Marcel, was found in a stable. Her throat had been cut and her body mutilated. In May 1895, Adèle Mortureux, aged 17, was treated in the same way. There were strong suspects for all these murders and, in the case of the last two, there were arrests – but nobody was sent for trial. In August 1895, 60-year-old Jean-Marie Morand was raped and killed in her lonely cottage while her son was in the fields. Like all the other victims, she had been disembowelled. The crimes had come at six-month intervals, but now Vacher struck again after only a week – a young shepherd, Victor Portalier, was repeatedly stabbed. This time a description of Vacher was circulated on the strength of people at the local farms reporting that this wretch had called on them begging for food.

It is difficult to understand how Vacher escaped capture, especially as next month he was disturbed by an approaching cart as he killed 16-year-old Aline Alise. The driver saw his bloodstained face and offered assistance, but Vacher claimed to have had a fit and fallen, and that he had recovered. The driver went on, and Vacher returned to mutilating the corpse. A week later he sexually assaulted and then killed another shepherd boy, aged 14.

Vacher was all but caught in March 1896 when he attacked 11-

51

year-old Alphonsine-Marie Derouet on her way to early morning mass. Her screams were heard by a gamekeeper who tackled Vacher, but could not capture him. However, the police now had a very accurate description of Vacher, although later that day a policeman on a bicycle stopped Vacher as he tramped along a road and, incredibly, did not recognize or detain him.

It is just as remarkable that, eight days later, Vacher was arrested for vagrancy, and still not recognized. After a few weeks in prison, he was free again. The killings were resumed: in September 1896, Marie Moussier, the 19-year-old wife of a shepherd, in October a 14-year-old shepherdess, Rosine Rodier. In May 1897 Vacher killed a 14-year-old fellow tramp, Claudius Beaupied, in an empty house although the body was not found until Vacher confessed to the murder six months later. In June it was the turn of 14-year-old Pierre Laurent, who was castrated.

On 4 August 1897 Vacher's atrocities finally came to an end. Mme Marie-Eugénie Plantier was out collecting pine cones with her husband and children when Vacher attacked her from behind. She got his hand from her mouth long enough to shout, at which her husband ran up, picked up a stone and smashed it into Vacher's twisted mouth. Vacher produced his scissors and wounded Plantier but, with the assistance of the latter's wife, children and a peasant working nearby Vacher was finally subdued. Two other peasants helped take him to the local inn, where he played his accordion to the locals while awaiting the police.

Vacher was charged with the killing of Portalier, and admitted all his previous crimes, pleading insanity and citing the incident with the dog. He was studied by a team of doctors headed by the famous Alexandre Lacassagne, who found him sane; with hindsight, it seems they were wrong. Vacher was sentenced to death on 28 October 1898 and on 31 December was dragged to the guillotine.

# Chapter Two

# COMPLEX MOTIVES

# Introduction

WHILE no serial killer could be considered normal, there are those whose motives are so complex that it is impossible for the ordinary person to imagine them with any clarity. Among the deeds described in this section are those of Peter Kürten, the Vampire of Düsseldorf, who drank blood; John Haigh, the Acid Bath Murderer, who claimed a similar taste – but may have been lying; and Neville Heath, who looked like an officer and had the air of a war hero but was a sadistic murderer who mutilated his victims.

Charles Manson's atrocities arose from a grudge against the rich, Charles Starkweather and his girlfriend killed from rage, while cousins Kenneth Bianchi and Angelo Buono encouraged each other in sexual depravity. The Zebra killings of the 1970s were racial: black killers and white victims. George Stephenson destroyed a whole family; anger and revenge were what pushed him over the brink.

Jim Jones was a paranoid preacher who not only murdered but had the power to persuade followers to commit suicide. Charles Schmid was a vain man who killed for bravado and boasted about it among his set. David Birnie killed as the end product of having the power to use women as playthings, while his wife aided and abetted him for her own satisfactions. Peter Sutcliffe had a mission to kill prostitutes, which might have arisen from revenge or from hearing 'voices' which controlled his movements.

Dennis Nilsen had the strangest motive – he killed 15 or 16 men for company – while Jacques Mesrine had the most dashing; his crusade against society became a quest for fame.

# Peter Kürten

A MILD-MANNERED, soberly dressed, intelligent man, Peter Kürten nevertheless caused terror in Düsseldorf in the late 1920s, and his deeds fascinated and horrified the whole world. A psychiatrist to whom he frankly related his crimes and his feelings after his arrest described Kürten as the 'king of sexual perverts'.

Kürten saw plenty of raw sex as a child because his father was a drunkard who violently forced himself on his wife in the presence of the children, of whom there were eventually 13. Kürten's sexual activity appears to have started at the age of eight, when a local dog-catcher showed him how to masturbate his dogs. He claimed to have committed his first murder at the equally tender age of nine, pushing a schoolfriend off a raft and holding down the head of a would-be rescuer, so that both boys drowned.

The family moved to Düsseldorf in 1894 when Kürten was 11. By the time he was 13 Kürten was practising bestiality with farm animals, and discovered his greatest satisfaction when stabbing a sheep while having intercourse. From then on, blood and sex were combined in his dreams and many animals of local farmers suffered. Kürten's father was imprisoned for the attempted rape of his own daughter and Kürten himself tried to have an incestuous relationship with the same unfortunate girl.

Kürten ran away from home at 14 after stealing from his employer and went to live with a prostitute, who taught him how to abuse her for her pleasure. He was subsequently imprisoned for two years for his theft, during which time his fantasies of blood and lust increased. On his release at the age of 16, he sexually assaulted a woman in the Grafenberger woods in Düsseldorf and then strangled her. However, although he left her for dead, she must have recovered because no crime was reported.

As Kürten's prison terms mounted up, so his fantasies took a revengeful twist, and he dreamt of poisoning whole schools of children. In his periods of freedom he enjoyed indulging in arson, and watching its victims' despair. His first proven murder occurred in 1913, when he was 29. He was burgling a tavern when he came across a 10-year-old girl, Christine Klein, asleep in bed. He strangled her and then cut her throat, leaving behind a bloodstained handkerchief bearing the initials 'PK'. Sadly, the girl's father was called Peter, and it was assumed the handkerchief was his. Suspicion fell on the father and then on his brother, Otto, with whom he had quarrelled bitterly the previous evening. The brother was tried for murder but acquitted on insufficient evidence. Not surprisingly the family never recovered from this trauma.

After spending most of World War I in prison Kürten went to Attenburg in 1921 and married there, his wife being an ex-prostitute who had reformed after shooting a man who jilted her. Kürten also managed to reform to some extent; he got a job in a factory, gave up petty crime and became an active trade unionist. However, he constantly relapsed into his old ways with sexual attacks on women and perversions with animals, only managing to avoid prison sentences for the former crimes because his wife testified to his good character. He later described the thrill of cutting off a swan's head and putting its neck in his mouth to catch the blood.

In 1925 Kürten returned to Düsseldorf, arriving while the city was enjoying a blood-red sunset, which he later said he took as an omen. His wife joined him a few weeks later, but if she had had a hand in his improved behaviour her influence was waning; between 1925 and 1928 he committed several attacks on women and a number of crimes of arson, and was imprisoned again. Between 1900 and 1928 his various spells in prison had totalled nearly 20 years. He was deliberately undisciplined when in captivity, seeking solitary confinement

*Police photo of Peter Kürten, the 'Düsseldorf Vampire'*

where he could enjoy his fantasies. Then in 1929, when he was 45, he embarked on the series of attacks which soon panicked Düsseldorf.

They began on 3 February, when he attacked a Frau Kuhn and stabbed her 24 times. Her screams saved her life – but only just. On 8 February he killed eight-year-old Rosa Ohliger, stabbing her repeatedly with a pair of scissors. In the evening he returned to the body and tried to burn it, using petrol. The body was found next morning under a hedge and it was evident that the scissors had been used in a sexual attack.

Five days later Kürten met a drunken man, Rudolf Scheer, going home from a beer cellar. He stabbed him repeatedly with the scissors and drank his blood. Soon afterwards he tried to strangle two women with a noose and their descriptions led to the arrest of a mentally handicapped man who confessed to the murders and was placed in a mental home. As if appreciating an escape, Kürten kept his worst impulses in for six months until August, when he began again, launching three separate attacks within half an hour on two women and a man as they walked home in the evening. They all survived his attack, but a domestic servant, Maria Hahn, was not so lucky; she allowed herself to be taken to some fields and was stabbed to death, after which Kürten drank her blood. Her naked body was not found for three months and Kürten later admitted that he had buried it twice, having dug it up six days after the murder with a view to crucifying it on a tree for all to see. He had the spikes with him, but found the task too difficult so reburied the body in a new place.

On 23 August Kürten met two stepsisters, Luise Lentzen, 14, and Gertrud Hamacher, five, returning across some allotments from the local fête. He gave the older girl some money and asked her to fetch him some cigarettes. While she was gone he strangled the younger girl and cut her throat, and when her stepsister returned she met the same end. Their bodies were found next day – the same day that another domestic servant, 26-year-old Gertrud Schulte, accepted Kürten's invitation to take her to a fair. On entering some woods, Kürten attempted to rape her. As she fought she cried, 'I'd sooner die', at which Kürten replied, 'Well, die then', and stabbed her repeatedly with a knife which eventually broke, leaving half of it in her back. She survived, and was able to describe Kürten as fortyish and pleasant-looking in a quiet way; in fact, Kürten was thought of as a dandy by those who knew him.

By now police knew they were searching for a man of unexceptional appearance who nursed a blood lust so strong that nobody in Düsseldorf was safe from a sudden savage and prolonged attack with a sharp implement. The world's newspapers compared the 'Düsseldorf Monster' with the unsolved case of Jack the Ripper. Although the police had descriptions of the Monster, and even óne victim who accused Kürten himself, the sheer volume of the information and clues handicapped them. Thousands of suspects were suggested to them by the public, and they interviewed around 10,000 people.

In September another servant, a class of young woman which seemed to fascinate Kürten, was bludgeoned to death with a hammer. Her name was Ida Reuter, and in November another servant, Elisabeth Dorrier, met the same fate. Two more women were attacked with a hammer but survived.

On 7 November Kürten reverted to the knife in killing a five-year-old girl, Gertrud Albermann. She had also been strangled but, for good measure, had been slashed 36 times. Her body was undiscovered for a couple of days and, perhaps in imitation of Jack the Ripper – whose case Kürten had studied – a newspaper was sent a map and a description of where her body would be found. Kürten also gave the location of the body of Maria Hahn, murdered three months before. These disclosures fanned the publicity and the fear surrounding the Monster.

Kürten was quiet now for another six months, until another domestic servant entered his life on 14 May 1930. Twenty-year-old Maria Budlick had lost her job in Cologne and took the train to Düsseldorf to find employment. She met a Frau Bruckner who gave her her address and offered to help her find accommodation, but that evening she failed to meet Frau Bruckner and accepted instead the assistance of a man who volunteered to take her to a hostel where she could get a bed. When the route led into Volksgarten Park, Maria, who knew of the Monster, became alarmed and resisted going further, despite the man's entreaties. A quietly spoken man came to her assistance and she was happy to allow him to find her a room instead. In the meantime she accompanied him to his flat and had a glass of milk and a ham sandwich with him before they took the tram to the hostel. Ironically, the last part of the journey was also through some woods – the same Grafenbergen woods in which Kürten claimed to have strangled a girl some 33 years earlier. This time Maria was not too worried about accompanying her new acquaintance – but her error nearly proved fatal. Kürten insisted on sex and, during intercourse, he began to squeeze the terrified Maria's neck.

Maria was lucky in that she was still conscious when Kürten reached a climax. He immediately became polite and concerned, as (he later confessed) was his normal behaviour after reaching satisfaction. He asked Maria if she could remember where he lived should she need his help again, and she said, 'No', a half-truth which saved her life. Kürten directed her to the hostel and left her.

Maria Budlick did not report her experience to the police, but she did write to Frau Bruckner to tell her of the traumatic encounter she had had. However, she misspelled Frau Bruckner's name, and it was a Frau Brugmann who received the letter and read it. She appreciated the implications and took the letter to the police, who went to see Maria Budlick in the hostel. By such strange coincidences was the first step taken in the apprehension of the Düsseldorf Monster.

Maria Budlick could remember the distinctive name of the street where she had been taken for a snack: Mettmannerstrasse. After some searching with the police she decided No. 71 was familiar, and the landlady showed them a room at the top of the block which she recognized. As they were returning downstairs Kürten entered the hallway and, on seeing Maria, turned pale and hurried out again. The landlady gave the police her tenant's name but, of course, there was still no proof that he was the Monster.

Frau Kürten was fetched from the restaurant where she was used to working until late at night (thus unwittingly giving Kürten the evenings unencumbered for his activities) but she could throw no light on the affair. She was, of course, resigned to Kürten's frequent gaol sentences – for sexual offences as well as burglary – so was only routinely worried about this latest development. Soon afterwards Kürten met her at the restaurant, and confessed to her that he was the Düsseldorf Monster. Frau Kürten took some convincing as, later, did the neighbours, who saw him as a gentle person who got on well with children.

Kürten arranged to meet his wife next day outside a church. She went to the police and led them to him, thus claiming the large reward offered for the capture of the Monster. Kürten was surrounded by armed police, whom he greeted with a smile, saying, 'Don't worry. There's no need to be afraid.' It is possible that this form of capture was planned by Kürten so that the reward would provide for his wife's old age.

Kürten was charged with nine murders and seven attempted murders. He admitted them all, and was fully cooperative in helping police and the chief psychiatrist to piece together the record of his crimes. He stood trial in April 1931, giving evidence from a cage; he was well-dressed and spoke in a matter-of-fact voice, helping the judge to present the facts. It was only when he began to cast aspersions on the morals of some of his female victims that the judge treated him without sympathy. Kürten confessed to 68 vile crimes, some not previously known to the police, all the details of which he could recall clearly. The recollection no doubt gave him renewed pleasure.

He was 48, and was considered sane and indeed clever. One witness said he was also a nice man. The contrast between his manner in the court and the events he was describing was genuinely shocking. He was found guilty, of course, and cooperated fully with the police psychiatrist before his execution by guillotine on 2 July 1931. He looked forward to a final 'pleasure to end all pleasures', he said – being able to hear for a split second the blood spurting from his neck, as it had from the swan he had beheaded in the park.

# Neville Heath

NEVILLE GEORGE CLEVELY HEATH was born in Ilford, Essex, in 1917, the son of a hairdresser who plied his trade at Waterloo Station and provided his family with a comfortable middle-class home. Neville was only a mediocre pupil at school, but came into his own at 18 when he was commissioned in the Royal Air Force. He was a good-looking young man with blond hair and a film-star cleft in his chin, was proficient at sports, became a pilot, and generally had the air of an aristocratic, insouciant man-about-town.

Alas, he lacked the income to indulge the role, and began embezzling mess funds and bouncing cheques to pay for the extravagances which he clearly regarded to be his rights. He deserted, was arrested and taken back to his station, escaped in a stolen car and was finally dismissed from the service. As a civilian he continued to offend, was sent to borstal when 19, and on his release enlisted in the Royal Army Service Corps. He was again commissioned but, while a captain in the Middle East soon after the outbreak of World War II, was cashiered for more financial frauds and put on board a ship bound for England.

However, Heath jumped ship at Durban and under the name Armstrong joined the South African Air Force. He married Elizabeth Pitt-Rivers, daughter of a prominent South African family, and soon had a son. In 1944 he was seconded to Bomber Command in England. In trouble again for issuing dud cheques, he returned to South Africa, where he was arrested for fraud. He agreed to a divorce from his wife, giving her custody of their son in return for £2000 and, soon afterwards, was deported to England. He arrived on 5 February 1946, and within five months was charged with murder.

Heath had shown minor signs of a liking for sadism from

schooldays – such as stamping on the fingers of a schoolgirl, and spanking another with a ruler. Sadistic practices among consenting adults are not often displayed to others, of course, but Heath had been in England for only 18 days when the manager of London's Strand Palace Hotel entered a bedroom because an electrician had heard screams from within. There was Captain James Cadogan Armstrong of the South African Air Force, otherwise Heath, beating a woman with a cane. She preferred no charges, although the police interviewed her, and the couple seemed on good terms later.

Armstrong's companion may have been Margery Gardner, a married woman who had left her husband and baby in Sheffield to seek fame in London. She wanted to be an actress but, at 31, was leading a precarious life, relying on casual men friends for meals and beds. She was a masochist, and her meeting with Heath provided both of them with some satisfaction. As for Heath, he was using the aliases of Blyth, Denvers and Graham as well as Armstrong, and passing himself off as an officer from the RAF or SAAF. He had the uniforms complete with wings to back up his deception, and was living by financial fraud again.

Margery Gardner certainly shared a night with 'Lieutenant-Colonel' Heath in May at the Pembridge Court Hotel in Notting Hill, where she was tied up and flogged, to the satisfaction of both parties. On 15 June, a 19-year-old girl, Yvonne Symonds, met 'Lieutenant-Colonel' Heath at a WRNS dance and was attracted to him. They booked into the Pembridge Court Hotel as Mr and Mrs N.G.C. Heath, although on this occasion Heath was well-behaved.

Yvonne Symonds went off to join her parents on holiday in Worthing and on the following Thursday, 20 June, Heath was back at Room 4 of the Pembridge Court with Margery Gardner. Both were drunk – they had been drinking together all evening, and Heath had also been consuming vast amounts of liquor ever since lunchtime. He left the hotel in the early hours of the morning.

At 2 pm next day the chambermaid entered the room, having

received no answer to her knock. It seemed to her that one bed had not been used and the other was still occupied. Feeling uneasy, she called the assistant manager, who pulled back the sheet a little to discover an unmistakably dead woman.

What the police uncovered when they arrived was a badly mutilated naked body. There were 17 deep lash marks caused by a diamond-patterned riding whip, her breasts had been bitten away and there was a seven-inch tear in her vagina, probably caused by a short poker in the fireplace. She had been bound hand and foot.

Heath, meanwhile, had followed Yvonne Symonds to Worthing, where he rang her hotel. He had been named in the newspapers as the man wanted for questioning and had to invent a story to cover himself; consequently, he told Yvonne that on the night of the murder he had met a friend, Jack, who was looking for somewhere to take a girl. Remembering he still had the key to Room 4 in the Pembridge Court Hotel (where he and Yvonne had stayed) he had lent the key to Jack. Some time later, Heath told Yvonne, he had received a call from a Chief Inspector Barratt informing him of the murder; he had gone to the hotel to help the police and had even seen the body. On being asked how the girl had died, Heath said: 'A poker was stuck up her. It must have been a maniac.'

Yvonne was convinced by Heath's manner of the truth of what he said. However, the Sunday papers carried the story that police urgently wanted to interview him, and she rang him back at the Ocean Hotel, where he was staying, to tell him her parents were worried. Heath said that he had hired a car and was returning to London immediately to help with police enquiries. Yvonne was never to see him again.

Heath did not go to London, however, but wrote to Scotland Yard, giving a story similar to that he had told Yvonne. He claimed he had lent his key to Mrs Gardner so that she could use his room until 2 am to go to bed with a man. She was to leave the hotel door open for Heath to join her later. At 3 am, he said, he had found her in the state in which the police had discovered her, and had packed his bags and left. He did not want to see the police because there would be a fraud charge against him, but he had the whip and was forwarding it separately, as there would be fingerprints on it other than his. He never did return the whip.

Heath's letter was postmarked Worthing, but by the time the police arrived there, interviewed Yvonne Symonds and visited the Ocean Hotel, Heath had gone, leaving a uniform and some medals. He was now Group Captain Rupert Brooke (an odd name for a handsome young man trying to blend into the background to choose), and was staying at the Tollard Royal Hotel in Bournemouth. On the sea front he met 19-year-old Doreen Marshall, a former Wren who was recovering from a spell of flu by having a holiday at the nearby Norfolk Hotel. Heath took her walking and invited her back to his hotel for tea.

That evening they had dinner, and a lot to drink. During the meal other guests noticed a change of mood in Doreen Marshall, who seemed upset. She and Heath retired to the writing room, where they remained under the observation of other guests, including a Mr and Mrs Phillips. At midnight, when the latter couple decided to retire, Doreen Marshall asked Mr Phillips if he would call her a taxi, which he did at the desk on the way up. However, soon after Heath cancelled it, telling the porter he would walk his guest back to the Norfolk Hotel. 'I'll be back in half-an-hour,' he said, which a still-unhappy Doreen Marshall changed to 15 minutes.

The porter waited for Heath till 4 am, then checked his room, to discover him sound asleep. Heath had used a ladder against the wall at the back of the hotel to climb in, he explained to the manager in the morning, claiming he had been playing a joke on the porter.

Doreen Marshall never returned to the Norfolk. A suspicious and observant Mrs Phillips, seeing Heath next day wearing a silk scarf, asked if she could see it closely, and noticed scratch marks on Heath's neck. Two days after Doreen Marshall's dinner with Heath, the manager of the Norfolk rang his counterpart at the Tollard Royal,

Mr Ivor Relf, to inform him of his guest's disappearance, and Mr Relf asked Heath if the missing Miss Marshall from Pinner might be his guest of earlier in the week. Heath laughed it off, saying his old friend did not come from Pinner. Nevertheless, the manager suggested Heath should go the the police, and with great bravado Heath rang the police to say he would come down to look at a photo of the missing girl to see if she were the one he had entertained to dinner.

'Group Captain Rupert Brooke' admitted at the police station that the girl was indeed the same, and related how he had seen her part of the way home and indeed had seen her again entering a shop the following morning. Completely at ease, and being as helpful as possible, he invented the name of an American army officer who, he said, was also her friend.

Heath was about to leave (and presumably rapidly disappear again) when there occurred one of those coincidences which often mark murder cases. Doreen Marshall's father and married sister arrived to aid enquiries. The two sisters were very alike and, on seeing this striking likeness, Heath was so moved that he began to shiver. The detective-sergeant interviewing him noticed this and suggested to him that Brooke and Heath were one and the same person. The murderer at first denied this but when it was pointed out that he looked very like the photographs of Heath he confessed to his identity.

Heath was detained for further enquiries. He asked if he could go with a policeman to his hotel for his jacket. An inspector went for it instead and found in the pocket a cloakroom ticket from Bournemouth West station dated 23 June. The suitcase was collected from the station and in it were found items of clothing, including a blood-stained scarf, and the diamond-patterned whip which had been used to such vicious effect on Margery Gardner.

A couple of days later Doreen Marshall's body was found. A young woman, Kathleen Evans, noticed her dog investigating something in the undergrowth at Branksome Dene chine, and disturbing a cloud of flies. When the same thing happened next day she brought her father

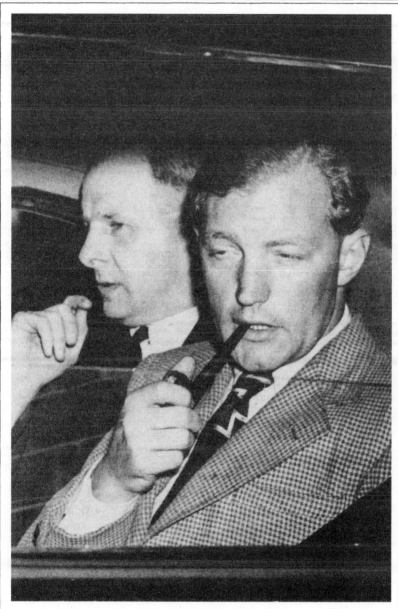

*Neville Heath being driven away from court under police escort*

to investigate. They found the naked body of Doreen Marshall with the hands tied and throat cut, covered by some of her clothes. Among her injuries were a bitten-off nipple and lines of deep, jagged cuts.

Heath was tried for the murder of Margery Gardner (at the time a person could be charged with numerous murders, but tried for only one at a time). He pleaded not guilty on the grounds of moral insanity. This defence relied on the fact that at the time of the crime the perpetrator was so mentally unbalanced as not to know that he was doing wrong. Heath was so clearly in control of himself that the jury took less than an hour to find him guilty.

He saw no one while awaiting hanging, but wrote to his mother to say that he would sit up during his last night to greet the dawn, which to him had happy associations of early aircraft patrols or late returns from nightclubs. His last dawn was 16 October 1946. When offered a traditional last whisky he replied, 'You might as well make it a double, old boy', continuing his impersonation of an officer and a gentleman until the end.

# Charles Starkweather
# and Caril Ann Fugate

CARIL ANN FUGATE'S family were unhappy about her boyfriend Charlie Starkweather, and with good reason. Charlie was 17 while Caril Ann was only 14, but that was only the beginning; though Charlie was small and slight, with thick glasses and bowed legs, he had a vicious and angry temperament. He lost his temper easily and would lash out at anyone without hesitation. Worst of all, he was excited by guns and always carried a rifle with him.

One Saturday afternoon in 1958 he was visiting Caril Ann's house in Lincoln, Nebraska, USA, when he quarrelled with her mother Velda, who said she was tired of him hanging around. During the heated exchange Velda slapped his face; when Charlie hit her in return, her husband Marion intervened and the teenager then shot them both. Their two-year-old daughter Betty was screaming in terror, so he cut her throat. Caril Ann apparently watched all this happening, then switched on the television and settled down in front of it. Charlie put Marion's body in the chicken coop and the others in the outhouse, Betty in a cardboard box and Velda with her body rammed partly down the lavatory.

The two teenagers stayed in the house for six days, putting a notice on the door which read 'Stay a Way. Every Body is Sick with the Flu.' Eventually relatives became worried and contacted the police. Though Caril Ann sent them away with a plausible story it was obvious to the lovers that discovery could not be far off, so they took off in Charlie's car.

The next of Charlie's victims was 70-year-old August Meyer, killed in his own living room after an argument with his unwelcome visitors. Charlie left his car and the two fugitives thumbed a lift from 17-year-old Robert Jensen and his girlfriend 16-year-old Carol King. Charlie drew his gun and forced them to drive to an abandoned school, where he took them into the cellar. Robert Jensen was shot six times in the head; Carol King was assaulted and then shot.

Two days later, Jensen's car was found in the driveway of business-man C. Lauer Ward. Inside the house, Ward's body lay in the hall; he had been shot in the head and stabbed. Upstairs were the bodies of Clara Ward and the housekeeper, 51-year-old Lillian Fencl; both had been bound and gagged, then stabbed to death. The family dog had had its neck broken. Charlie and Caril Ann had made their escape in Ward's limousine.

In Wyoming, they looked for another car. Charlie saw shoe sales-man Merle Collison at the roadside, taking a nap behind the wheel of his car. He woke him and told him to get out of the car and, when Collison did not obey immediately, shot him nine times, only to find that the car would not start. Another motorist, seeing two young people apparently with car trouble, stopped to help. When Joseph Sprinkle, an oil company employee, found himself looking down the barrel of a rifle, he managed to grab it. Charlie lunged at him but Sprinkle had a powerful physique and they were both on the ground, fighting desperately, when Deputy Sheriff Bill Romer arrived on the scene.

Caril Ann ran to Romer, shouting at him to stop Charlie before he killed again. Charlie managed to escape in Ward's car and a frantic chase ensued. The limousine, pursued by police cars, raced through towns at over 160 km (100 miles) an hour and, when they were unsuccessful at catching up with him, the police began firing. Eventually Charlie screeched to a stop and surrendered: his ear had been cut by flying glass from his shattered rear window and the sight of his own blood had thrown him into a panic.

In the trial that followed, no convincing explanation emerged for

Charlie's murderous temperament. He was the third of eight children, seven of them boys, and the rest of the family seemed normal enough. He may have inherited his temper from his father, but the two were never close and he had far more love for his mother. He was always teased about his physical appearance by his schoolmates and even as a child was subject to black moods. By the time he reached his mid-teens he had already developed a hatred of the world that seemed to extend to everyone except his mother and Caril Ann. A year before the murder of her parents he had held up a petrol station near her home, abducting the attendant, 21-year-old Robert Colvert, and shooting him in the head. The crime would probably have remained unsolved but for his later killing spree.

Caril Ann always claimed that she had been terrified of him, and had been forced to go along in fear of her life. Charlie flatly refused to agree that she had been his captive and claimed that she had participated in the killings, saying: 'If I go to the chair, she should be sitting on my lap.' Caril Ann Fugate was sentenced to life imprisonment: Charles Starkweather went to his death in the electric chair on 25 June 1959.

# Charles Schmid

TUCSON is a diverse city; a centre of commerce and of the food-processing industry, it is popular too with tourists and retired people. It is also the university town of Arizona, and supports a large floating population of students. In the early 1960s it was a place where drugs, alcohol and easy sex were available, and there developed an underground teenage society whose activities were based around these. One of the leaders of this society was Charles Schmid who, in 1964, was 22 years old.

Schmid was a bizarre character. He was only 160 cm (5 ft 3 in) tall, and wore high-heeled cowboy boots into which he tucked pads to give him an extra centimetre or two. He was red-headed, but dyed his hair black to present a meaner appearance. He also used make-up, and even affected an artificial mole on his cheek. His behaviour was wild and his stories were wilder. Teenage girls hovered around him, attracted by his easy arrogance, and he was called the 'Pied Piper of Tucson'. His parents were well off, he even had his own 'pad' – a shack-like building at the foot of his parents' garden – and owned a souped-up battered car. One of his tales was that he ran a ring of prostitutes, to whom he had taught 100 different ways of having sexual intercourse. He found a job in the nursing home his parents owned for one young admirer, Mary French, and persuaded her to pay her wages into his bank account.

It was in this atmosphere of 'anything goes' that on the night of 31 May 1964 Schmid told his companions Mary French and John Saunders that he had the urge to kill a girl – any girl – and that they should all do it that very night. Mary French went in search of 15-year-old Alleen Rowe, and asked her to join them for a drive in

Schmid's car. Alleen had told her mother previously that she had been invited to join a 'sex club' and was clearly anxious to become part of the in-crowd, so she was not slow to accept the invitation.

The four drove into the desert, where French stayed in the car while Schmid and Saunders took Alleen to a quiet spot. Schmid raped the girl and calmly told Saunders to hit her over the head with a rock. Before Saunders could obey the terrified girl ran for it, so it was Schmid himself who chased and caught her and smashed in her skull. They buried her in a shallow grave and returned to their drinking, Schmid telling Mary French that he loved her. A strange aside to the story is that Alleen's father, in another part of the country, dreamt about his daughter being murdered, and phoned his wife to tell her of the dream.

Schmid had bragged to his companions beforehand that he could literally get away with murder, and now his boast was that indeed he had. The news, of course, spread in teenage society and many claimed later that Alleen Rowe's fate was common knowledge, but none of this reached the ears of any responsible persons, or if it did it was dismissed as just rumours. So far as the police were concerned, Alleen was just another missing person.

In 1965 Schmid became friendly with a handsome blonde girl, 17-year-old Gretchen Fritz. Schmid, who boasted of the freedom with which he distributed his own sexual favours, was beside himself with misery when the flighty Gretchen rang to tell him she had just made love with somebody else. However, Gretchen later became infatuated with Schmid, who soon found her something of a millstone round his neck.

In mid-August 1965 Gretchen took her 13-year-old sister with her to a drive-in movie, and then went to visit Schmid in his shack. Schmid strangled both sisters and dumped the bodies in the desert. Again, be could not keep quiet about his daring; he boasted to Richard Bruns, a 19-year-old friend. Bruns demanded to see the bodies as proof, so Schmid drove him into the desert, where they buried the bodies more securely.

Once more the sex-and-drugs teenage crowd of Tucson heard the stories but they kept them to themselves, even when undercover police tried to join their circles. Schmid himself, when questioned by outsiders, maintained that the two sisters had run away to California.

It was inevitable that sooner or later there would develop a weak strand in this web of deceit and insider knowledge. It was Richard Bruns who cracked; he acquired the notion that his own girlfriend, whom he knew Schmid had approached unsuccessfully, would be the next on the death list and he began to have terrifying nightmares about it. On 9 November, three months after the double murder, he could stand it no more; he was in Columbus, Ohio, while his girlfriend was still back in Tucson, in reach of Schmid. Bruns went to the police in Columbus and said he could tell them of several murders that had taken place in Tucson.

On 11 November, Schmid, Saunders and French were all arrested and, when the last two turned state's evidence, Schmid's fate was sealed. In any case, Bruns was able to show the police where the two skeletons were. Alleen Rowe's body was never found. Schmid was sentenced to death for the murder of the Fritz girls, and to 55 years in prison for the rape and murder of Alleen Rowe. Saunders received life imprisonment and French five years for their parts in the murder of Alleen Rowe. The picture of Tucson teenage society which emerged at the trial flabbergasted the older citizens of the town.

Capital punishment was subsequently abolished in Arizona for some years so Schmid avoided the death penalty, receiving two terms of life imprisonment instead. He escaped from the Arizona State Prison in November 1972 with another triple murderer and they stayed on a ranch, holding the owners hostage, for a day or two. However, when they split up they were soon recaptured.

# Jacques Mesrine

JACQUES MESRINE developed a simple ambition: to be the most famous criminal in the world. Possibly he succeeded. His crimes certainly contained more flair and daring than anybody else's. The public half-admired him, but to the French authorities he was simply 'Public Enemy Number One'.

Mesrine was born near Paris in 1937, and was noted at his schools (he was expelled twice) more for his energy and aggression than for his intelligence. At 18 he married a beautiful black girl from Martinique named Lydia, who was expecting another man's baby, but he would not accept being tied down and was divorced after being conscripted into the army at the age of 19. In Algeria he proved a brave fighter, and won the Military Cross. Life afterwards seemed dull, so he joined the OAS, a right-wing organization opposed to Algerian independence, and took to crime, being sentenced to three years in prison for burglary in 1962. He was still only 25 but had already made a second marriage to a Spanish girl called Soledad, with whom he had a daughter, Sabrina (who was to remain devoted to him through everything) and two sons. On his release after a year, he took a job in an architect's office but, on being made redundant, went back to crime, despite his wife's pleas that he should keep on the right side of the law. In 1966, he left his family (whereupon Soledad returned to Spain) and lived with a prostitute, Jeanne Schneider, who adored his bravado and became a perfect partner in crime. In November 1967, while staying at a hotel in Chamonix, they brought off the audacious armed robbery of a wealthy Arab, a fellow guest. However, Mesrine's flamboyance was becoming a trademark and a manhunt was mounted in France, so in February 1968 he and Jeanne moved their operations to Canada.

There they worked for a 69-year-old crippled millionaire, Georges Deslauriers, as chauffeur and housekeeper. When they were dismissed they kidnapped him for a $200,000 ransom, but a drugged drink Mesrine gave him failed to work, and Deslauriers found his crutches and escaped. They then made the acquaintance of a wealthy widow, Evelyne le Bouthillier, who was subsequently murdered. The pair fled to the USA but were caught and brought back. Mesrine escaped from prison while awaiting trial for murder and released Jeanne, but they were recaptured. Acquitted of the murder, Mesrine received ten years and Jeanne five for the kidnapping.

The expensive new prison – with more warders than prisoners – was said to be escape-proof but, after a year, Mesrine led three others out in a spectacular escape which was front-page news in Canada. With his fellow-escapee Jean-Paul Mercier, Mesrine determined to win more glory by returning to the prison and freeing the others but they were intercepted by a police car and after a gunfight were repulsed.

Next they successfully robbed a Montreal bank, then, on being surprised by forest rangers while having target practice in some woods, they killed the rangers and took their guns.

Mercier was accompanied by his girlfriend Suzanne and Mesrine offered to free Jeanne to join them too, but in view of the murders and the subsequent manhunt she decided to serve her sentence. Mesrine found himself a new girlfriend, the beautiful 19-year-old Jocelyne Deraiche, and the foursome moved to Venezuela via the USA. With papers obtained through the OAS network they set up headquarters near Caracas, intending to raid US banks from there. However, Interpol was on their trail and, while Mercier and Suzanne (who needed an operation) returned to Canada, Mesrine and Jocelyne flew to Spain and, from there, drove back into France.

Mesrine continued his marauding from several bases in Paris, on one occasion wounding a police officer after a gunfight in a bar. He was captured in March 1973 using a flat rented from a judge – a typical piece of bravado. He boasted – no doubt falsely – of 39 murders and was once again top news in France, especially when he promised to be free in three months. What the police did not know was that he had studied the courthouse at Compiègne to which he was brought on 6 June and a pistol had been smuggled into the lawyers' lavatory. Mesrine acquired it and forced his way out with the lawyer as hostage. A friend was waiting in the courtyard with an Alfa Romeo, and Mesrine escaped in a hail of bullets which wounded him in the arm.

With Jocelyne, Mesrine now moved to a flat near the police headquarters in the seaside resort of Trouville, where he befriended a policeman. Among his accomplishments was, of course, a mastery of disguise. Eventually the homesick Jocelyne, who was too conspicuous with her Canadian accent, returned to Canada where she was subsequently imprisoned for helping Mercier (serving a term for the murder of the forest rangers) escape. Mesrine continued his audacious robberies in Paris, usually committing two on the same expedition, to maximize profit without undue risk. He even visited his sick father in hospital, disguised as a doctor. He cultivated an image of gallantry and was charming to a female cashier who was scared when she pressed an alarm button accidentally; he assured her that he liked music while he worked. Finally, in September 1973, his driver was captured and the police discovered Mesrine's hide-out, where he was recaptured in a blaze of publicity.

Mesrine was not tried for 3½ years, during which time he wrote a book and smuggled it out for publication, causing the French government to bring in a new law prohibiting criminals from profiting by their offences. At the trial, in May 1977, he was again the star, at one stage removing from the knot of his tie a plaster impression of the keys of his handcuffs. The court was electrified but the judge, whom he had ridiculed, was not so amused. He was sentenced to 20 years.

La Santé, in Paris, was another 'escape-proof' prison. On 8 May 1978 Mesrine was in the interview room awaiting his lawyer, when, from a ventilation duct, he produced pistols, a knife, tear gas and a rope. Meanwhile a fellow prisoner, François Besse, put a guard out of action by squirting soapy water into his eyes. A third prisoner, Carman Rives, was released, and warders in the staff office were overpowered. The three convicts donned the warders' clothes and told workmen fitting new grilles to the windows to move the ladders to the outside wall. With these and the rope they scaled the wall, but Rives was shot dead by police. Mesrine and Besse hijacked a passing car and escaped.

A huge manhunt for Public Enemy Number One was launched after this sensational escape. Mesrine continued his daring and quixotic raids with Besse as an ally. In Deauville they were both injured in a shoot-out with police, Besse badly so, but by taking hostages, commandeering cars and even stealing a rowing boat they got to Paris while police helicopters scanned the route.

Mesrine then robbed a company which had won libel damages over his book, and a plan to kidnap the judge who had sentenced him failed only because of the inexperience of his helpers. Foiled of this personal revenge, Mesrine kidnapped a rich industrialist, Henri Lelièvre, an operation which realized 6 million francs and gave him the means to relax in London for a while.

In August 1979 an anti-Mesrine squad was formed in Paris as the authorities realized that Mesrine was becoming a national anti-hero, undermining the law. In September Mesrine met a journalist named Jacques Tillier and wounded him as a warning, believing him to be an informer. Tillier could provide sufficient details of Mesrine's accomplice, Charly Bauer, for police to identify and find him, and soon police knew Mesrine's hide-out. The whole block and much of the surrounding area was staked out by plain-clothes police.

On 2 November 1979 Mesrine emerged with his girlfriend, Sylvie Jeanjacquot, and her white poodle. They drove off in a BMW. Soon they found a blue lorry, with tarpaulin covering the back, cutting across them to turn right. Another lorry was behind. Suddenly the tarpaulin was thrown back and four police marksmen fired 21 shots point-blank at Mesrine. A car pulled up alongside and another police-man fired a shot into Mesrine's head, although he was already dead; Sylvie Jeanjacquot and her dog were severely wounded. Minutes after the attack was launched the police were literally dancing with joy in the street.

# Charles Manson

SHARON TATE, wife of the film director Roman Polanski, was spending a quiet evening with friends in her Hollywood home. She was eight months pregnant and while her husband was away in Europe, Voytek Frykowski, a writer, and his girlfriend, coffee heiress Abigail Folger, were staying with her. On the evening of 9 August 1969 Sharon's ex-lover Jay Sebring and a friend of Frykowski, 18-year-old Steven Parent, had joined them for a quiet drink. All five were brutally butchered that night by members of Charles Manson's 'family', obey-ing their leader's commands.

Two girls – Susan Atkins and Patricia Krenwinkel – and an ex-football star, Tex Watson, broke into the house though the nursery prepared for the baby while a fourth member of the family, Linda Kasabian, stayed on watch outside. 'I am the Devil and I'm here on the Devil's business,' Watson announced to the shocked group of friends. Sebring tried to tackle him, but Watson shot him through the lung, then pursued Frykowski, who tried to run for it. He knifed him in the back, shot him twice, then battered him over the head with his gun butt. Sharon Tate and Abigail Folger were both screaming in panic; Abigail ran out into the garden pursued by one of the women, who stabbed her over and over again. Sharon Tate was the last to die and as she pleaded desperately for the life of her unborn baby Susan Atkins laughed, 'Bitch, I don't care!' All three joined in the savage attack that followed, when Sharon Tate was stabbed 16 times, in the neck, chest, back and the womb. Afterwards a towel dipped in her blood was used to write the word 'Pig' on the living room wall.

The group then went back to report their success to Manson, though it was only when they heard the report on television that they knew who they had killed. Susan Atkins was thrilled to find that one of their victims was as famous as Sharon Tate. The senseless brutality of the murders sent shock waves through America, reinforced two nights later when supermarket owner Leno LaBianca and his wife were killed in a similar manner. Rosemary LaBianca was stabbed 41 times, her husband 12 times and the word 'War' was cut into his abdomen. The words 'Death to Pigs' and 'Helter Skelter' were written on the walls in blood.

The killers were only identified when Susan Atkins, while in custody on a charge of car theft, told her cell-mate about her involvement with the Tate–LaBianca killings. This was a valuable piece of information for a remand prisoner trying to bargain for release and it was soon passed back to the investigating officers. What they heard led them to the hippie group led by the magnetic Charles Manson, who demanded unquestioning obedience from his followers.

Manson was born in Ohio in 1934, the illegitimate son of a prostitute who was gaoled for beating up and robbing her clients. By the age of 11 he was already a juvenile delinquent and was sent to reform school. Sentences for armed robbery, pimping and car theft ensured that he spent much of the next 21 years behind bars. By the age of 32, when he was at last free, he was confused and bitter, unable to adapt to normal life: 'I didn't want to leave gaol but they insisted,' he said.

He spent his first few days and nights of freedom riding on buses

*Charles Manson during the Tate–LaBianca trial*

but eventually gravitated to the Haight-Ashbury district of San Francisco, then the centre for the 'flower power' hippie movement. He found himself in his element, taking hallucinogenic drugs and practising free love; he grew long hair and a beard, developed an interest in hypnotism and the occult and began to see himself as a Messiah. He gathered a group of young people around him and made the headquarters of the 'family' in abandoned shacks behind a ranch in the Californian desert. Sex orgies and drug-taking were commonplace; alcohol and contraceptives were banned. Women were subservient and had to submit sexually to any man who wanted them. All the members of the group were completely dominated by him. 'He is the king and I am his queen,' Susan Atkins was to say later. 'The queen does what the king says . . . Look at his name, "Man's Son" – now I have visible proof of God, proof the church never gave me.'

He had such command over his followers that he was able to direct them to commit crimes, beginning with theft and car stealing, progressing to terrorizing rich people in their homes and eventually to murder. He drew up a 'hit list' of wealthy and privileged people as well as those he imagined had slighted him, and his code-name for the day of reckoning, when all scores would be settled, was 'helter skelter', taken from a Beatles record.

In July 1969 he sent three of his followers to rob and kill musician Gary Hinman who was thought to keep a large amount of cash in his house. Though Hinman was tortured the money was never found, but he was forced to sign over his two cars to the group before he was stabbed and left to bleed to death. Soon afterwards a member of the group was stopped while driving one of Hinman's cars and arrested. Manson announced, 'Now is the time – helter skelter.' Within a week, the seven brutal murders had taken place.

Manson went on trial with Susan Atkins, Patricia Krenwinkel and another female follower, Leslie Van Houten, who had taken part in the LaBianca killings. It was the first of many trials involving members of the Manson family: there were 84 witnesses and it lasted over nine months.

Linda Kasabian, who had turned state's evidence, was a crucial witness. She had lived in 11 drug-oriented communes before she joined the Manson family and felt that she belonged at last, believing that Manson was 'the Messiah come again'. She told how, when she was left on watch outside Sharon Tate's home, she heard loud screaming, then saw the wounded Frykowski crawling towards her: 'He had blood all over his face . . . and we looked into each other's eyes for a minute . . . and I said, "Oh god, I am so sorry. Please make it stop." And then he just fell to the ground in the bushes.'

Manson showed his power over the women of the family by coercing the three girls into confessing to the murders, declaring that he was innocent. When the lawyers for the girls would not cooperate and refused to question them, the girls insisted on telling their stories verbatim. The judge ruled that the jury must leave, so that this testimony could later be edited and the inadmissible parts removed before they heard it. The girls countered by refusing to testify unless the jury was present.

Manson then decided to take the stand and, in the absence of the jury, spent 90 minutes expounding his philosophy. His 'family' he said, 'were just people that you didn't want, people that were alongside the road; I took them up on my garbage dump and I told them this: that in love there is no wrong'. He was bitter about a society that has discarded him long ago and now regarded him as a fiend. 'I don't care what you do with me,' he declared. 'I have always been in your cell.' Once Manson had had his say, he told the girls not to testify and, of course, they obeyed.

The prosecutor, in his summing up, called Manson 'one of the most evil, satanic men who ever walked the face of the earth'. All four defendants were found guilty and sentenced to death but, as the California Supreme Court voted to abolish the death penalty for murder in 1972, their sentences were commuted to life imprisonment.

# The Zebra Murders

THE TERRIFYING activities of the Black Muslim group calling themselves 'Death Angels' were highlighted in San Francisco, USA, in 1973–4, when 15 white victims died at the hands of black killers: hence the nickname of 'Zebra murders'. The murderers were aspiring members of the group and were simply fulfilling their initiation rites, which meant killing a specified number of 'white devils', men, women and children alike. The victims were chosen at random on the street, in telephone booths or stores, or standing at a bus stop. They had never seen their killers before and had no chance to protect themselves.

The first attack was on Richard and Quita Hague, who were walking down a San Francisco street in October 1973 when several black men jumped out of a van and bundled them into the back. Quita was raped and hacked to death with a machete. Richard, too, was attacked with a machete but in spite of serious wounds, he lived. In the same month Frances Rose, aged 28, was driving along a city street when a black assailant opened the passenger door of her car and shot her. A few weeks later a grocery store owner was tied up and shot in the head.

In December there were six killings, including that of an 81-year-old man. The same guns were used in several of the murders and the police were by now fairly certain that they were looking for a group of killers working together as would-be members of the 'Death Angels'. There was already a horrifyingly long list of unsolved murders in the same pattern in California: over 130 men, 75 women and some 60 children were already likely victims of the murderous group.

Four people were killed within a couple of hours on 28 January: two men and two women aged between 32 and 69. A fifth, 23-year-old

Roseanne McMillan, who survived her wounds, said that a smiling black man had approached her, said 'Hi', then taken out a gun and fired. The last two murders, and three more attempted ones, came in April. A young couple were gunned down on their way to a grocery store: 19-year-old Thomas Rainwater died instantly while 21-year-old Lindy Story was partially paralysed for life. Two more young men were wounded on Easter Sunday and the last death came on 16 April 1974, when Nelson Shields received three bullets in the back.

The full-scale investigation mounted by the police, stopping and questioning thousands of blacks and searching them for weapons, inflamed racial feelings and produced no tangible results. The break-through came only when Anthony Harris, one of the group of killers, volunteered a confession and named eight other Zebra murderers. All were arrested, but four were later released because the evidence against them would not stand up in court. The remainder – Jesse Cooke, Larry Greene, Anthony Harris, J. C. Simon and Manuel Moore – were charged with murder. Two of them, Harris and Moore, had met while in prison and had decided before their release to earn member-ship of the 'Death Angels'.

The trial began on 5 March 1975 and established a record as the longest in California's legal history, running until 9 March, 1976. Over 180 witnesses gave evidence, chief among them Anthony Harris, who spent 12 days on the stand. All four were found guilty and sentenced to life imprisonment. The fully-fledged members of the Death Angels, those who had already reached their killing total, were never caught.

# Peter Sutcliffe

OVER a period of five years a sadistic killer committed so many violent crimes on women in the area from Leeds to Manchester that women turned out on the streets to demonstrate against the impotence of the police to catch the killer. When the police received taped messages purporting to come from the killer taunting them on their inability to catch him, the ingredients of a sensational case were in place. The savagery with which the killer mutilated his victims' bodies led to him being called the 'Yorkshire Ripper'.

The realization that there was a maniac at large developed as the attacks increased in number. The first occurred on 5 July 1975, when Anna Rogulskyj was attacked in Keighley. On 15 August 1975 Olive Smelt was assaulted in Halifax. Both women were hit on the head with a hammer and slashed with a knife, but both survived after brain surgery.

Wilma McCann, a 28-year-old prostitute, was not so lucky; she was killed with a hammer 90 m (100 yd) from her home in Leeds on 30 October 1975 and then stabbed several times. Some three months later the body of another prostitute, Emily Jackson, aged 42, was found in the same condition, except that the wounds inflicted after death were even more horrific – 50 lacerations caused by a knife and a Phillips screwdriver. A wellington boot had stamped on her, so the police knew the killer's shoe size. This second murder was also in Leeds, and the police acknowledged the two were linked.

In May 1976 a woman survived an attack in Leeds, and the next murder was not until 5 February 1977 when the body of Irene Richardson, a 28-year-old part-time prostitute, was discovered in a playing field by a jogger. The details were as before, with the careful arrangement of her boots on her thighs contrasting with the way her body had been slashed with a knife.

It was now that the name 'Yorkshire Ripper' was applied to the killer, and Leeds prostitutes began to live in fear. The next killing was in nearby Bradford; Patricia Atkinson, a 32-year-old divorcee, was murdered in her home in the vice district. As well as the identifying atrocities being present, her sheets showed the imprint of a wellington boot of the same size as before.

George Oldfield, Yorkshire's most experienced detective with 31 years in the force, was put in charge of a massive murder hunt. The public really became involved towards the end of June 1977 because the next victim, back in Leeds, was a 16-year-old girl on her way home from seeing friends. Sadly for her, the route took her near the red-light district. The outcry against the killings was now deafening.

With a huge police operation involving over 300 officers in progress, another woman was attacked in Bradford in July 1977. She survived but, unfortunately, the description she gave of her assailant proved to be unlike that of the Ripper. From now on the Ripper was not to strike consecutively in the same town and the next murder was across the Pennines in Manchester. Jean Jordan, a 21-year-old prostitute, was struck 11 times and killed near some allotments but, as the Ripper dragged the body to some bushes, he was disturbed by the arrival of another car and fled. The body was not discovered, and he returned to it eight days later to search for the new £5 note he had given her, which he realized might be a giveaway. He could not find her handbag and, in frustration, attacked the body savagely with a piece of broken glass, trying to remove his hammer trademark by cutting off the head. He failed. The body was found next day, and the £5 note soon afterwards.

The bank that had issued the note was traced, and all the employees of companies which had been supplied notes from the batch to pay wages were interviewed. Among them was Peter Sutcliffe, who was seen twice but aroused no suspicions.

A woman was attacked in Leeds in December, and on 21 January a prostitute, Yvonne Pearson, aged 22, was murdered on waste ground at Bradford. Her body, which had been jumped upon as well as suffering the usual mutilations, was not discovered for two months. Ten days after this murder, Helen Rytka, an 18-year-old prostitute who practised in tandem with her twin sister, was killed viciously in a Huddersfield woodyard. A short time later, the Ripper returned to the still undiscovered body of Yvonne Pearson and placed a newspaper, dated four weeks after her murder, beneath her arm. He possibly made the body more visible, too. In May, a 41-year-old prostitute Vera Millward was murdered in Manchester.

In August Peter Sutcliffe was interviewed by the police twice more, once because his car registration number was on a list compiled of vehicles in Leeds and Bradford, and once when police were checking tyre marks. His rare blood group, B, and small shoe size (seven) were not checked against what the police thought they knew of the Ripper. By now the police had interviewed thousands of men, and the reward for information stood at £15,000.

The Ripper was now quiet for 11 months, but the murders resumed in April 1979 in Huddersfied with an attack on a 19-year-old building society clerk, Josephine Whitaker. The murder of such a young girl after the long break provoked another outcry. In June the police broadcast a tape they had received, apparently from the Ripper, which followed three letters that had arrived since March 1978; it had been the flaps on the envelopes that had given away the Ripper's blood group. The voice on the tape taunted George Oldfield with his failure to catch him and promised another victim in September or October. Experts studied the accent, and from now on it was assumed the Ripper came from Sunderland. The tape was broadcast around pubs and clubs in Leeds and Bradford, while parts of the letters were published in the hope that a member of the public would identify the writing.

Oldfield had a heart attack in July as the pressure told on him, and

Sutcliffe was once again interviewed, as his car had been recorded in the relevant Bradford area on 36 occasions. However, Sutcliffe was not from Sunderland, and escaped detection again. A month later a student from Bradford University, 20-year-old Barbara Leach, was killed while taking a walk at night. It seemed the Ripper was not now waging a campaign against prostitutes, but was attacking girls merely for being out in the evening.

The Ripper did not strike for nearly a year after this, during which time the police concentrated again on the £5 note. The number of companies which might have issued it was reduced to three. Sutcliffe was interviewed four more times during this period.

In August 1980 Marguerite Walls, a 47-year-old civil servant who had been working late in the office, was on her way home in Leeds when she was killed. In October the Ripper attacked Upadhya Bandara, a doctor from Singapore but, having put a rope around her neck, he inexplicably apologized and left her. On Guy Fawkes night he knocked down a 16-year-old girl but her boyfriend heard her scream and the Ripper was chased off.

Less than a fortnight later another student was killed. Jacqueline Hill got off a bus near the Leeds University hall of residence in which she lived when the Ripper struck. By now the five-year lack of success in catching the Ripper had become a scandal, and a 'super squad' was formed.

It was routine police work that finally caught the Ripper. On Friday, 2 January 1981, two policemen saw a possible prostitute climb into a car in Melbourne Avenue, Sheffield. They decided to investigate. The driver, calling himself Peter Williams, asked if he could relieve himself in some bushes and was allowed to, but his purpose was to hide a knife and hammer behind an oil storage tank. While he was away the policemen discovered the car plates were false, and took 'Peter Williams' and the prostitute, Olivia Reivers, to the police station, where 'Williams' went to the lavatory again, and hid a second knife in the cistern.

*Peter Sutcliffe on his wedding day*

The arrested man admitted his name was Peter Sutcliffe and was held overnight. Next day, the Ripper squad was called. It was established that Sutcliffe's blood group was B, and the police discovered he had been interviewed often during the investigation. All day Saturday he was questioned, and then kept another night. Meanwhile Sergeant Bob Ring, one of the policemen who had brought Sutcliffe in, heard that the Ripper squad were interviewing him in depth, and suddenly realized the significance of the man's wish to relieve himself at Melbourne Road. Hurrying back there, he searched around and found the hammer and knife.

On Sunday afternoon, after several hours of talking, it was suddenly sprung on Sutcliffe that the hammer and knife had been found. Sutcliffe straight away admitted that he was the Yorkshire Ripper and made a long statement, which took 17 hours, explaining his motives.

Sutcliffe had been a small, weak baby when he was born on 2 June 1946, the oldest of the five children his parents would have. His black eyes were his most startling feature. He was intelligent but was small and was bullied as a child. Later he had little success with women, although he was extremely vain. Among his menial jobs was that of a grave-digger at Bingley Cemetery; because of his beard, his colleagues nicknamed him 'Jesus'. He met a dark, pretty, 16-year-old Czech girl, Sonia Szurma, and courted her for seven years before they were married in Bradford in 1974.

Some time around 1969, two events took place which had a great effect on Sutcliffe. His mother, whom Sutcliffe adored, was dramatically exposed by his father in front of the whole family after Sutcliffe senior discovered she was having an affair with a neighbour, a policeman, an event which Sutcliffe's father afterwards said he thought had turned his son's mind. The second significant event was that Sutcliffe went with a prostitute after a row with Sonia. Humiliatingly, he was unable to achieve intercourse, and was furthermore cheated by the girl who failed to give him £5 change from a £10 note. This inspired his first attack on a prostitute; he found her two weeks later and hit her over the head with a sock filled with stones.

There was a similar attack in 1971, in the red-light district of Bradford, when he was out driving with his best friend, Trevor Birdsall. On the way home, he admitted to Birdsall what he had done. Birdsall was also with him on the night in 1975 that Olive Smelt was attacked, and at one stage he told his wife that he suspected Sutcliffe was the Ripper.

Sutcliffe's defence to the charge of 13 murders and seven attempted murders was based on insanity. He claimed that God had spoken to him from a particular headstone while he was working at the cemetery, and had instructed him to go out and kill prostitutes. 'Cleaning the streets' was how he later explained it to his brother.

The Attorney General, Sir Michael Havers, was said to be ready to accept a bargain plea of manslaughter, believing him to be suffering from paranoid schizophrenia, but Mr Justice Boreham threw that out, no doubt on the grounds that only a full-scale trial would satisfy the public after such a traumatic five years. Coincidentally, Sonia had been diagnosed as schizophrenic after a breakdown two years before their marriage; this handicapped Sutcliffe's defence, as the jury were invited to believe that Sutcliffe's 'symptoms' were merely copied from Sonia, who had imagined she was a second Christ.

Many of the investigative mishaps were aired at the trial. At T. and W. H. Clarke, the road haulage company where he worked, colleagues had jokingly referred to Sutcliffe as the Ripper because of the number of times he had been questioned by the police. In his cab was a handwritten note which read: 'In this truck is a man whose latent genius if unleashed would rock the nation, whose dynamic energy would overpower those around him. Better let him sleep?' Sutcliffe even revealed that on one occasion, when he was asked about the size seven wellington boots which had left their imprint at two murders, he was actually wearing them – but the policeman interviewing him had not noticed.

Despite the medical evidence, the jury found Sutcliffe guilty on all counts and on 5 May 1981 he was sentenced to life imprisonment, with the recommendation that he should serve at least 30 years.

An intriguing unanswered mystery concerns the tape message, of which Sutcliffe denied all knowledge, and which sent the police so drastically on the wrong trail (they had 50,000 responses to its broadcast). In 1993 a North Shields widow, Olive Curry, revealed that when Sutcliffe was arrested in 1981 she recognized him as a man she had met often in 1978 when she worked in the canteen at the North Shields Fisherman's Mission (the haulage company I. and W.H. Clark confirm Sutcliffe was often in the area at that time). Sutcliffe, said Mrs Curry, was always with a friend he called Carl or Trev. Mrs Curry had heard the tapes and, on seeing Sutcliffe, realized that the voice was that of Sutcliffe's friend. She said that she had informed the police of this in 1981 but had heard no more. She subsequently wrote to Sutcliffe about this and visited him in prison; Sutcliffe wrote hundreds of letters to her, stopping only when she revealed her story to the press. Sutcliffe then himself wrote to the *Sunderland Echo* to deny he had an accomplice. However, Mrs Curry remains convinced, and perhaps there is a final twist to the story to come.

# Jim Jones

UNLIKE most mass murderers, Jim Jones did not kill with his own hands. However, in his efforts to create an earthly paradise for his followers he was ready to order the deaths of anyone who opposed his will and finally, when he saw that his religious empire was doomed, he ordered the 900 cult members to commit mass suicide. Perhaps he had set out as a benign religious leader who would create a better and fairer society but, as he felt the joy of power over his congregation, it had all gone disastrously wrong.

Jim Warren Jones had founded the People's Temple in a run-down area of Indianapolis, USA, in the late 1950s, preaching a gospel of racial integration that would create a classless society. As his congregation grew he launched himself into the profitable faith-healing market, healing the sick and crippled by the dozen and raking in the dollars. Eventually he set up a new Temple in downtown San Francisco, using the support of prominent politicians and often preaching to crowds of 5000 or more.

Then came the defections, with ex-members of the Temple claiming that Jones was forcing his followers to sign over all their money to him. They exposed his faith cures, describing how they had pretended to be blind or wheelchair bound, only to jump up when Jones laid hands on them, crying that they could see or walk for the first time. They also told stories of Jones presiding over bizarre sex rituals and claiming the right to take any woman in the congregation to his bed. He ordered youngsters who did not show sufficient respect to be beaten or tortured with electric cattle prods.

Eventually the tide of criticism threatened to swamp Jones and his Temple so he led his followers to a new home in Guyana, setting up a

*Jim Jones*

community on a tract of savannah grassland surrounded by jungle, where there would be no one to interfere. However, a year later a California Congressman, Leo Ryan, pressured the US State Department to persuade the reluctant Guyanese government to let him go to Jonestown and interview the cult members. Ryan had received many reports from his constituents that young people were being held in the commune against their will and beaten and abused if they did not obey Jones's orders, so he was determined to discover the truth for himself. He arrived at Jonestown on 17 December 1978 with a group of reporters and cameramen, to find the perimeters of the remote settlement patrolled by armed guards. Jones explained that they were necessary to keep out bandits. The cult members looked gaunt and hungry but most still professed complete devotion to Jones and his ideals. When Ryan gave a personal guarantee of protection to anyone who wanted to leave, only 20 commune members volunteered.

Jones knew that if one of his congregation returned home, the truth about Jonestown would emerge, and he could not allow that to happen. As the party was preparing to leave from Port Kaituma airport, 18 km (8 miles) from Jonestown, they were ambushed. A tractor emerged from the bush on to the tarmac and gunmen opened fire from it, moving in to shoot victims already lying on the ground at point-blank range. Congressman Ryan was killed instantly and NBC reporter Don Harris died as he took the full force of the blast from an automatic rifle. Cameraman Robert Brown, who had continued filming after the massacre began, only stopped when fatally hit by a bullet. A young photographer from the *San Francisco Examiner* also died in the hail of bullets.

According to an eye-witness, once Jones heard that some members of Ryan's party had escaped and realized that the authorities would soon take action, he decided that his followers should take part in one final ritual: mass suicide. He had always told them that this was the only way out if the existence of the commune was threatened and over 900 men, women and children gathered to hear him talk about the beauty and dignity of death.

'We were too good for this world,' he told them. 'Now come with me and I will take you to a better place.'

The elders of the Temple produced large vats of cyanide mixed with Kool-Aid, a popular soft drink, and the mixture was ladled out by the commune's doctor and nurse. Members lined up to collect the lethal mixture, singing gospel songs. Babies died first, as parents spooned the poisoned drink into their mouths, then the children, then finally the adults drank, wrapping their arms round one another to stay close in death.

When Guyanese soldiers arrived next morning they found Jones's body sprawled across the altar, a bullet through his brain. They also found a number of bodies lying near the trees at the edge of the clearing, with bullets in their backs; many of those who tried to flee had been executed before they could reach safety.

# Kenneth Bianchi and Angelo Buono

THE FIRST victims of the 'Hillside Strangler' were found bound, raped and strangled on the hills above Los Angeles in October 1977. Both 19-year-old Yolanda Washington and 15-year-old Judith Miller were prostitutes and their deaths caused little public interest. At first the police thought they were looking for a killer of street women but their ideas changed rapidly with a string of murders in November: seven more bodies were found and only one, Jill Barcomb, was a prostitute. The others were a waitress, four students and two schoolgirls, 12-year-old Dollie Cepeda and 14-year-old Sonja Johnson. Three of the bodies were found together on 20 November, thrown naked on to a rubbish dump so that the boy who found them thought they were discarded fashion mannequins. All had been tied up before being strangled and police now knew that they were looking for two murderers, for the girls had been raped by two different men.

In December, the naked body of call-girl Kimberley Martin was found on a vacant lot in the city; she had disappeared after going to meet a client who gave a fictitious telephone number. One of the tenants in the apartment block she had visited, 26-year-old Kenneth Bianchi, told the police that he had heard screams.

The last of the set of murders was that of Cindy Hudspeth, a 20-year-old waitress whose body was found in the boot of her car, which had been pushed over a cliff in February 1978. She was naked and, like the other girls, had been raped by two men. After that everything went quiet, the female population of Los Angeles began to relax and the police hoped that the killings were over. But the killers were to surface again in Bellingham in the state of Washington where two girls, Diane Wilder and Karen Mandic, were offered a job minding a house for a few hours while its alarm was repaired and were later found strangled, their bodies thrown in the back of Karen's car. Karen had told her boyfriend that they had been hired by Kenneth Bianchi and though he denied all knowledge of the girls, a search of his home turned up a number of items linked to the victims and he was arrested.

At first Bianchi denied everything, then he took refuge in claims of multiple personality: he was completely innocent and it was his alter ego, Steve, who had killed the girls. Eventually, at a sanity hearing in October 1979, it was decided that Bianchi was shamming and that he should be indicted for murder. At that point, Bianchi decided to plead guilty and agreed to testify against his partner in crime, his cousin Angelo Buono, in return for a life sentence to be served in California, rather than Washington's harsh Walla Walla prison. He protested that he was full of remorse for his actions: 'In no way can I take away the pain I have given others, and in no way can I expect forgiveness from others.'

Bianchi, who was something of a charmer with a history of lying and stealing, was the subservient half of the partnership, hero-worshipping his cousin Buono who was 17 years his senior, oversexed and brutal and never happier than when he was ill-treating women. In the 1970s the cousins went into business together as pimps. They promised a 16-year-old girl called Sabra Hannan work as a model then forced her, by beatings and threats of death, to act as a prostitute. Later they recruited a 15-year-old, Becky Spears, terrorizing her and forcing her to submit to all manner of sexual acts.

Intent on broadening their operation, they paid an experienced prostitute for a list of clients, only to find that it was false. They set out for revenge but, as they could not find the prostitute who had cheated on them, they settled for her friend Yolanda Washington. They found raping and strangling her such a great experience that they wanted to repeat it over and over again. Bianchi, who had always cherished an ambition to join the police force, had often posed as a policeman to corner his victims. They had picked up Judith Miller on the pretence of arresting her for prostitution, and had told the two schoolgirls that they were investigating a burglary in the neighbourhood and needed to question them.

It seems that by early 1978 Buono was tired of the killing games and even more tired of Bianchi, and when Bianchi's common-law wife decided to move back to her home town of Bellingham, Buono persuaded him to follow her. If that had been the end of the 'Hillside Strangler', the murderers might never have been caught, but Bianchi found life flat and dull without the stimulus of raping and killing and thought that carrying out a couple of murders alone and unaided would earn him respect from his cousin. With typical carelessness, he chose as his victim Karen Mandic, who worked in the store where he was employed as a security guard.

Once in gaol, Bianchi hatched a plot to clear himself. A writer, Veronica Compton, had asked for help with a play about a female serial killer and through letters and visits revealed an obsession with torture and murder. She happily agreed to Bianchi's plan to prove that the Hillside Strangler was still at large: she would drive to Bellingham and strangle a woman, then leave behind some of Bianchi's sperm, which had been smuggled out of prison in a rubber glove. Fortunately, her selected victim proved too strong for her, and she was arrested and sentenced to life imprisonment.

Buono's trial lasted for two years; Bianchi alone spent five months in the witness box, contradicting himself over and over again and even claiming that he was innocent after all. Buono's lawyer argued that Bianchi was solely responsible for the murders and was only implicating his client for the sake of a plea bargain.

The jury remained unconvinced and Buono was found guilty and sentenced to nine terms of life imprisonment. Bianchi was held to have violated the terms of his plea bargain and was sent to Walla Walla prison, where he was to need special protection from the other prisoners.

In pronouncing sentence, the judge told Bianchi and Buono: 'I am sure you will probably only get your thrills from reliving over and over again the torturing and murdering of your victims, being incapable, as I believe you to be, of feeling any remorse.'

# Dennis Nilsen

DENNIS NILSEN was an intelligent, shy man who felt that all his life he had suffered rejection in one form or another. Usually extremely lonely, he liked making friendships and helping others less well off than himself, and extended his concern to animals. He liked to expound his caring views – he hated Thatcherism – but at the same time possessed a dominant personality that demanded admiration and acquiescence. Events and circumstances combined with this strange and complex personality to make him the serial killer with possibly the highest number of victims in Britain.

Nilsen's sense of rejection began early. He was born on 23 November 1945 in Fraserburgh, Scotland, fathered by a Norwegian sailor who came to Scotland in 1940 when Norway was overrun by the Germans. His father was a hard drinker and, though his parents married, Dennis did not see much of him. The person who meant most to him in his early life was his grandfather, Andrew Whyte, with whom he and his mother, brother and sister lived. He was left there after his mother divorced and remarried – his first experience of rejection. In 1951 his grandfather died, and the six-year-old Dennis, without preparation, was invited to see the corpse. It was a shattering experience which shaped his life, and united images of love and death in his mind.

Nilsen rejoined his mother but left home as soon as possible and at the age of 15 joined the army catering corps, where he became a good-looking, amusing companion, albeit too retiring to make close friendships. He photographed his closest acquaintance feigning death in action. It was the first sign of fantasies about death, and also perhaps of a mental instability which had shown itself in his mother's forebears. He had a girlfriend for a while and thought about marriage, but was too shy to propose and broke off the relationship. He enjoyed his 11 years in army catering which, incidentally, gave him a skill in dissection which he was to use again.

Nilsen left the army because he didn't like the British treatment of the Irish and joined the police, where he saw plenty of dissected corpses, which fascinated him. He had homosexual tendencies which made it difficult for him to ignore the aggressive and routinely intolerant views of many officers on the subject, and he left after about a year. He subsequently joined the Department of Employment and worked at a Job Centre, where he met many young men living a lonely life. His fantasies about death had now reached the point where he would colour his lips blue, smother his body in talc to give it a white appearance and lie looking at himself in the mirror.

When Nilsen was 30 he met a much younger man, David Gallichan, and for two years they shared a garden flat at 195 Melrose Avenue, Cricklewood. They acquired a dog, Bleep, adopted a stray cat and led a happy and orderly life. It was not a sexual relationship, but Nilsen was devastated when, in 1977, Gallichan took a job in Devon and moved away. Nilsen once more felt rejected and began to spend much of his free time drinking.

On New Year's Eve 1978, Nilsen met an Irish teenager in a pub and took him home. They became insensibly drunk. In the morning Nilsen awoke first, and knew that when the youth awoke, he would become another of those who would leave him. Picking up his tie, he strangled him until he was practically dead, then finished him off by holding his head in a bucket of water. He than carried the body to the bathroom, washed it tenderly and thoroughly, dried it carefully and dressed it in

*Dennis Nilsen* (left)

fresh underclothes. He lived with the corpse for a week then placed it under the floorboards, where it stayed for an amazing eight months, with, according to Nilsen, very little decomposition. After that he took it down the garden and burned it, together with some rubber to disguise the smell.

Nilsen was amazed at getting away with murder and panic-stricken at the same time; he determined to reform and give up drinking. Yet just three months later he attempted a similar murder with a Chinese man named Andrew Ho, who managed to break free from the strangulation attempt and went to the police. Nilsen was again amazed that the police accepted his explanation that Ho's allegations were merely Ho's attempt to get even after they quarrelled.

A young Canadian, Kenneth Ockenden, was Nilsen's next victim, on 3 December 1979. Because he was expected home for Christmas and had disappeared suddenly from his hotel, Ockenden was the only one of Nilsen's victims for whom there was a well-publicized search. The details of the killing followed what became a pattern. After killing Ockenden Nilsen carefully washed the body, dressed it in fresh underwear and kept it for a couple of weeks, watching television in the evening with the body beside him on the bed. He undressed the body, wrapped it in curtains and placed it under the floorboards when the time came to sleep.

After a fortnight, Nilsen cut up the body and kept parts under the floorboards and parts in a wooden garden shed where he built a pile of bricks into a sort of tomb. He would daily spray inside the shed with disinfectant, and burn the fragments piecemeal.

Nilsen now killed more frequently. He usually met his victim in a pub, took him home where they both got drunk, then Nilsen would strangle him with one of his ties, wash and dress the body and finally chop it up for the shed and the fire. Between May 1980 and May 1981 there were nine more victims. The last at Melrose Avenue was an epileptic, Malcolm Barlow, whom Nilsen found sitting on the pavement near the house in September 1981, his legs having given way.

He took him in for coffee and called an ambulance for him. Next day, Barlow was waiting on the doorstep when Nilsen returned from work. Nilsen asked him in and strangled him, it being easier than calling an ambulance again. At the time, there were parts of six bodies already under the floorboards.

Soon afterwards Nilsen, a sitting tenant in the flat, was offered £1000 to move, and accepted. He had one final bonfire and, in October 1981, moved to an attic flat in 23 Cranley Gardens, Muswell Hill, another of London's more respectable districts. Some of the people who died at Melrose Avenue were never identified and had Nilsen died or changed his way of life, nobody would ever have known about the murders.

Nilsen did intend to reform: many stayed with him and lived, especially in his early days at Muswell Hill. The first murder there was in March 1982, when the victim, John Howlett, put up such a fight that he nearly overpowered his killer. Nilsen chopped up the body and boiled chunks of it in a big black pot. In May Carl Stotter did escape. He was to go to the police after Nilsen's arrest, as were two more men who had escaped Nilsen's murder attempts.

Late in 1982 Nilsen killed a man who fell asleep while eating an omelette. Parts of the body were boiled and stored while others were gradually flushed down the lavatory. The last victim was Stephen Sinclair, on 26 January 1983.

A week later the residents of 23 Cranley Gardens complained that the drains were blocked. On the evening of 8 February a plumber came to inspect. What he found 3.5 m (12 ft) down under the manhole cover outside seemed to him to be about 40 pieces of nauseating human flesh. He came back next morning with his boss, to find only some small pieces of flesh and bone. The police were called.

During the night Nilsen had played his last card, going down the manhole and removing the flesh. He had thought of covering it with chicken flesh, but could not buy enough. He went to work next day wearing the scarf of his last victim, Stephen Sinclair. As he left the office, where he was now supervisor, he told the staff that tomorrow he would be either dead or in prison. They thought it a strange joke. When he got home, the police were waiting to interview him.

The interview wasted little time on niceties. 'What has happened to the rest of the body?' asked the inspector. 'In there,' said Nilsen, pointing to the wardrobe. Inside were two bin liners containing human remains. In the car on the way to the station the inspector asked: 'Are we talking of one body or two?' 'Fifteen or 16 altogether,' replied Nilsen. This matter-of-factness contrasts with his concern for his faithful dog, which was put down a week after the arrest.

Nilsen made a detailed statement: he had an attentive captive audience at last. Later, in prison, he wrote a full and frank description of a murderer's feelings. At his trial the defence argued that the circumstances of his upbringing had left him with a severe personality disorder, but Nilsen himself insisted that he was sane and he was convicted by a majority of 10–2 of six murders. He was sentenced to life imprisonment on 4 November 1983.

# David and Catherine Birnie

DAVID BIRNIE was a slim, dark-haired weak-looking man with a strikingly long nose. He did not look the sort to frighten anybody, yet his slight frame contained an almost insatiable sexual appetite – sex six times a day was his ideal. This excessive libido, coupled with a wife who became thoroughly dependent upon him and was prepared to help him indulge his violent desires, led to five weeks of horror in 1986 which shook the people of Western Australia and which, but for the courage of a teenage girl, could have been even worse than it was.

Both David and Catherine Birnie had been deprived of normal family affection as adolescents. David was the eldest of five children. His parents' marriage broke up in 1961 when he was ten and the children were placed in institutions, whereupon he lost touch with both his mother and father. At 15 he worked in some horse-racing stables, but was sacked after approaching a young female colleague wearing nothing but a stocking over his head. He had known Catherine, who was the same age, as a child, and now they began a series of burglaries together which led to their being placed in juvenile detention.

Catherine's mother had died when she was young and she had been taken to South Africa by her father, who soon sent her back to Australia to live with her grandparents in Perth. It seems she rarely met other children and, after she had the unnerving experience of seeing her grandmother have an epileptic fit in the street, she was moved to an uncle and aunt in Lathlain. Here she met Birnie. By the age of 15 they were lovers and she was pregnant when they embarked on their burglaries.

After their release from detention they went their separate ways and each got married, Catherine settling down with the son of a family for whom she worked as a domestic help. Her life seemed to have turned out happily for her and as the years went by she had six children.

However, in 1983, Catherine met Birnie again and once more they became lovers. In February 1985 she left her family and went to live with Birnie in Willagee, Fremantle, where he worked in a car-wrecker's yard, and sold tyres from his home. They began to talk of kidnapping girls for Birnie to rape.

Their first crime was not planned, however. A 22-year-old psychology student, Mary Neilson, came to their bungalow on 6 October 1986 to buy tyres for her car. Birnie produced a knife and forced his visitor into the bedroom, where Catherine watched while he raped her. Afterwards they took her to the Glen Eagle National Park, where Birnie raped her again before strangling her with a nylon cord. Both of them then mutilated her body before burying it in a shallow grave. The Birnies were encouraged by the success of this episode to advertise in the local paper for a 'young person, preferably female, 18 to 24 years old, to share a single-bedroom flat', but it is not known if the ad brought any response.

Two weeks after the murder the Birnies gave a lift to a 15-year-old hitchhiker, Susannah Candy. She was taken to the bungalow and kept for several days, during which time Birnie raped her repeatedly. He forced her to write two letters to her parents in which she was made to say that she was safe and well but needed a few days to sort out some problems. It was Catherine who eventually strangled her, perhaps being jealous of the attention Birnie had been paying her. She too was buried in the Glen Eagle park.

A few days later the Birnies found their third victim – Noelene Patterson, a 31-year-old air hostess with whom they were already acquainted, having helped her decorate her home. Noelene's car ran out of petrol and the Birnies, who were passing, helped her push it to a service station.

They then forced her into their own car at knife-point and took her back to the bungalow in Willagee. She was kept there for three days, a slave to Birnie's desires, but again Catherine became jealous at the interest Birnie showed in his new plaything. She insisted Noelene be killed, and Birnie gave her a large number of sleeping pills and strangled her while she was unconscious. She, too, was taken and buried in the Glen Eagle park.

On 4 November, less than a month after their first victim had knocked on their door, the Birnies picked up another hitchhiker, 21-year-old Denise Brown. She was taken at knife-point to the house, chained to the bed and repeatedly raped by Birnie during the next two days. She was then taken to a plantation of pine trees near Wanneroo, and raped again before being killed. Birnie actually stabbed her while raping her and, failing to kill her at first, accepted a bigger knife from his wife. Even then the girl tried to get out of the grave they had dug, and Birnie was forced to kill her with an axe.

Only three days later, the Birnies dragged a 17-year-old girl into their car and took her to the bungalow. She was chained to the bed and raped twice by Birnie. While he was at work next day, however, Catherine made the mistake of leaving the room while the girl was unchained. The half-naked girl opened a window and escaped, burst into a supermarket and sobbed out her story. Police were soon at the house and the Birnies were arrested.

They soon confessed to the murders and showed the shocked police the graves. Catherine spat on the grave of Noelene Patterson, still unable to overcome her jealousy. Both pleaded guilty at the trial, Catherine admitting involvement in all the crimes – she had photographed the rapes and the corpses.

Birnie's young brother, who himself had been imprisoned for molesting his little niece, told the press that, after a temporary split between David and Catherine in 1984, he had given in to his brother's demands for sodomy. As a reward, a couple of months before the murders began, he was allowed sex with Catherine on his twenty-first birthday.

Clearly Catherine was dedicated to, and dominated by, David Birnie. They both received life sentences, and in David's case the judge said he should never be released.

# George Stephenson

IN 1987 George Stephenson was found guilty of murdering the Cleaver family in their home in Hampshire, England, where he had left them bound and helpless, then set fire to the house so that they would be burned alive. It was an act of 'indescribable brutality and cruelty' said the judge, Mr Justice Hobhouse, and he told Stephenson: 'You showed no mercy and deserve none.'

The bodies of 82-year-old Joseph Cleaver, his wife Hilda, who had been confined to a wheelchair for 14 years, and 70-year-old nurse Margaret Murphy had been found in the master bedroom, so badly burned that they had to be identified from dental records. Thomas Cleaver, aged 47, had managed to crawl out of the bedroom in search of air, but had been suffocated by smoke. His wife Wendy, age 46, had been beaten, raped and strangled: her body had been doused with petrol but remained unburned.

The story that unfolded in court was one of revenge and greed. Thirty-five-year-old Stephenson had been employed as a handyman at Burgate House, the Cleavers' imposing mansion in extensive grounds beside the River Avon, but had been sacked three weeks before the murders, so he decided to avenge himself. On 1 September 1986 Stephenson and two companions, George and John Daly, entered the house while the family were at the dining table. They always dined promptly at 8 pm and Stephenson knew that the front door was left open at this time, in case friends cared to drop in.

All three men carried pickaxes and they shepherded four members of the family into the main bedroom and tied them up before they dragged Wendy Cleaver into the next room, where she was raped by all three men and finally throttled. The intruders then searched for the safe but failed to find it and had to make do with cash and jewellery worth less than £100, as well as three shotguns and the family stock of liquor. Before they made off they set fire to the master bedroom, intending to burn down the house. However, the plan misfired; the house was so solidly built that the fire failed to penetrate much beyond the room itself and the murders were discovered when staff arrived next morning.

Stephenson was an immediate suspect and when his picture was shown on television he went to the police. At first his story was that he had told some bikers about the Cleavers and their money on the day of the murders, but forensic evidence was to link him to the scene. At the trial, Stephenson maintained that he had not realized that anyone had died until he saw the television broadcast: 'It was like a mirror; I was looking at myself. Up until that moment I hadn't any idea what had happened. I was expecting the police to contact me because I thought I would get pulled for a burglary.'

The three men pleaded not guilty, with John Daly withdrawing his alleged confession to the murder of Wendy Cleaver. They failed to convince the jury and Stephenson received four life sentences for murder – though he was found not guilty of killing Wendy Cleaver – and the judge recommended that he should serve at least 25 years. John Daly was sentenced to life imprisonment and George Daly to 22 years.

# Chapter Three

# FOR MATERIAL GAIN

# Introduction

GAIN is not a common motive among serial killers; most of those who commit murder over and over again enjoy the act itself or have some deep psychological need to kill. But when someone kills for financial advantage – to benefit from a will or from insurance policies or because they have already squeezed the victim dry and need to dispose of the evidence – the act of killing is no more than a necessary chore.

Outwardly such killers are often respectable members of the community, so they may remain undiscovered for a long period. Beneath the apparent normality, however, they are a special sort of people who rank human life as unimportant compared with gaining the money that will enable them to fulfil their desires. Once they have killed and got away with it, they see no reason why they should not repeat such a successful exercise.

One of the most repugnant aspects of murder for gain is that the murderers find their most profitable campaign plan is to prey on the vulnerable, winning the confidence of the lonely or desperate: Marcel Petiot convinced Jews in Nazi-occupied France that he was their passport to freedom only to kill them for their possessions, and Raymond Fernandez advertised in 'lonely hearts' columns, convincing women that they had at last found happiness when all that awaited them was certain death.

# George Joseph Smith

GEORGE JOSEPH SMITH seemed to have hit upon a foolproof way of making money – killing his wives and collecting the insurance. Unfortunately he was quite unable to show a little restraint: by bumping off one wife the day after the wedding he was clearly going to draw attention to himself.

Smith was born in Bethnal Green, London, in 1872 and spent his years between nine and 16 in a reform school, which signally failed to reform him because he became a small-time crook, always in and out of prison. His one asset was a capacity for charming women, which was partially derived from his hypnotic eyes. In 1898, as Oliver Love, he married 16-year-old Caroline Thornhill and put her to work as a servant in well-to-do houses so that she could steal. She was soon caught and imprisoned, whereupon he disappeared. However, she later met him by coincidence and denounced him; he served a prison sentence in his turn while she emigrated to Canada.

In 1908, under his real name, he bigamously married Edith Pegler, and remained true to her. He set her up in a home in Bristol, and always returned from his trips 'dealing in antiques' with money for her. Some of this money came from his marriage, as George Rose, to a Miss Faulkner in October 1909 in Southampton. He took his bride to the National Gallery, where he left her for a minute to go to the lavatory. She didn't see him again nor the £300 he took with him together with other possessions.

On 26 August 1910, Smith met and married 33-year-old Miss Bessie Mundy at Weymouth. He was Harry Williams at the time; she was an heiress worth £2500. Smith found that this money was too tied up for him to get it, so he took the £138 that was available and departed, leaving a note for the former Miss Mundy claiming that he had caught a social disease from her, and had to go away to recover. She herself went to live in Weston-super-Mare and, by coincidence, bumped into Smith one day on the front. Such was Smith's persuasive charm that she immediately agreed to live with him again.

In 1912, therefore, they went off to begin a new life at Herne Bay, although in Bessie's case it was not to be a long one. As soon as they arrived Smith bought a second-hand bath, knocking half-a-crown off the price by haggling. Then he and his wife made out wills in each other's favour. They then visited a Dr French about Bessie's 'fits' – although so far as she was concerned she had only a mild headache. The doctor was called twice more two days later, but Bessie seemed all right. Next day, however, the doctor was called to certify her death, as she had drowned in her bath. A policeman and a neighbour were there to aid the stricken husband and, 'drowning during an epileptic fit' was the verdict. The whole operation had taken a week. Smith collected over £2500 and he and Miss Pegler invested in a shop and other property. Smith, by the way, did not pay for the bath; he returned it as unwanted after all.

In November 1913 Smith used his real name again to marry Alice Burnham, a plump 25-year-old nurse, at Portsmouth. Her father (as did most men) took an instant dislike to Smith, which was enhanced when Smith demanded from him £104 that he was looking after for his daughter. Smith had to resort to a solicitor to get it, but he had insured Miss Burnham's life for £500. His treat for her was a trip to Blackpool.

One day the landlady, Mrs Crossley, ran a bath for the couple as they took a walk. The next thing she knew water was coming through the ceiling and Smith was knocking at the front door with some eggs he had just 'bought for breakfast'. Pointing to the water, Mrs Crossley urged him to hurry upstairs. He found Mrs Smith had died in her bath.

The landlady was not impressed by Mr Smith, who had happily played the piano while the inquest arrangements took place, and then treated his late wife to the very cheapest of funerals. When he left, she

*George Joseph Smith – the murder of Alice Burnham*

wrote in her card-index: 'Wife died in bath. We shall see him again.' The inquest verdict was accidental drowning.

A few months later Alice Reavil married Oliver James at Woolwich. She proved to be lucky. Smith left her in Brockwell Park six days later, taking £78 plus her furniture, including a piano, and those clothes she wasn't actually wearing.

Less than three months after this a clergyman's daughter, Margaret Lofty, married John Lloyd in Bath. Her life had already been insured for £700, and when the couple searched for lodgings in Highgate they had been particular in finding rooms with a bath. With those formalities out of the way Smith was able to take his new bride to the local doctor on her actual wedding day to seek advice about her 'fits'. Next morning they saw a solicitor about her will in his favour. That evening the new bride took a bath.

The landlady heard the splashing while, in the front room, the groom played the harmonium – the tune was the hymn 'Nearer My God to Thee'. Ten minutes later the husband was at the front door. He had 'slipped out for some tomatoes for tea' and forgotten his keys. The bride did not live to enjoy the tomatoes; alas, she was found drowned.

It was a week before Christmas. The inquest was begun but adjourned until 1 January 1915, and the conclusion was that the bride had fainted; giving rise to a verdict of accidental drowning. Unfortunately for Smith, the *News of the World* loved the story, and 'Bride's Tragic Fate on Day after Wedding' made the front page.

Alice Burnham's father and Mrs Crossley, the Blackpool landlady, both noticed that the details were exactly the same as the case of 13 months before. They wrote to the police, and it was not long before bodies were exhumed, other cheated women came forward, and Smith's history was pieced together. Smith was charged with three murders, but under the law could be tried for only one. The prosecution chose Bessie Mundy. Smith claimed accidental death, which allowed the prosecution to cite the other cases as evidence of 'system'. It was proved by experiment (an experiment which came uncomfortably close to the real thing) that it was simple for Smith to drown his brides by lifting their legs with one arm and holding down their heads with the other. The jury took 22 minutes to find him guilty.

Smith had shown a macabre sense of humour by playing 'Nearer My God to Thee' while his last wife took her bath. Another example came at his trial, when his Bristol 'wife' tearfully told how he had advised her not to buy a bath because it is well-known that 'women often lose their lives through weak hearts and fainting in a bath'.

The last laugh was on Smith, though. He was hanged on 13 August 1915 – a Friday. His only legal wife – the one who had emigrated to Canada – had turned up to give evidence at his trial and joyfully remarried the day after he died.

# Henri Landru

IT WAS World War I that enabled Henri Landru to launch upon a highly organized career deceiving women and relieving them of their wealth. In the case of at least 11 of them, he relieved them of their lives as well.

Landru was born in Paris on 12 April 1869. After a Roman Catholic education he became a sub-deacon of the church, and was conscripted into the army. In spite of his supposed piety he seduced Marie Catherine-Remy, a laundress and distant relation, and she had a daughter. Landru married her two years later and had three other children, supporting his family by working as a salesman and second-hand furniture dealer.

From 1904 he increased his profits with petty fraud and served two or three prison sentences before, in 1914, being sentenced in his absence to four years. The war began at the same time and the petty criminal was not pursued. Landru noticed another benefit of the war: the plenitude of young women suddenly detached from their menfolk. He exploited this situation to the hilt, both sexually and financially.

Landru used a time-honoured way to meet widows he wanted to free of their inhibitions and inheritances – the personal newspaper advertisement. Claiming under various names to be a widower in his forties, affectionate and with a comfortable income, he sought a widow with a view to matrimony. At least the age was accurate.

A Madame Celestine Buisson answered just such an advertisement from a Monsieur Fremyet. She was so overwhelmed by him that she sold her furniture, asked her sister, Mlle Lacoste, to look after her illegitimate son and, in August 1917, went to live with him in his villa at Gambais, 40 km (25 miles) outside Paris. In May 1918, not having heard from her sister since, Mlle Lacoste wrote to the mayor of Gambais asking if he could inform her of Mme Buisson's whereabouts.

It so happened that the mayor recalled a similar letter received some weeks previously from a Mme Pelat, asking the mayor to help her trace her sister, Mme Anna Colomb, who had gone to live in Gambais some time earlier with her fiancé, M. Dupont. The villa both correspondents described sounded like the Villa Ermitage, owned by M. Tric, who rented it to M. Dupont. The mayor strolled over. The place was empty, but a neighbour could describe M. Dupont. The mayor, intrigued by the coincidence, replied to Mlle Lacoste and advised her to talk to Mme Pelat, who had shared a similar experience. This letter proved to be a vital step in the apprehension of Landru. Mlle Lacoste did as suggested, and it was not long before the two women who had lost their sisters realized that Dupont and Fremyet were the same. After all, could there be two charmers with remarkable bald heads and pointed red Assyrian beards taking widows from Paris to Gambais? They went to the police.

The police were very interested. They were already looking into the disappearances of women who had answered 'lonely hearts' advertisements – including one Mme Jeanne Cuchet who, according to her relations, had gone to join her fiancé at a villa at Vernouillet, taking her 16-year-old son with her. Mme Cuchet's fiancé was called Raymond Diard, and since Vernouillet was the railway station for the village of Gambais, police assumed that Fremyet, Dupont and Diard were one and the same. The Villa Ermitage was searched, but nothing untoward was discovered.

There then occurred an amazing coincidence. On the very day that Mlle Lacoste had been interviewed by an Inspector Belin, she saw the suspect walk into a china shop in the rue de Rivoli, arm in arm with a young woman. She watched him order a tea service and leave his card and she tried to follow him home, but lost him after bumping into him in her eagerness to follow him on to a bus. She immediately rang Inspector Belin.

The inspector, fearing Mlle Lacoste might have been recognized by the man, began a hurried but lengthy process of finding the manager of the shop which was now closed for the day, then the relevant salesman, then returning to the shop for the card. It belonged to a Lucien Guillet, of 76 rue de Rochechouart. The inspector found Guillet had just left the flat with his friend, and had to wait four days before the couple returned and he was able to make an arrest.

While Belin searched the flat, his assistant, Inspector Riboulet waited with Guillet in the police car. He noticed Guillet trying to drop something out of the window, a black notebook. The book contained the names of 283 women, including those of Buisson and Colomb. Belin meanwhile found the name 'Landru' on an envelope in the flat, and the real identity and police record of the suspect were discovered.

Despite perfect circumstantial evidence in the form of articles and documents belonging to the missing women that were found in a garage rented by Landru, it was difficult to find any firm evidence of murder. Another thorough inspection of the Villa Ermitage found only a heavy-duty iron stove. Neighbours told stories of vile-smelling smoke occasionally coming from the house, about which they had complained, but no human remains were found.

Landru's meticulously kept notebooks and accounts enabled police to guess the whole story. There were letters from 169 of the 283 women named in the black book. Many of the women were traced and admitted they had succumbed to Landru's charms and had subsequently been swindled. Eleven women were listed together on one page of the black book and the police estimated that they had all died at Gambais. Part of the circumstantial evidence for this belief included accounts which showed the purchase of one return and one single ticket for their trips to Gambais.

Landru's activities were not solely aimed at financial gain – he also took great pride in his success with women, as was made evident during his appearances before magistrates over the next 2 years. His asides, his protestations of gallantry and the need to preserve a lady's

Henri Landru and his 'wives'

honour when refusing to detail his dealings with her, amused Paris, which gave him many names, of which Bluebeard became the most popular – Bluebeard being a figure in a fairy tale popular in France who kept the corpses of previous wives locked in a room as he kept marrying and adding to their number.

Landru's trial began in November 1921. His sole defence was that 11 women said to be dead were, so far as he knew, alive. 'Prove they are dead', was the gist of his argument. If the public was entertained by the confident show he put on, the judge was less captivated. At one point Landru asked a woman spectator looking for a seat if she would care to have his. The jury found him guilty, but they too proved sympathetic and pleaded that he be spared the death penalty. The judge ignored them and Landru faced the guillotine on 25 February 1922.

Throughout his philandering and swindling, Landru had supported his family. He publicly apologized to his wife for his 283 acts of infidelity. He also maintained a deep feeling for his latest companion, with whom we had bought the china – the beautiful Mlle Segret, who was 29 at the time of his arrest. She had broken off an engagement to a soldier to live with him and her love for him was not destroyed by the disclosure of the horrifying crimes he had committed. She left France on his execution but in 1965, soon after a film about him had been released, she reappeared and sued for libel at the representation of her. She had been working as a governess in the Lebanon but it had been assumed she was dead, and the judge awarded her only 10,000 francs. However, now that she was again in the public gaze, the 72-year-old woman found life intolerable and one day she threw herself into a moat and drowned.

In 1963, a framed drawing Landru made in his cell while awaiting execution was taken from the frame. A message found on the back, which read 'It happened in the house', has been regarded by some as a confession.

# Fritz Haarmann

IT WOULD be difficult to imagine more sickening crimes than those of Fritz Haarmann. Haarmann picked up young boys in the unsettled days after World War I and murdered them, according to him, by biting through their throats. He then cut up the bodies and sold the flesh on the black market as meat for human consumption. Eventually about one body a week was being sold.

Haarmann was born in Hanover on 25 October 1879. He was weakly and was sent to a military school to be toughened up, but was subsequently diagnosed as epileptic and released. He was then put into an asylum after being caught molesting children, but escaped. After that he drifted into crime and served periods in prison, where he spent the duration of the war. On his release he continued his small criminal activities – including selling meat, which was scarce, on the black market – and at the same time got on the right side of the police by becoming a paid informer.

Haarmann was homosexual and as Hanover became a centre of attraction for youths with no jobs or prospects and, because of the losses of the war, in many cases without even a father, Haarmann had an endless supply of boys to satisfy his desires. At the railway station he would always find a lost soul willing to accompany him to his basement room for warmth and a snack. Haarmann, with his police connection, even shrugged off being caught practising his sexual deviances – there were far too many other problems for the police in this shifting, desperate society.

It is not known when Haarman first began to kill the boys. Probably it was at first for the purpose of robbery. The murders accelerated in 1919 when he met a homosexual 20 years his junior who became both

125

a sexual and criminal partner. This man, Hans Grans, was elegant and witty and dominated Haarmann. They shared a flat, where Grans treated Haarmann as if he were a servant. Grans would sometimes select a victim because of some possession, such as a jacket, that he coveted.

Haarmann, for his part, was happy to take the risks of picking up the boys and, once the killing became a habit, realized that his butcher's trade was a good way to get rid of the bodies. He expertly filleted them, chopped them into choice cuts and threw the skulls and other bones into the River Leine. Haarmann developed a taste for his own product, which drove him on to acquire more, while, if his customers noticed the peculiar flavour of the meat – well, practically all the meat available at the time had something wrong with it. One woman was known to have taken meat bought from Haarmann to the authorities, where it was analysed by the police expert. She was told that it was as good a piece of pork as could be obtained in the city!

The end drew near for Haarmann in May 1924, when a human skull was fished out of the Leine. Soon there were three more, and a dredge of the river was organized which turned up some 500 human bones. On 22 June Haarmann was arrested for attempting to molest a boy named Fromm and, while he was in custody, police searched his flat. Items belonging to missing boys were found, plus human blood on the walls.

By now Haarmann had grown tired of his oppression by Grans and confessed, taking pleasure in implicating his partner. Haarmann's trial began on 4 December 1924. He was accused of 27 murders of boys and men whose ages ranged from 10 to 23, but most were between 16 and 18. The dates of the murders ranged from 12 February 1923 to 14 June 1924 – a week before Haarmann was arrested. Haarmann denied some of the murders, but admitted there must have been many more before February 1923 – he was prepared to admit to 40, and clearly couldn't remember them all.

Nearly 200 witnesses were called, most of them relatives identifying the belongings of victims. Haarmann was unrepentant, chatting to the judge, telling Grans to confess, and turning the 14 days into a vulgar show. He shouted at and argued with the witnesses, telling one boy's father that he would never have looked twice at such an ugly boy.

Haarmann could not face a return to an asylum – he demanded the death penalty and, on 20 December, was beheaded. Grans, who was certainly a partner in murder, if not in selling the flesh, received a life sentence and served 12 years.

# Henri Girard

HENRI GIRARD was a clever poisoner who, instead of employing the usual well-known deadly poisons, decided to dispose of his victims by giving them natural illnesses, such as typhoid fever. It was a hit-and-miss method as some recovered, and it turned out not to be as detection-proof as he had hoped.

Girard's father was a prosperous chemist in Alsace who, in the 1880s, moved his family to Paris in order to accept an appointment there. The teenaged Henri was enrolled at boarding school but, after being expelled from two establishments for theft, was sent to a reform school. At 18 he joined the army, where he again disappointed, losing his rank as an NCO. On his return to civilian life he indulged in an easy-come easy-go lifestyle of many mistresses and days spent at the races, which entailed first stealing from his father and then dabbling in wine-selling, bookmaking and selling insurance. He was what used to be called a rake, and was extremely popular.

After a fraudulent share-dealing scheme earned him a year in prison, he decided his business partner, one Pernotte, could be more useful to him dead than alive. So, in 1909, he insured Pernotte's life (without the knowledge of Pernotte's family) with two companies for several thousand francs. Pernotte, his wife and two sons soon developed typhoid fever. On feeling better they went away to convalesce, but M. Pernotte did not quite recover despite, or because of, an injection which Girard, who had convinced him of his medical knowledge, gave him.

Pernotte died, at which eyebrows were raised, but Girard nevertheless collected his money and continued his rake's progress. He was living at Montreuil-sous-Bois, just outside Paris, and one of his neighbours was a Monsieur Godet. At Girard's suggestion the two men took out a joint insurance policy, so that if one died the other would benefit. One day, after lunching with Girard, Godet was taken badly ill with typhoid fever. He eventually recovered, but decided not to see Girard again.

Girard was called up into the army when war broke out in 1914, and his raffish lifestyle made him as popular as ever. He continued to try to repeat his successful coup, and insured the life of a fellow soldier named Delmas, who also developed typhoid fever after lunching with Girard. Luckily for him, he had the resources of a military hospital to help him recover.

Girard now turned to another friend, a post-office employee named Duroux. Duroux was flattered by the attentions of his dashing, well-off new friend, and enjoyed a meal at his flat with no ill-effects, to the surprise of Girard, whose technique was clearly not yet perfect. However, two bouts of illness after eating in restaurants with Girard persuaded Duroux to give his friend a wide berth from then on.

Girard married, moved into Paris and for his next victim turned to Mme Monin, an ex-milliner who made hats for his wife, taking out four policies on her life. When she called one evening Mme Monin was given a glass of the wine Girard and his wife were enjoying before they went out. Mme Monin reached home only with the help of policemen and a taxi, for she collapsed in the Metro soon after leaving Girard's house. She died that evening. Girard collected on one policy immediately and on two more after some difficulty, but one company declined to pay. No poison was found in the body of Mme Monin, but Girard was detained while enquiries were made.

Girard's flat was found to contain extensive equipment for bacteriological research. There were also extensive notebooks, from which it was clear he was experimenting on ways of extracting poison from mushrooms and other fungi, and diaries with notes of the condition of his victims.

Police also obtained admissions from his wife that she had stood in for Mme Monin when the medical tests were made for the insurance policies on Mme Monin's life, and a statement from a former mistress of Girard's that the meal given Duroux was thought to be so lethal that she and Girard sent away the servant and washed up the dishes themselves, using large quantities of disinfectant.

Examinations of Girard pronounced him sane and he was committed to stand trial in October 1921, but he died in prison beforehand. He had been clever enough to make himself his last victim.

# Dr Morris Bolber

DR MORRIS BOLBER was not a *bona fide* medical practitioner but among the Italian community of Philadephia, USA, in the 1930s he made a comfortable living selling his useless potions. Especially popular with the local housewives was a draught made from ginger beer and saltpetre which was supposed to lessen their husband's sexual drive.

In 1932 he had an idea for increasing his income substantially when Mrs Giacobbe, the grocer's wife, confided in him that her marriage was miserable because her husband was always chasing other women. On the pretence of giving her his special urge-damping potion he supplied her with an aphrodisiac, with instructions to add it to her husband's food every day, with the object of making sure that she became even more disenchanted with her husband. He then arranged for an Italian tailor, Paul Petrillo, who had as few moral scruples as the 'doctor' himself, to seduce the unhappy Mrs Giacobbe.

Petrillo then began to work on his new mistress, convincing her that if only her husband was eliminated they could marry and live happily – especially if she had insured her husband's life for $10,000.

Mrs Giacobbe showed little reluctance. One winter night when her husband came home drunk and passed out on the bed she and Petrillo stripped him and left him lying under the open window so that he caught pneumonia. Even then he might have survived, had not Dr Bolber added a little poison to his medicine. After that, the widow Giacobbe was in no position to refuse when he demanded half of the insurance money.

Everything had gone according to plan and Bolber saw a rich future ahead. He recruited Petrillo's cousin Herman to the team, so that they could spread the net wider. It was Herman who became the lover of Mrs Lorenzo, whose husband was a building worker. Lorenzo was not insured, so Herman impersonated him, arranging a substantial policy. Herman then arranged a temporary job on the same building site as Lorenzo and waited for the right opportunity to push him off a roof.

The third victim was a fisherman named Fierenza and once again one of the Petrillos impersonated him for the benefit of the insurance agent, so that Fierenza himself had no idea that when he died he would be leaving his widow a good-sized nest-egg – to be shared with her evil partners in crime.

In 1933, with a number of murders already to his credit, Bolber joined forces with Carino Favato, known as the 'Philadephia witch', who was reputed to have poisoned three husbands and to be willing to dispose of any unwanted man for a small fee. She had plenty of useful contacts, thus enlarging Bolber's potential market, while he was able to introduce her to the benefits of insuring the victim first.

By then Bolber had decided that contriving so many 'accidents' was becoming too risky and he worked out a new way of killing off unwanted husbands so that their deaths appeared to be from natural causes. He used a canvas bag filled with sand, which would first knock the man out. More blows with the heavy bag would then induce a cerebral haemorrhage without leaving any sign of violence.

Over five years, Bolber and his associates killed some 30 people and enhanced their bank accounts considerably. They might have gone on in the same way indefinitely if Herman Petrillo had not bragged to an ex-convict friend that he had found a sure-fire way to make money: murdering for insurance. The ex-convict, Harrison, evinced great interest and tempted Petrillo into expanding on his methods. Harrison then went straight to the police and told all he knew.

The murderous gang was arrested and each member, anxious not to take the blame alone, was eager to talk about the part the others had played so the police soon built up a fat dossier of crimes. The wives who had been so willing to see their husbands killed were brought in for questioning; some were eventually tried and imprisoned but many were granted immunity in return for turning state's evidence. Doctors who had performed medical examinations for insurance policies identified Herman Petrillo as the man who had posed under various pseudonyms.

After a lengthy trial, Bolber and Favato received sentences of life imprisonment while both Petrillos were sentenced to death and executed in the electric chair.

# Marcel Petiot

DR MARCEL PETIOT was legally sane but, in the words of a psychiatrist, 'chronically unbalanced'. Extremely intelligent, he cared nothing for the views of others. Both his parents had died within eight years of his birth in Auxerre in January 1897 and he was brought up by aunts and uncles; he was clever at school but sadistically cruel to animals.

In World War I Petiot was wounded at the front and showed signs of mental disorder, eventually being discharged as unfit. However, he obtained a medical degree and set up in practice at Villeneuve, where he married a rich, good-looking woman and was elected mayor. He was subsequently given a suspended sentence when irregularities in council funds came to light, and people recalled earlier allegations of theft and, more seriously, his being questioned in an unsolved murder and arson case, and the disappearance of his housekeeper and mistress, who had become pregnant.

In 1933 the family moved to Paris, and it was discovered that the house they had lived in had been wired to the local mains to give him free electricity. Allegations concerning the supplying of drugs and the carrying out of abortions began to surface. In Paris Petiot built up a big practice in the rue Caumartin with false credentials, and was then charged with assault on a store detective who had caught him stealing books. He pleaded insanity, making use of his army discharge record as he had done before, and was found not guilty, but then voluntarily spent seven months in a mental institution. He nevertheless was able to accumulate several properties in Paris (partly by means of cheating the tax authorities) and then embarked on profiting from the desperate circumstances of the German occupation of France in the early 1940s.

Under the guise of working for the Resistance, Petiot let it be known that he could help those in danger from the Nazis, such as Jews and patriots, to escape to Spain. He had suppliers and helpers, who included Raoul Fourrier, a barber, René Nézoudet, an old friend, and Maurice, his younger brother. Petiot, masquerading as 'Dr Eugene', quoted a cheap rate but, in addition to this, his customers had to bring enough jewellery, cash and so on for the journey and to establish themselves in a new place. Of course, the strictest secrecy had to be kept.

Petiot used one of his properties for the operation: 21 rue le Sueur, off the Bois de Boulogne. One day a neighbour was annoyed by the vile black smoke and smuts which were coming from the chimney and investigated. There was a note pinned to the door: 'Away for a month, send mail to 18 rue des Lombards, Auxerre'. The police were called, and obtained from the concierge the Paris phone number of the owner, Dr Petiot. He was contacted and said he would come round. When he didn't turn up the fire brigade were called to break in – and what they and the police found inside shocked even wartime Paris.

The fire was coming from a stove in the basement. All around it were skulls, bones, mounds of rotting flesh. The place was a factory to get rid of bodies. One of the policemen went outside, pale, to phone for senior officers and met Petiot arriving by bicycle. Petiot told him

133

that the place belonged to the Resistance, that the bodies were of Germans and traitors, and that he must hurry away to destroy files which mustn't reach the hands of the Germans. He was allowed to go and vanished.

In the outbuildings behind the main entrance was the doctor's 'consulting room' and, separated from it by a narrow corridor, was a triangular room, the death chamber. It was later deduced that Petiot drugged his clients (possibly with an injection 'necessary for the journey') and took them through a soundproof door to the triangular waiting room, which had another reassuring set of doors and a push-button summons in the opposite wall. These, however, were false. There was a row of iron rings set into one wall so that Petiot could chain up his victims, and a spyhole through which, from the outside, Petiot could watch his victims die, presumably either from gas or poison. Further search of the premises revealed two lime pits in which numerous other bodies were decomposing.

Petiot's wife and brother were arrested. It was the latter's address that had been pinned to the door, and his role emerged under interrogation; he had supplied the quicklime in which the bodies were disposed of. In May 1943 Petiot had been arrested by the Gestapo and his brother, visiting the premises in his absence, had discovered the nature and size of the operation and refused to deliver any more quicklime. Petiot, on his release in January 1944, was forced instead to use the stove which had caused his discovery. (Petiot had apparently been very brave in the hands of the Gestapo, who were trying to discover the 'escape-route' that had come to their notice; it is not known how much they knew of Petiot's activity, but of course had they discovered he was murdering would-be escapees they would have considered him on their side.) A neighbour's story of suitcases being removed from 21 rue le Sueur led police, through Petiot's brother, to another friend whose attic contained 45 suitcases full of clothing belonging to Petiot's victims.

In the chaotic days after the liberation of Paris in August 1944

*Luggage belonging to the victims of Dr Petiot*

Petiot, thickly bearded and calling himself Henri Valeri, joined the Resistance and helped round up collaborators, but was recognized on 31 October by colleagues and handed to the police. His trial began on 18 March 1946. He was brave, clever, witty and brilliantly defended. He claimed to be a genuine Resistance hero, that he had indeed killed a number of people but they were all Germans or collaborators spying for the Germans. He claimed that the Gestapo, after his arrest, went to No. 21 and discovered his activities. They released him, he said, after filling the house with corpses themselves. Because there were collaborators in the police, he was forced to get rid of the corpses. It was a story that in the unreal atmosphere of occupied Paris seemed plausible to some and, in 1963, a book published by a man who was a British agent in Paris at the time argued that Petiot was indeed in the Resistance.

The jury didn't believe Petiot and, on 4 April, he was found guilty of 25 of the 27 murders he was charged with. On 25 May 1946 the blade of the guillotine fell on his neck.

# John Haigh

WAS John George Haigh a common con man with an exaggerated idea of his own learning and cleverness, or was he a badly disturbed man who enjoyed drinking blood? Stories of vampirism kept Britain fascinated in 1949 when Haigh was arrested and charged with murder.

The story centred round the Onslow Court Hotel in London's fashionable South Kensington. Haigh, a dapper man with a neat moustache, charming smile and immaculate hair, who wore smart clothes and highly polished shoes, had been staying in Room 404 for two years. A wealthy widow, 69-year-old Mrs Olive Durand-Deacon, whose husband had been a colonel in the Gloucestershire Regiment, had lived in Room 115 for seven years. They dined at neighbouring tables.

On 14 February 1949 the courtly John Haigh, then 39, invited Mrs Durand-Deacon to visit his factory in Crawley, Sussex. She had expressed interest in manufacturing artificial fingernails, and Haigh said he could help her. In fact Haigh merely rented occasional use of a glorified storeroom, which Mrs Durand-Deacon was to discover when Haigh drove her there in his racy Alvis on the following Friday, picking her up not from the hotel but at the Army and Navy Stores in Victoria.

On arrival Haigh produced a revolver and shot his guest expertly through the neck. He then poked her 89 kg (14 stone) body into a 205 litre (45 gallon) drum, stood the drum up with difficulty, then strolled round to Ye Olde Ancient Priors' Restaurant for poached egg on toast and tea. After his repast he returned to the storeroom and, wearing a rubber apron, gloves and a gas mask and using a stirrup pump, filled the drum with sulphuric acid before driving back to London, leaving the acid to do its work over the weekend.

On Saturday he discovered, to his temporary discomfort, that Mrs Durand-Deacon had mentioned her proposed trip with him to a friend at the hotel, Mrs Constance Lane, so his avoidance of being seen driving off with the wealthy widow had been in vain. He had to tell Mrs Lane that Mrs Durand-Deacon had not kept the appointment and quickly sold his victim's watch and jewellery. By Sunday, Mrs Lane was talking about reporting her friend's disappearance to the police. Haigh drove her round to the station, pointing out that his story would be of use to them. The affable and helpful Haigh impressed the police with his concern.

However, as enquiries gently meandered on, Sergeant Alexandra Lambourne had an uneasy feeling about the too-smart, too-charming Haigh and voiced it to her superiors. Instead of rebuffing her, they investigated his background and found convictions and imprisonments for fraud and theft. They decided to inspect the premises at Crawley. Haigh had already emptied the drum on the Sunday after the murder, but in a hatbox they found various ration books, passports, diaries, a revolver and some bullets. There was also a dry-cleaning ticket which proved to be for Mrs Durand-Deacon's fur coat. Soon Mrs Durand-Deacon's jewellery turned up at a dealers and later that day Haigh was invited to return to the police station.

Haigh was inventing a story to explain the finds when the senior detectives were called from the room. Alone with an Inspector Webb, Haigh suddenly asked: 'What are the chances of anyone being released from Broadmoor?' He had decided that he would plead insanity and get sent to the institution for the criminally insane.

Haigh, who knew but misunderstood the phrase 'corpus delicti', thinking it meant there had to be a body before murder could be proved, told the officer that Mrs Durand-Deacon no longer existed. He said she was sludge at the Crawley works. Haigh then gave the astonished officers a long matter-of-fact statement, in which he told what

*John Haigh arriving at court*

had happened to Mrs Durand-Deacon, with the additional detail that, after killing her, he had made a careful incision in her neck, drawn off a glassful of blood, and drunk it. He then went on to explain his possession of ration books and documents in the names of McSwan and Henderson.

Donald McSwan was the son of a man who had employed Haigh as an amusement arcade manager in the 1930s. In September 1944, after they had renewed acquaintance, Haigh took him to his basement flat in Gloucester Road, near the Onslow Court Hotel, killed him and disposed of him in acid, as with Mrs Durand-Deacon. A year later he did the same, separately, with McSwan's parents, Donald and Amy. He forged signatures to gain power of attorney over the family's affairs, and sold their property for his own profit. Exactly three years later, in September 1947, he answered an estate agent's advertisement and made an offer for the house of a Dr Archibald and Rosalie Henderson. The deal did not come off, but he started a friendship with the couple and, in February 1948, he killed them and dissolved their bodies in acid at the Crawley workshop. By clever forgery he again allayed suspicion and realized their property assets. In the case of all five murders, said Haigh, he had drunk his glassful of warm blood immediately after the killings.

The police went back to the Crawley workshop. Sunk into about 2 sq m (20 sq ft) of garden was a greasy sludge, about 7.5 cm (3 inches) deep. Professor Simpson, the police pathologist, discovered among it three gallstones and plastic items which the acid had not dissolved. Among these were the strap of Mrs Durand-Deacon's red plastic handbag, and, vitally, her false teeth, which could be positively identified by her dentist.

The game was up for Haigh, but his stories of vampirism had reached the newspapers and caused a sensation. By linking pictures of his arrest with a story of the murders of the McSwans and the drinking of blood, the *Daily Mirror* was fined for contempt of court and its editor went to prison. Haigh was sure that he would be declared insane, and the life story he told was to reinforce the idea of his madness. His parents were Plymouth Brethren, and he was brought up in a house enclosed by high walls, where newspapers, radio and friends of his own age were not allowed. His father had a blue scar on his forehead as a result of being hit by a chip of coal in the colliery where he was foreman, and told Haigh that this was the mark of Satan; his mother, to whom Haigh was devoted, was said to be an angel, with real wings.

In spite of his odd childhood he won a choral scholarship to Wakefield Grammar School and sang in the choir at Wakefield Cathedral. After school, he found work tiresome. At 25 he married a waitress who was also a photographer's model, but when four months later he was imprisoned for fraud, he was never to see her again. When he came out of prison, he lived by fraud and theft. In 1944, the year he set up his own engineering company, he had a car accident in which he had swallowed some of his own blood. This had revived schoolboy dreams of crucifixes which dripped blood and awakened his lust for blood to drink.

While in prison Haigh was observed drinking his own urine, but only one of the medical experts who examined him believed him to be insane – the others concluded it was all an act. He was tried at Lewes in July 1949 and the jury found him guilty after only 15 minutes' retirement. He was hanged on 10 August 1949, 17 days after his fortieth birthday. Four years later his trial judge, Sir Travers Humphreys, retired – and went to live at the ill-fated Onslow Court Hotel.

# Raymond Fernandez
# and Martha Beck

RAYMOND FERNANDEZ had been earning his living by fleecing women who answered 'lonely hearts' advertisements when he met Martha Beck through a contact sheet provided by Mother Dinene's Friendly Club. When he arranged to meet her he hoped to add her to his list of victims but it was soon obvious that, as a divorcee with two children, she had no money to give him. However, he felt able to explain his line of business to her, whereupon she offered to become his accomplice. With her assistance his confidence tricks became more lucrative – and more deadly.

Fernandez and Beck were both social misfits and as soon as they met, like called to like. Fernandez, the son of Spanish parents, served in Franco's forces during the Civil War and earned a reputation as a hero. In 1945 he left his Spanish wife behind and sailed for America on an oil tanker. During the voyage a hatch cover fell on his head, putting him in hospital for 10 weeks and leaving him with scarred brain tissue. After that it seemed that his personality changed; he became ruthless and cunning and believed that he had psychic powers, so that he could make any woman do his bidding.

He certainly had little difficulty in convincing scores of women that he was the man they had been waiting for all their lives and charming their money out of their bank accounts into his. He had already deceived some 100 women when he took a middle-aged teacher, Mrs Jane Thompson, on holiday to Spain. The couple travelled as man and wife but after a fierce quarrel Mrs Thompson was found dead in their hotel room. Her death was ascribed to gastro-enteritis but later doubts were raised when it was found that her 'husband' had bought the drug digitalis from the chemist's two days earlier. By this time Fernandez was already back in the USA, showing Mrs Thompson's elderly mother a forged will that showed that the apartment in which she had lived with her daughter now belonged to him.

It was soon after this that Fernandez met 26-year-old Martha Beck. On her application form for the Friendly Club she claimed that she was 'witty, vivacious and oozed personality'. She was also a woman whose outsize bulk and voracious sexual appetite frequently made her a figure of fun. Physically, she had matured early and at the age of 13 had been raped by her brother. She trained as a nurse and by the time she met Fernandez she was superintendent of the Pensacola Crippled Children's Home. Incurably romantic, she was looking for her ideal man and she immediately fell head over heels in love with Fernandez. He was less willing to commit himself but he found her an exciting bedmate, joining with enthusiasm in any and every perversion they could devise.

Together, they looked for likely victims but their first joint venture was a failure. In February 1948 Fernandez married a retired teacher, Mrs Esther Henne – though the marriage was, of course, bigamous – and took her to his New York apartment, where she was introduced to his 'sister', Martha. Esther became uneasy when he pressed her to sign over her pension and insurance policies to him and, when she heard rumours about the untimely death of Mrs Thompson, she decided to go home to Pennsylvania. She took legal action to recover $500 she had already given to Fernandez.

Martha's presence was useful in reassuring women that Fernandez's intentions were honourable but she loved him too much to allow him a free hand. She was happy to see him woo and wed women but did all she could to prevent him from consummating the marriage. In Cook County, Illinois, Fernandez married Myrtle Young from Arkansas. He managed to persuade her to part with $4000 but she became angry when she found herself sharing a bed with Martha rather than with her husband, supposedly because of his shyness. She laid down an ultimatum: either Martha left or she did. Martha fed her a dose of barbiturates and while she was still reeling from the drugs the couple put her on a bus to Arkansas. She collapsed on the journey and died soon afterwards.

Fernandez had corresponded for some time with a 66-year-old widow, Janet Fay, who was delighted with his sensitivity and sympathy with her religious views. She went to stay with Fernandez and Beck in an apartment they had rented on Long Island. Trustingly she made over a sum of $7000 to Fernandez, as well as signing over her insurance policies. Then she had a row with Martha, who hit her over the head with a hammer. Fernandez panicked but Martha stayed cool and after she had cleaned up the blood they stuffed the body into a trunk, which they buried under a layer of concrete in the basement.

In February 1948 the couple were staying with a young widow, Delphine Downing, and her three-year-old daughter Rainelle in Grand Rapids, Michigan. Fernandez had corresponded with her under the name of Charles Martin, describing himself as: '38 years old, brown eyes, dark hair, weight 165 lbs, height 5 ft 8 inches. Never married. Perfect health. Am considered fair looking and kind.' When she met Fernandez, Delphine fell under his spell, as so many women had before her, but she delayed any plans for marriage until she was certain of his affections and once more Martha was consumed by jealous rage as Fernandez seduced his latest victim.

It was never certain how Delphine Downing met her death but it seems likely that she decided against marriage after all, whereupon Martha added barbiturates to her food and, once she was drugged, Fernandez shot her. Afterwards little Rainelle cried so much that Martha drowned her in the bath. Both bodies were cemented into the cellar floor and neighbours were told that Delphine had taken her daughter away on holiday. The neighbours remained uneasy and the police were notified. When they arrived Fernandez and Beck welcomed them in but their smiles faded when detectives discovered a

*Raymond Fernandez and Martha Beck*

newly laid patch of cement and unearthed the bodies of Delphine and her daughter.

The state of Michigan, where the pair were arrested, did not operate the death penalty but New York did, and the murder of Janet Fay had been committed there. Public feeling against the callous 'Lonely Hearts Killers' contributed to the decision to hold the trial in New York. The decision filled Martha with fear but surprisingly Fernandez, who had always been the weaker of the two, said: 'They ought to kill me. I've done a terrible thing and I'm not afraid of the chair.'

Though they were suspected of no less than 20 murders, they confessed to only three – of Janet Fay, Delphine and Rainelle Downing – and pleaded not guilty by reason of insanity. Martha's disastrous childhood was detailed and Fernandez's head injury was blamed for his irrational state of mind. Press coverage was harsh and intolerant and evidence about their torrid sex lives ensured that the case stayed in the headlines. There was never any doubt about the verdict and they were both found guilty of first-degree murder and sentenced to death.

While waiting on Death Row, Martha's only concern was whether her beloved Fernandez still loved her. A few hours before the time set for execution, he sent her a note saying: 'I would like to shout my love for you to the world.' Martha told the wardress: 'Now I know that Raymond loves me, I can go to my death bursting with joy.' In her last statement from prison she once again stressed her deep feelings for him: 'My story is a love story, but only those tortured with love can understand what I mean . . . in the history of the world, how many crimes have been attributed to love?'

The Lonely Hearts Killers went to the electric chair at Sing Sing on 8 March 1951 and newspapers gleefully reported the struggle by prison staff to fit Martha's huge bulk into the electric chair. So strong was public feeling against her that few people reading the account of her undignified last moments had any sympathy to spare for the 'overweight ogress'.

# Perry Smith and Richard Hickock

RICHARD HICKOCK heard about the wealthy Clutter family when he was serving time in Kansas State Penitentiary, USA. His cell-mate Floyd Welles had worked on Herb Clutter's farm and reckoned that his employer normally kept $10,000 in his safe. Hickock questioned Welles closely about the household and discovered that 48-year-old Clutter was a prosperous wheat farmer, a well-known and respected member of the community, who lived with his nervous, highly-strung wife Bonnie and two of his children, 16-year-old Nancy and 15-year-old Kenyon. As he served his sentence, Hickock had plenty of time to plot how to turn the information to his advantage.

On the night of 15 November 1959 Hickock and his accomplice Perry Smith followed Welles' directions to the Clutter farm at Holcomb, Kansas, where four members of the family lay sleeping. Herb Clutter heard the intruders and came downstairs to be faced with two armed men demanding the money from his safe. Mildly and politely, he pointed out that he had no safe but Smith and Hickock dragged him from room to room as they searched.

Then they went upstairs, ignoring Clutter's plea not to disturb his invalid wife, and herded the four members of the family into the bathroom. Except for Kenyon, all were in their nightclothes; he had hurriedly dressed in jeans and T-shirt, though his feet were bare. The robbers decided that it would be safest to leave each of the Clutters in a separate room while they searched further. First they trussed up Herb Clutter and left him lying face down on a cardboard box in the boiler room, then Kenyon was bound and left in the downstairs recreation room. The two women were tied up and left lying on their beds.

The robbers' search was fruitless and by the time they realized

*The Clutter family. The picture shows (clockwise) Mr Herb Clutter, teenagers Kenyon and Nancy, and Mrs Bonnie Clutter*

there was no $10,000, both men were angry and frustrated. They went into a huddle and decided that leaving the Clutters alive to identify them was just too risky. The killing began with Herb Clutter: Smith stabbed him in the throat then, when he did not die quickly enough, shot him in the head. His wife, son and daughter were all shot as they lay helpless. Only Nancy, whose mouth had not been taped, was able to plead for her life, but in vain. The robbers made off with $50 and Kenyon's radio.

Once news of the murders broke, Floyd Welles told police what he knew and the police hunt for the fugitives was on. Some six weeks later, Smith and Hickock were apprehended driving a stolen car in Las Vegas. 'Perry Smith killed the Clutters and I couldn't stop him,' said Hickock. 'He killed them all.' Though Smith at first maintained that Hickock had killed the two women, he later confessed that he had acted as executioner. He said of Clutter: 'He was a nice gentleman . . . I thought so right up to the moment I cut his throat.'

The prosecutor at their trial exhorted the jury not to be 'chicken-livered' about bringing in a guilty verdict. After they had found both men guilty on each of the four counts of murder and sentence of death had been passed, Smith said to Hickock, 'No chicken-livered jurors they', and both men laughed heartily.

It took almost five years for the two killers to exhaust the legal appeals procedure but both were finally hanged on 14 April 1965.

# Captain Julian Harvey

MURDER for gain is an unforgivable crime, the more so when, for example, a bomb is placed on a plane or a train is derailed in an attempt to kill one person, with no concern for the deaths of all the other victims unknown to the murderer.

The person who commits this crime is more properly a mass murderer than a serial killer. Captain Julian Harvey was one such, but it was suspected after his death that it was not his first exercise in sacrificing others for his main purpose, so he could be called a possible serial killer too. It was the emphatic and unexpected way in which he was exposed that makes his case interesting.

Julian Harvey was born in 1916, and, after a career as an officer in the US Air Force, during which he reached the rank of lieutenant-colonel, he began operating a ketch, the *Bluebelle*. On 8 November 1961 he set sail from Fort Lauderdale, Florida, with his wife Mary and the Dupperault family, consisting of Mr Arthur Dupperault, his wife, and three children: 14-year-old Brian, 11-year-old daughter Terry Jo and seven-year-old Renee.

Five days later Captain Harvey was found adrift in a dinghy, which also contained the drowned body of little Renee. He said that the *Bluebelle* had caught fire and blown up the day before, when they were some 80 km (50 miles) from Nassau. The flames had been so fierce that he had been unable to reach his wife or any of the other passengers before he had had to leave the boat. He had fished Renee's body from the sea, but everybody else had disappeared. There was no hope for them.

Although Captain Harvey had shortly before taken out a double-indemnity policy on his 34-year-old wife, nobody considered that the

*Terry Jo rescued from her raft after her three-day ordeal at sea.*

case could be other than a tragic accident at sea. Harvey was attending a coastguard hearing four days later when amazing news reached the inquiry – one of the passengers, 11-year-old Terry Jo, had been rescued from a cork raft.

Terry Jo's story was quite different from Captain Harvey's. She had seen Harvey slaughter her parents, her brother and his own wife. She had seen the bodies of her mother and brother, she said, covered all over with blood. She had been on deck when Harvey opened the vessel's sea-cocks to allow the ketch to sink, but had managed to get away on the raft before the ship had gone down.

On learning of the girl's rescue, Harvey did not wait to hear the story she told. He left the hearing shaking his head, went back to his Miami motel room and wrote a suicide note before slashing his wrists with a razor blade. He was buried at sea.

It was discovered afterwards that Harvey's first wife had also died violently and not alone. In 1945 Harvey had been driving a car containing his wife Joan and also her mother, Mrs Myrtle Boylen, over a river bridge in Florida when it crashed through a railing into the water. He told the investigators that he had been thrown clear, but that the two women had been drowned in the car. Could Captain Julian Harvey have twice killed other people in order to cover up the murder of his wives?

# Roy Fontaine

ROY FONTAINE was a con man and jewel thief who pulled off some brilliant coups yet always got caught sooner or later. He became a serial killer late in life, more or less by accident.

He was born Archibald Hall in Glasgow in 1924. When he was 16, he was seduced by a woman 24 years his senior. She took him to expensive hotels, and he developed a liking for elegant living. His criminal life probably began with cheating while collecting for the Red Cross; he was imprisoned at 17 for theft, and a year later for housebreaking. Classed as mentally unstable, he was twice sent to mental hospitals, from where he escaped for the 28 days which, under Scottish law, established him as capable of looking after himself. However, in 1944 he was certified insane after more housebreaking and detained indefinitely. He was released in 1946, only to be given a two-year gaol sentence for forgery and housebreaking, after asking for 51 other offences to be taken into account.

In 1951 he obtained his first job as a butler, a calling he was to find a lucrative one for his criminal activities. Among his successful impersonations were a stand-in for his unknowing employer at a royal garden party, a rich Arab in full dress to con jewellers and a wealthy American, which last led to a civic reception as guest of the Lord Mayor of Torquay. However, he was sentenced to 30 years in 1956 for a string of offences. Released on parole in 1963, he was hardly out before being sentenced to ten years in 1964. He escaped daringly but was caught after two years and had five years added to the original ten. Paroled in 1973, he married in September but, a year later, was imprisoned again until 1977.

So Roy Fontaine, as he preferred to be known (Joan Fontaine was his favourite film star), had spent most of his life in prison when his brilliantly forged references won him a job as butler to Lady Peggy Hudson at Kirtleton Hall, just over the border in Scotland. On his recommendation a new gardener, David Wright, started work there six weeks later. Wright had had a homosexual relationship with Fontaine in prison and had plans to blackmail him but, in September 1977, suggested instead that the two of them rob Lady Hudson. Fontaine rejected the idea, having bigger plans, but while Lady Hudson was away Wright stole an expensive ring. Fontaine traced it to Wright's girlfriend and retrieved it, but that night Fontaine was woken by a rifle shot fired into the headboard of his bed by a drunken Wright. Next day, when the two went shooting rabbits, Fontaine waited until Wright's gun was empty and then shot him, burying him in the bed of a stream and covering him with pebbles. During the rest of his time in the employ of Lady Hudson, who was told Wright had taken a job elsewhere, Fontaine built more and more stones over the grave. But this lasted only a week before Lady Hudson received an anonymous letter exposing him, and sacked him.

Fontaine took a cottage at Newton Arlosh, near Carlisle, and, in November 1977, secured a post as butler with Walter Scott-Elliott and his wife in Sloane Street, Chelsea. Scott-Elliott was 82, a charming man but often vague because of the drugs he was forced to take. Soon the Scott-Elliotts trusted Fontaine enough to give him blank signed cheques to pay the bills. They were so rich that, while taking advantage of this, Fontaine wanted more from them. He had met an old friend, Mary Coggle, an Irish mother of nine from two failed marriages, who was living partly as a forger of credit cards at Kings Cross. With her and one of her friends, petty thief Michael Kitto, Fontaine planned to defraud his employers.

Fontaine took Kitto to the house at 10.30 pm on 8 December 1977 when he thought Mrs Scott-Elliott was staying in a nursing home for a few days, but she returned early and surprised them in her bedroom. Fontaine, in panic, knocked her down and they had to suffocate her to stop her screaming. Mr Scott-Elliott, who woke, was told his wife had had a nightmare and meekly went back to bed. The following day Fontaine and Kitto put Mrs Scott-Elliott's body and many valuable antiques in the boot of a hired car and took it to Fontaine's cottage near Carlisle. Kitto was 'chauffeur', Fontaine was in the passenger seat, and Mary Coggle with wig and the deceased's fur coat was in the back with Scott-Elliott, impersonating his wife and keeping him well supplied with pills. Next day they drove into Scotland, buying a spade on the journey, and near the village of Braco they buried Mrs Scott-Elliott in a ditch behind a stone wall skirting the road.

For the next couple of days they stayed in Fontaine's cottage and planned their tactics. After persuading Scott-Elliott to sign three blank cheques, they decided he must be killed. On 13 December they drove back into Scotland and, after 322 km (200 miles), stayed the night at the Tilt Hotel, Blair Athol. Next day they drove on, with Scott-Elliott thanking the manager for a 'nice stay'. At Glen Afric, when Scott-Elliott wished to leave the car to relieve himself, Kitto and Fontaine killed him and buried the body in some bushes. On the way back to the cottage they stayed the night in Aviemore, and in Perth and Edinburgh they sold antiques. Trouble arose when Mary Coggle refused to give up the mink coat, which Fontaine considered too dangerous to keep. She invited him to make love to her on it in an attempt to soften him into letting her keep it but, although he accepted, it didn't work. In the course of a row Fontaine struck her repeatedly with a poker, and the two men finished her off by suffocation. Dressing the body in shirt and trousers, they drove next just over the border to Middlebie and dumped it in a stream. They were getting less careful. In the next fortnight they returned to the Scott-Elliotts' house and removed their remaining valuables for disposal, sending notes to friends of the Scott-Elliotts to postpone suspicion.

On 13 January 1978 Fontaine's brother Donald Hall, 17 years younger, was released from a prison in Cumbria after a three-year sentence. The two went to meet him and took him to the cottage at

Newton Arlosh. Fontaine was not keen on his brother, whom he considered a cheap and uncouth criminal, and took exception to Hall's curiosity about Fontaine's new wealth. They argued and, on 15 January, Kitto helped Fontaine kill his brother with chloroform. Next day, in a hired car on which they had changed the number plates, they returned again to Scotland, this time with Hall's body in the boot. They stopped for the night at the Blenheim House Hotel in North Berwick.

The body of Mary Coggle had been found on Christmas Day and the hotelier, John Wight, was suspicious of the two men travelling light in the snow. While they ate he rang the police, who ran a check on the car number plate and found it false. They arrived at the hotel as Fontaine and Kitto were enjoying their brandies, and took them and the car to the station for questioning.

Fontaine escaped from the police station by climbing through a lavatory window, but having found a taxi he asked to be driven from hospital to hospital, saying he was looking for his wife, who had had an accident. Inevitably, at a road block he was captured and returned to the station. It could hardly have been a serious escape bid.

At the station Fontaine was told of the discovery of the body in the boot. Asking for a glass of water, he took some pills which he had concealed in his rectum, but the suicide attempt was foiled with a stomach pump after a dash to Edinburgh Royal Infirmary. Kitto cracked and began to confess. Fontaine followed suit, and the bodies were gradually found, including that of David Wright. Two days after his first attempt, Fontaine tried suicide again but was saved as before.

Fontaine and Kitto were tried twice, in both England and Scotland, for the murders committed in the respective countries. Both men were sentenced to life imprisonment, in Fontaine's case without the possibility of parole, in Kitto's case with a minimum of 15 years to be served.

# Chapter Four

# GANGSTERS

# Introduction

GANGSTERS can be among the most callous and matter-of-fact killers. In the gang wars of American Prohibition, taking an enemy 'for a one-way ride' or giving him 'a concrete overcoat', the better for his body to sink, was business – no personal animosity was necessarily felt. In fact the man to be bumped off was often an erstwhile colleague, who had just happened to back the wrong gang-boss.

The gangsters in this section are not like the serial killers in other sections, although some of them undoubtedly got a taste for killing for its own sake. Bonnie and Clyde liked the thrill and Al Capone killed for personal satisfaction when he had hundreds of employees who would do it for him. The members of Murder Inc. took a professional pride in their executions and treated murder as just another job.

# Al Capone

AL CAPONE is the personification of the Chicago gangster popularized in Hollywood films of the 1930s and beyond. He was the head of a mob which more or less owned Chicago, including the police and the law, and he was personally responsible for more than 500 killings.

Capone was born in 1898 in the slums of Brooklyn, the son of a barber from Naples. He left school after beating up his teacher and became a gangster, impressing the older Johnny Torrio, who hired the podgy teenager as a bouncer in a saloon-cum-brothel. In a fight over a woman with Frank Gallucio, another hood, Capone received the long scar on his left cheek which earned him the nickname 'Scarface', the title of one of the films about him.

In 1920 Torrio went to Chicago to help his uncle Big Jim Colosimo to run the brothel business there, and he took Capone with him. When the Volstead Act was passed and the prohibition of liquor opened up great bootlegging prospects for gangsters Colosimo was slow to act, so Torrio decided to eliminate his uncle and Capone took care of the murder.

Torrio's empire grew until there was only one rival for the 'ownership' of Chicago. This was the North Side gang, mainly Irishmen led by Dion O'Banion, a florist. In 1923 O'Banion sold Torrio a brewery and then had it raided by the police, causing Torrio's arrest. Later in the year, Mike Merlo, who ran the illicit liquor manufacturing business under Torrio's protection, died, and the mob ordered $100,000 worth of flowers for the funeral – mostly from O'Banion. Three of Capone's men, under the pretence of buying flowers, shot O'Banion in his shop.

After O'Banion's funeral all-out war existed between the two groups, during which as many as 1000 gangsters lost their lives. Torrio himself was shot, his life being saved only by the jamming of a gun held to his head. After nearly dying in hospital he retired, and the 26-year-old Capone was in charge. His organization employed over 1000 men, paying out $300,000 per week. He was nevertheless not above killing personally, especially to make a point, as when 'Ragtime Joe' Howard, a bootlegger, mistreated his book-keeper. Capone approached Howard in a crowded bar and shot him six times in the head. There were 'no witnesses'.

Liquor, gambling and prostitution were Capone's main concerns, and he was popular; he kept his workforce happy by loyalty, which was returned. He survived numerous murder attempts, including being shot at by the men who nearly killed Torrio, an attempt at poisoning and, most spectacularly, when his headquarters in the Hawthorn Hotel in Cicero, Illinois, was sprayed with machine guns by eight carloads of men from the O'Banion gang. Over 1000 rounds were poured in, but Capone escaped by lying on the floor surrounded by bodyguards.

Capone got away with machine-gunning Chicago's assistant attorney from a speeding car – the gangster trademark – and was never held for long on any charge. Two actions probably prompted the beginning of the end for Capone just when it seemed he was untouchable. The St Valentine's Day massacre in 1929 was meant to eliminate Bugs Moran, the leading light in the O'Banion gang. Capone's men, dressed as policemen, went to a meeting called by the opposition in a garage and, lining the seven gangsters present against a wall, machine-gunned them down. Moran himself was late, saw the fake police car, and escaped. Three months later, at a lavish banquet, Capone denounced three of his men, including two of his top gunmen, as traitors. Taking a club from under his chair, Capone walked round the table and battered the three to death, with nobody lifting a finger.

The public were sickened by these events and the federal government found a way of getting Capone by charging him with income tax

*Al Capone winks at reporters as he arrives at the Chicago court for sentencing*

evasion. 'I didn't know you paid tax on illegal earnings', was his confident attitude, but the jury he had carefully fixed were replaced at the last minute and he was sentenced to 11 years' imprisonment, first at Atlanta and then in Alcatraz. His health rapidly deteriorated through paresis, a paralysis of the motor functions derived from syphilis. After his release he had eight years of luxurious freedom in his mansion at Palm Beach, but his mind had completely gone. He died peacefully in 1947, aged 48.

# Murder Inc.

MURDER INC. was the name given by newspapers to an outfit designed to keep order for the syndicate that divided up crime in the United States in the 1930s. Lucky Luciano and Meyer Lansky were the leading gangsters who formed the syndicate, which was a collection of the younger Mafiosi and the Irish and Jewish gangs that proliferated in the Prohibition Era.

The aim was to control and eliminate the gang warfare that had caused so many deaths in the Capone/O'Banion era, a control that became especially necessary after the repeal of the Volstead Act and the end of bootlegging. The gambling, prostitution, drugs, loans and other racketeering businesses were to be divided up, shared and practised for everybody's mutual benefit. Of course, the old gangs were not always agreeable when it came to allocating spoils, and even when demarcations existed the lines could be crossed, so it was necessary for the heads of the syndicate to have a 'law enforcement' arm. This was a troop of killers who would kill only for business and only on the orders of the syndicate. This was Murder Inc. – a private assassination army.

Lucky Luciano was the most influential figure in the development of organized crime in the USA – in fact, he was the man who did most to add the description 'organized' to crime, and to make the syndicate 'bigger than US Steel'.

He was born Salvatore Luciana near Palermo in Sicily in 1897 and entered the USA in 1906. He offered smaller kids at school 'protection' from bullies – they either paid or he beat them. One who wouldn't pay was Meyer Lansky, a Jewish kid born in 1902 in Grodno, Poland. They fought, then became lifelong allies. While both became

*Lucky Luciano at his Naples home, 1958*

gangsters, Lansky joined up first with Bugsy Siegel to form the Bug and Meyer gang, which both hijacked liquor and sold protection to bootleggers. They would kill for a price and were, therefore, the forerunners of Murder Inc.

Luciano and Lansky worked to form the syndicate during the 1920s. By eliminating 'Joe the Boss' Masseria and Salvatore Maranzano, the old-style Mafia chiefs, they were in a position to put their plans into operation. Lansky, well-read, studious, devious, clever with money, and Luciano, ruthless, fearless and with a flair for organization, made a perfect complementary pair. Among other 'directors' of the newly formed syndicate were Joe Adonis, an Italian who controlled bootleg liquor in Manhattan and who was unofficially second-in-command to Luciano, New Yorker Dutch Schultz, the king of the numbers racket (an illegal gambling pastime which made huge profits), Louis Lepke, a union racketeer who took control of the garment industry, and Frank Costello, an Italian who looked after the bribery for the syndicate, paying out thousands of dollars to politicians, judges and police. He was known as the Prime Minister of the Underworld.

Lepke, a man who loved violence, was the operating head of Murder Inc., with Albert Anastasia as his second-in-command. Anastasia, known as the Lord High Executioner, could be said to live solely for killing and was also called the Mad Hatter. Below these two were lieutenants like Abe 'Kid Twist' Reles, Louis Capone and Mendy Weiss. Orders for a killing came down through these men to killers like Pittsburgh Phil (alias Harry Strauss), Frank Abbandando, Happy Maione, Buggsy Goldstein and Vito 'Chicken Head' Gurino, who practised by shooting heads off chickens.

No killing was carried out without the approval, explicit or by implication, of the board of directors. A killing was called a 'hit' and the killer the 'hit-man'. An order for a killing was a 'contract' and the victim was a 'bum'.

It was a superb organization in that if a killing were necessary the contract could be given to a hit-man far removed from the directors or the bum. The killer and victim might be from different parts of the country and unknown to each other. The hit-man would arrive, do his job and disappear – how could the law trace the murder back to Luciano or another director?

The professionalism and singleness of purpose of Murder Inc. could allow Bugsy Siegel to promise 'we only kill each other'. The highest-ranked criminal to be killed by Murder Inc. was Dutch Schultz, himself a director of the syndicate. Schultz wanted to eliminate Thomas E. Dewey, the prosecutor who was later just beaten in the election for President of the USA, and when this idea was rejected by the board he set up a plan to do it himself. It was about to be put into operation when Albert Anastasia, in whom he had confided, reported it to Luciano. The board put out a contract on Schultz, and he was shot, with his three companions, at a chop house in Newark, New Jersey.

The number of hits carried out by Murder Inc. in the 1930s is thought to be about 500. Of the founder members mentioned here, Albert Anastasia was shot dead in 1957, with the approval of Meyer Lansky, as he sat in a barber's chair at the Park Sheraton Hotel, New York. Lepke, Weiss and Capone were executed in 1944 for a contract killing. Pittsburgh Phil, the most prolific killer, whose own score possibly surpassed 100, was sent to the electric chair in 1941 for just one of his hits. Abbandando went to the chair in 1942.

The reason many of these original members of Murder Inc. were executed by the state was that in 1940, Abe Reles was picked up on a murder charge with other members of Murder Inc. and word got around that one of them was about to talk. Frightened of being informed upon, Reles, whose own score of killings was about 30, decided to get in first and gave the authorities their first knowledge of Murder Inc.

Reles' testimony allowed 49 murders to be solved, and he was a star witness in numerous trials. In November 1941 he was due to give evidence on Anastasia and Bugsy Siegel but, although he was always guarded by six policemen, he 'fell' out of a hotel window. Twenty years later Luciano revealed that it had cost Costello a bill of $50,000 to the police department to check whether the singing canary could also fly.

# Bonnie Parker and Clyde Barrow

BONNIE and Clyde are famous from song and screen, where their image has been idealized so that they appear as a glamorous young couple defiantly escaping the Depression and taking on the world's old fogies. In truth, they were a naive pair of killers of limited intelligence who were rather despised and resented by real gangsters like John Dillinger.

Clyde Barrow was born on 24 March 1909 on a farm at Telice, Texas, one of eight children. He was a sadist, thief and truant who was sent to approved school at nine, and committed his first adult crime, car stealing, at 17. At 21 he met petite, blonde 19-year-old Bonnie Parker, who had married one Roy Thornton at 16, only to lose him to a 99-year prison term for murder.

Clyde and Bonnie hit it off at once, but Clyde was soon arrested for burglary and car thefts and sentenced to two years' imprisonment. Bonnie smuggled in a gun and Clyde escaped, only to be caught in Ohio and given 14 years at Eastham, Texas, a brutal establishment which hardened him and confirmed him in his homosexuality. After 20 months Clyde persuaded a fellow prisoner to chop off two of his toes in the hope of gaining an early parole, and was released on crutches.

Bonnie and Clyde now teamed up on robberies, but soon Bonnie was caught stealing a car and was under arrest when Clyde and his associates, who included a vicious gunman named Ray Hamilton, killed a jeweller and two lawmen. On her release, Bonnie joined Clyde and Hamilton – who, in truth, was a more accomplished criminal than Clyde. He also had wide sexual tastes, and slept with Clyde as well as with Bonnie, who was insatiable in her appetite for sex. The pressures of the triangular relationship often caused Hamilton to drift away, and finally he left for good.

A jaunt during which they pulled off a string of small robberies, then a $3000 raid in Texas, earned Clyde the nickname of the 'Texas Rattlesnake' and Bonnie the description of his 'quick-shooting accomplice'. In Sherman, Texas, Bonnie shot dead a storekeeper who came at her with a meat-cleaver. In November 1932, the pair held up a filling station where they kidnapped the attendant, 16-year-old William Daniel Jones who, on learning their identity, eagerly agreed to join them. He worshipped Clyde and no doubt fulfilled Hamilton's role as far as Bonnie was concerned, but he was not really callous enough for the gangster role and subsequently described his 18-month association with them as 'utter hell'.

On Christmas Day 1932, Clyde shot dead a man who surprised them stealing his car. They killed a deputy sheriff in escaping from a police trap at Dallas, and holed up in Joplin, Missouri, where they were joined by Clyde's brother, Buck, his mentor in crime newly released from prison, and Buck's wife Blanche.

Suspicious neighbours informed on them and the police investigated in force. Clyde saw them arriving and shot a policeman dead. All except Blanche, who ran off up the road clutching her dog and screaming, got away from the house by crashing the car out of the garage, scattering police. They picked up Blanche and made their escape. Clyde and Jones suffered slight wounds, but two policemen were dead and another was badly injured.

As well as numerous guns in the house, police found film which, when developed, showed Bonnie and Clyde posing with guns and draped around the bonnet of their car. The pictures were widely published in the newspapers. In one Bonnie was shown smoking a cigar, which led to her being referred to as Clyde's 'cigar-smoking moll' – a description which considerably annoyed both of them, as Bonnie had borrowed the cigar from Buck. A chief of police they later captured was released to tell the world this news, and the indignant

*Bonnie Parker and Clyde Barrow pose for the camera, in a picture found by police in one of their hideouts*

pair wrote to the papers. Bonnie even circulated her poems, which the papers also published, fanning the legend which was growing up around them.

They were now often obliged to sleep in the cars they stole. Bonnie was badly burned when the car crashed into a gorge in Texas, and a local farmer who helped them eventually guessed who they were. However, they managed to escape again and Bonnie was able to get treatment at Fort Smith, Arkansas.

Buck and Blanche joined them again as the bank raids continued, and a newly appointed marshal was shot dead in Fayetteville, Texas, where they robbed a store, a raid which netted only $50. In Platte City, Missouri, they fought their way out of another police ambush, but Buck was shot in the head and Blanche badly injured by glass. They didn't get far and were soon surrounded again, being forced to fight for three hours, during which Buck was hit again. Incredibly, Bonnie, Clyde and Jones got across a river and escaped; while Blanche stayed with the dying Buck.

All three remaining members of the gang were injured, and had to lie low again. Jones then left – he had had enough. Three more inquisitive policemen were killed by Bonnie and Clyde when the travels and the raids resumed, but the end was approaching. With hardly anyone to turn to for help, they made contact with Henry Methvin, a convict who was himself on the run after escaping from prison with their old ally Ray Hamilton. But Methvin betrayed them to earn his own freedom, and six Texas Rangers were waiting when Bonnie and Clyde turned up to keep an appointment with him.

Thirteen kilometres (8 miles) from Gibsland, Louisiana, the pair were driving along in their Ford V-8 Sedan in relaxed fashion, Clyde barefooted and Bonnie munching a sandwich, when over 160 bullets smashed through the windscreen. It was 9 am on 23 May 1934. Crowds arrived in no time to look for souvenirs, and a procession of sightseers' cars followed the towed wreck which carried their mutilated bodies back to town.

# Chapter Five

# THRILL KILLERS

# Introduction

THRILL killers enjoy murder as the ultimate sado-sexual act or because the very act of killing gives them a buzz of excitement they cannot obtain any other way. Usually their victims are strangers – not viewed as people but just bodies used for gratification.

They often seem to graduate from lesser sex crimes – one commits minor assaults on women during the course of robberies, then moves on through rape to murder, another interferes with teenage boys, then begins abducting and killing them – but as they feed their unnatural lust the need for more extreme experiences grows . . . until only sexual acts culminating in murder will satisfy their need. The first murder may provide such of frenzy of pleasure that it has to be repeated, often at more and more frequent intervals.

Such killers are often acting out an elaborate sexual fantasy that they have spent years creating and the thrill is closely tied up with ideas of dominance: the victims of the 'Trailside Killer' were shot while kneeling, as though begging for their lives, and Dean Corll strapped young boys to his 'torture board' to torment them, sometimes for days, before they were finally killed.

The vast majority of thrill killers – or, come to that, serial killers of any kind – are men, but occasionally a man and woman come together and spark off some dark compulsion in one another. Then, like child-killers Myra Hindley and Ian Brady, they stimulate one another to commit acts that they might never have contemplated alone.

# Earle Nelson

THE NUMBER of women raped and murdered by Earle Leonard Nelson is unknown, but in the 16 months alone from February 1926 to June 1927 his victims numbered at least 20. Among the names given him during this spell was the 'Gorilla Murderer'.

Nelson was born in 1897 in Philadelphia. His 20-year-old mother suffered from a venereal disease contracted from his father, and died before he was a year old. He was brought up by his aunt Lillian Fabian, who was devoutly religious and said her nephew would be a minister one day; he certainly did become obsessed with the Bible.

At ten he was hit by a trolley car, suffering terrible injuries which left him with a hole in his head that caused intermittent pain throughout his life. As a teenager he alternated Bible-mania with acts of violence, and in 1918 he was committed to a mental asylum after raping a young girl in Philadelphia. He repeatedly escaped from the asylum and remained free from 1919 when, using the alias of Roger Wilson, he married a schoolteacher. Constant lecturing from the Bible and accusations of infidelity finally gave Mrs Wilson a nervous breakdown which sent her to hospital, where Nelson visited her and attempted to rape her. He was ejected from the hospital and disappeared.

What Nelson did for the next six years is unknown. The series of murders which brought him to the public's attention began on 20 February 1926. On that day Miss Clara Newman, a 60-year-old lodging-house owner in San Francisco, was visited by her nephew. He thought she was out until he pushed open a lavatory door and found her naked body propped on the seat. She had been badly assaulted and strangled with her own pearl necklace. The removal of a 'To Let'

notice from the window suggested that she had been killed by somebody looking for a room. Two weeks later a very similar murder was
committed at a lodging house in San José, and there were three more
in June and August in the same San Francisco-Oakland area.

The killer then moved to Portland, Oregon, where three landladies
were murdered on consecutive days in October. In November his
victims were in Oregon City, San Francisco and Seattle, in December
he killed in Council Bluffs, Iowa, and around Christmas time two
women died in Kansas City. The second, 28-year-old Mrs Germania
Harpin, had an eight-month-old daughter, whom the killer throttled
with a piece of rag.

The killer's method was clear: he would enquire at houses showing
a 'To Let' sign and if the landlady who invited him in was alone he
would strangle and rape her, often hiding the body under a bed.
Sometimes he took jewellery, and it was through this that the first
description of him was produced. The Portland police published
details of some of the stolen jewellery and were brought items three
landladies had bought from a young man who had stayed with them.
They proved to belong to Mrs Florence Monks, who had been killed in
Seattle. The description the ladies gave of the pleasant, quiet,
religious young man was that he was short, blue-eyed and dark-
complexioned. He had a slightly simian jaw. This last detail, and the
ferocity of the killings, led to the 'Gorilla' tag, although other papers
called him the 'Dark Strangler' or the 'Phantom'.

In 1927 the trail of bodies led through Philadelphia, Buffalo,
Detroit and Chicago. In June the killer crossed into Canada, taking a
third-floor room in Smith Street, Winnipeg, where the landlady was
a Mrs Catherine Hill. The next day Mr and Mrs Cowan, a couple
staying in the same house, reported their 14-year-old daughter Lola
had disappeared. Then, in another part of town, William Patterson
came home to find his wife Emily missing and informed the police.
That night, as he knelt to pray, he saw her hand under the bed and
discovered her dead body.

Recognizing the Gorilla Murderer's trademark, the Winnipeg police checked all lodging houses. Mrs Hill mentioned the lodger who had just left, Roger Wilson, a Bible-loving man. The police asked to see his room, and under the bed, giving off a terrible stench, was the mutilated body of Lola Cowan, where it had lain for three days.

The net was tightening on Nelson, because he had changed his clothes at the Pattersons' house, and changed them again at a second-hand shop, so it was known he was wearing corduroys and a plaid shirt. An attempted strangulation in a boarding house at Regina, some 480 km (300 miles) to the west, gave police a clue as to the direction Nelson was taking, and a full-scale hunt was launched between there and the border with the States. He was picked up by two officers, Constables Gray and Sewell, 19 km (12 miles) from the border. He gave his name as Virgil Wilson, and looked so innocent that he was left alone in the gaol, handcuffed to the bars, while the officers phoned Winnipeg to check details. In 20 minutes he had picked two locks to escape. But the police were now on to him, and when they spotted him again next day they made no mistake.

Nelson killed at least 20 women, and there were other killings, particularly three in Newark, New Jersey, which bore his mark. He was tried in Winnipeg for the Canadian murders only and although he was supported by his aunt and former wife in a plea of insanity, after four days was found guilty. 'I am innocent before God and man,' he said from the stand. 'I forgive those who have wronged me. God have mercy!' He was hanged on 13 January 1928.

# Gordon Cummins

IN 1942, London was suffering night after night from the raids of German bombers. From sunset to sunrise it was illegal to show any light which would indicate the target to a bomber, and each evening householders put up their special blackout curtains. In February there occurred a series of murders which earned a young aircraftman the title of the 'Blackout Ripper'.

The murders were first discovered in the early hours of 9 February 1942, when a woman's body was found in a brick-built air-raid shelter in Marylebone. She was identified as Miss Evelyn Hamilton, a 42-year-old chemist. Her silk scarf had been bound round her nose and mouth as a gag, and she had been strangled. Her handbag was found nearby. The only clue to her killer was a bruise on her throat which led police to believe her attacker was left-handed.

The following day the body of Mrs Evelyn Oatley was found in her apartment in Wardour Street, Soho. She was an ex-Windmill girl who used the name Nita Ward, and had taken to a little prostitution. Hers was a sex murder. Her naked body had been thrown across her bed. Her throat was cut, and her belly and sexual organs had been savagely attacked with a tin-opener; this lay nearby and showed left-handed fingerprints, as did part of a mirror found in the flat. Mrs Oatley had been last seen in Piccadilly Circus, hailing a taxi with a man.

The two murders caused a frisson of anxiety among London women, particularly those who needed to go out into the dark evening streets. Three days later the neighbours of Mrs Margaret Lowe told police they were worried that they had not seen her. Mrs Lowe was a prostitute who, under the name of Pearl, operated from a flat just off Tottenham Court Road. Police forced the door, and under a quilt on the bed found her naked body. She had been strangled with a silk stocking. Her lower body had been severely mutilated by a variety of instruments which lay scattered around, including a bread knife, other knives and a poker. There were more fingerprints, and confirmation again that the killer was left-handed.

Detectives were still examining the body when they were informed of another, in Sussex Gardens, Paddington. Mrs Doris Jouannet, the wife of a hotel manager, was found dead. Her husband, as was his habit, had slept at the hotel and found her on his return home in the morning. It was a similar case: the naked body sprawled across the bed, the tightly knotted scarf round the neck, the sadistic slashing of the genital area.

The police then turned to two other events that had happened on the same evening as Mrs Jouannet's death. A young married woman, Greta Heywood, had been bought a drink by a good-looking, charming airman in Piccadilly. As they left the pub and went into the dark street, he pulled her into the doorway of an air-raid shelter and began to throttle her. She dropped the torch which most people then carried, and its noise attracted a passer-by. The airman fled but left behind his gas mask, on which was stencilled his RAF number – 525987. Two hours after this attack, Mrs Margaret Mulcahy also met a young airman in Piccadilly, and took him to her apartment in Southwick Street, Paddington. Then, she told police, he tried to strangle her, but she was too strong and screamed and kicked to such effect he ran off. He left behind an RAF belt. Mrs Mulcahy lived just round the corner from Mrs Jouannet.

It was a matter of a few minutes routine to discover the owner of RAF number 525987 – he was 28-year-old Aircraftman Gordon Cummins, stationed at St John's Wood. He was immediately arrested. The fingerprints tallied, and a cigarette case and fountain pen belonging to two of his victims were found in his billet.

As was the practice of the day, Cummins was charged with one murder only – that of Mrs Oatley. There was a major hiccup at the trial when the jury was asked to inspect fingerprints; the superintendent who investigated the case pointed out to the judge that they were from one of the murders not being tried. The judge was forced to halt the case, appeal to the discretion of the press, and restart the trial with a new jury days later. The jury pronounced a verdict of guilty, and the Blackout Ripper was hanged on 25 June 1942.

# John Christie

JOHN REGINALD HALLIDAY CHRISTIE was an inadequate youth who suffered a trauma as a teenager when unable to perform the sexual act with a more experienced girl. As a result of this episode he became known among his circle as 'Reggie No-Dick'. In later life he always found it easier to have sex with passive, unconscious or possibly even dead women, and this led to him becoming one of Britain's most notorious murderers.

He was born on 8 April 1898 in Halifax, and was a clever, studious boy. However, at 17 he was caught pilfering and sacked from his job as a clerk with the police, whereupon his father, a disciplinarian who was remote from his children, turned him from the house. After this he drifted around, sometimes sleeping on his father's allotment, until he was called up in World War I, during which he suffered a dose of gas poisoning which left him with a quiet voice.

Christie married in 1920 but, as his record of petty crimes built up, his wife Ethel left him. He was convicted in 1929 of an attack on the prostitute with whom he was living. Eventually he pleaded with his wife to return and, in 1933, she did. They moved to London, took a flat at 10 Rillington Place, Notting Hill, and, in 1939, he became a war reserve policeman. He was at last in his element, as the uniform gave him the air of authority he craved.

In August 1943 Constable Christie met a 17-year-old part-time prostitute, Ruth Fuerst. She had a cold, and he told her he had an ideal cure for a blocked nose. Ethel was away and Christie took Fuerst to 10 Rillington Place. There the cure involved her putting her head under a cloth and inhaling the steam from a bowl of boiling water and friar's balsam. Unknown to Fuerst, it also contained a tube which was connected to the gas; it was by this means that Christie rendered his victim unconscious. Christie committed rape on the insensible Fuerst and then strangled her. When his wife returned unexpectedly he had to relinquish the body and surreptitiously bury it at night in the garden.

In October 1944, when Mrs Christie was again away, Muriel Eady became Christie's second victim. By now he had refined his technique, using an inhaler in the form of a jar of perfumed water, with again, a tube leading to the gas. Eady's body joined that of Ruth Fuerst in the back garden.

In 1948, Timothy and Beryl Evans had moved in upstairs as Christie's subtenants, and Beryl had given birth to a baby, Geraldine. Beryl and Geraldine were murdered in November 1949. Evans was hanged for Geraldine's murder, although many years later he was given a posthumous free pardon. Not all experts are in agreement about these two murders, but the most generally accepted version of events is that Mrs Evans required an abortion, which was then illegal. Christie persuaded the mentally subnormal Evans that he could perform it, and would do so during the day while Evans was at work. Christie's first-aid manuals would have helped him persuade Evans of his credentials. Mrs Evans was perhaps 'helped to relax' with Christie's inhaler. He then raped and strangled her.

When Evans returned from work he was told by Christie that his wife had died during the operation. They carried her body to an empty flat, and Christie impressed on Evans that they were both implicated in breaking the law. Evans was persuaded that the best course would be for Christie to hide the body in a drain outside the house and place the child with a couple he knew, while Evans went back to Wales for a while. Evans duly sold his furniture and left to stay with relatives, but three weeks after the murders went to the police in Merthyr Tydfil and related a version of events. This was that he had returned home from work and found his wife dead after she had tried to give herself an abortion. He said he had disposed of the body down the drain. Police investigated and found the drain cover impossible for one man to lift and the drain empty. On being confronted with this news, Evans implicated Christie and told the latter's version of events.

The police went back to Rillington Place and found a stolen brief-case – sufficient grounds for them to arrest Evans for the time being. They also met Christie, who told them that Evans had had rows with his wife. Another closer search was made of the premises when, it is said, Christie's dog unearthed a bone in the garden and Christie was forced to kick earth back over it and take the dog indoors. In the outside washhouse the bodies of mother and baby were found, the baby with one of Evans' ties around her neck. Evans, who had been in custody for 3 days, then made a further confession, admitting both killings, and was charged.

At Evans' trial, where he was accused of murdering his baby, Christie gave impressive evidence for the prosecution. Evans retracted his contradictory confessions and maintained Christie had killed both his wife and child, persisting in this story even after being found guilty. He was hanged on 9 March 1950.

How much Ethel Christie knew of all this was never established. On 14 December 1952 Christie murdered her – by his own account as a mercy killing, for he said she was suffering convulsions. He kept the body in bed for two days, then hid it under the floorboards.

In the next three months three more women were killed. The bodies of Kathleen Maloney, 26, and Rita Nelson, 25, were wrapped in blankets and propped up in a cupboard in the kitchen. Hectorina MacLennan, 26, also ended up there, sitting on a pile of rubbish, her bra strap hooked to one of the other bodies to keep her upright. Christie wallpapered over the door of the cupboard to disguise its existence. A fortnight after the last murder he left, illegally renting his flat to subtenants who paid three months in advance (£7.13s) but were evicted by the landlord next day.

The top-floor tenant, Beresford Brown, was told by the landlord he

*10 Rillington Place, home of John Christie*

could clean up the kitchen and use it himself. On the third day after Christie's departure Brown decided to put up a bracket to hold a shelf for his radio and discovered the door beneath the wallpaper. Behind this, he saw a near-naked body.

After removing the contents of the cupboard, which included a large can of air freshener, police soon found a fourth body – that of Ethel Christie – beneath the living-room floorboards, and then the two in the garden which they had missed four years earlier. By now a human bone was propping up the fence. A warrant was issued for Christie's arrest and a policeman found him staring into the Thames near Putney Bridge. He had been living rough for ten days.

Christie was charged with murdering his wife and admitted murdering all the six women whose bodies had been found, plus Beryl Evans, though not baby Geraldine. He pleaded insanity but was found guilty and hanged on 15 July 1953.

After the trial there was an immediate outcry about the conviction of Timothy Evans. Mr Scott Henderson QC was appointed to carry out an enquiry into a possible miscarriage of justice before Christie's execution took place. He found that the evidence was overwhelming that none had occurred. However, investigative journalism – particularly on the part of Ludovic Kennedy, who disclosed in a book published in 1961 that Evans' defence had been deprived of crucial evidence in the form of the worksheets of men employed in the house at the time of Beryl Evans' death, provoked a further review in 1966 by Mr Justice Brabin. The worksheets had since disappeared but Brabin's review concluded that Evans, on probabilities, had not killed his child but had killed his wife. In October 1966 Evans was granted a free pardon and his body was reburied in consecrated ground.

# Heinrich Pommerencke

IN 1959 a wave of fear spread through the young women of southern Germany, for the 'Beast of the Black Forest' was on the loose and he might pounce on any lone female at any time.

The body of 18-year-old Hilda Knothe was found hidden in the bushes in a park in Karlsruhe. She had been brutally raped, the clothes literally ripped off her body, and her throat had been slashed with a razor. A month later an 18-year-old beautician, Karen Walde, was raped and battered to death with a rock.

In June, 21-year-old student teacher Dagmar Klimek was taking a nap in an empty railway carriage when a man slipped in quietly from the corridor and threw himself on her. Waking with a start, she fought back, whereupon he opened the carriage door and threw her out onto the line. He then pulled the communication cord to stop the train and ran back down the track to where Dagmar lay unconscious. He dragged her into the undergrowth and tore off her clothes, raped her, then stabbed her to death.

Only five days later a woman was looking out of the window of a train pulling out of Rastatt station when she saw a girl running down the road, chased by a tall young man in a grey suit. When he caught up with her he pulled her off the road into the woods. The woman assumed that this was natural horseplay between a girl and her boyfriend until, a couple of days later, she heard a radio report that Rita Walterspacher, an 18-year-old secretary, was missing. Her report led to a police search and Rita's body was found hidden under a pile of brushwood. She had been raped and strangled and, just like the other victims, her clothes had been torn off with brute force.

The day after Rita's disappearance a young man called in at a tailor's shop in Hornberg, near Rastatt, to collect a suit that he had ordered earlier. When he had tried it on, he asked the tailor if he could leave his old clothes and the parcel he was carrying in the shop while he did some other errands. He left them in a corner but once he had gone the tailor decided to move them into the back room. When he picked up the parcel he realized that it felt suspiciously like a gun, so he reported it to the police. Sure enough, they found that the parcel contained a sawn-off shotgun. This was a particularly interesting find, as a sawn-off shotgun and been used in a robbery in a local railway station the day before, as well as in several other similar robberies in the area. When the young man, Heinrich Pommerencke, came back to collect to his property he was arrested.

As the police questioned him, they realized that there was a correspondence between the areas in which the burglaries had taken place and those where rape and murder had occurred. Moreover, Pommerencke fitted the description given by women who had been attacked but had managed to escape and that of the train passenger who had seen Rita Walterspacher with her assailant. Quite soon, Pommerencke was confessing to both the burglaries and the rape-murders.

He was born in East Germany in 1937 and spent a solitary childhood; he never made a single friend, he said. When he reached his teens he was too shy and awkward to find himself a girlfriend, though he was tormented by violent sexual urges. By the age of 15 he was hanging around dance halls and making attempts at assaulting girls who left alone, though he usually ran away at the first scream. Later he graduated to rape and at one time he was forced to flee to Switzerland to avoid imprisonment for sex crimes.

He explained that sexy films made him so tense that he needed to relieve his frustration by 'doing something to a woman.' It was after seeing *The Ten Commandments,* where he watched half-naked women dancing around the golden calf, that he followed Hilda Knothe into the park and committed his first murder.

Pommerencke seemed genuinely revolted by his actions, saying,

'Everything I did was cruel and bestial. From the bottom of my heart I would like to undo all this.' This led some psychologists to believe that his apparent stupidity in leaving his gun behind in the tailor's shop may have fulfilled a subconscious need to be caught and punished.

At the time of his trial for 4 murders and 12 attempted murders, as well as 21 rapes and 35 other counts, Pommerencke was only 23 years old. He was sentenced to 6 life sentences, adding up to at least 140 years in prison.

# Harvey Glatman

PHOTOGRAPHY is a glamorous profession, and Harvey Glatman saw it as the way to get some beautiful women in his power. Three of them were to die horrible deaths before the fourth proved to be as tough as he was.

Glatman was born in 1928 and was a pampered mother's boy. When he reached his teens he had several brushes with the law, and was imprisoned in New York for attacks on women and in Colorado for aggravated assaults on them. In 1945 he was imprisoned for a long spell for robbery, and the authorities decided he needed psychiatric treatment. His mother, who doted on him, paid for treatment for five years and, in the 1950s, sent him to a television repairman's school and then set him up with a TV repair shop in Los Angeles.

Glatman, an unattractive weedy-looking man with large jug ears, took an interest in photography and looked round for an attractive model to hire. Calling himself Johnny Glynn, he made an appointment with 19-year-old model Judy Dull. On 1 August 1957 Judy arrived at his 'studio' in Melrose Avenue, Hollywood. She stripped and Glatman took some nude photographs of her. Then he produced a gun and raped her. After this he made her dress and said he needed bondage pictures for a detective magazine. He tied her hands behind her back while she sat in an armchair, tied her legs together, fitted a gag in her mouth and pulled up her dress to take his provocative photographs.

Despite her desperate promises to say nothing about the session, Glatman could not let his model go. When it got dark he took her into the desert near Indio, strangled her, then buried her.

On 9 March 1958 Glatman made a date with a pretty 24-year-old divorcee, Shirley Bridgeford, whom he met through a 'lonely hearts' club, where he used the name George Williams. He drove her to the desert outside San Diego, and raped her several times. She too was photographed tied up and gagged and clearly in great distress. Finally, Glatman strangled her and covered her body with scrub.

Ruth Rita Mercado was a 23-year-old Los Angeles stripper and model who advertised in the newspapers. Glatman called on her on 23 July 1958, forced his way into her apartment, and tied her up. He took several photographs, and then drove her out into the desert towards San Diego. They spent the night in the car, and next day Glatman raped her several times and took more photos of her tied up. She played along with him, humoured him and asked him to let her go to feed her parrot. 'I liked her,' said Glatman later, but her tactics did not save her. He strangled her as night fell again.

Lorraine Vigil, a 27-year-old dark-haired Latin girl who advertised through a model agency, was Glatman's next intended victim. She was suspicious and wanted a chaperone present but, on 27 October, he persuaded her to accompany him in his car to his apartment. Instead of driving there he sped out on the Santa Ana freeway, turned down a side road, pulled up and produced a gun. Miss Vigil screamed and struggled and the gun went off, searing her thigh. This disconcerted Glatman enough for the brave Miss Vigil to get a hold of the gun. As

*Harvey Glatman (right), with police, stands over the bones of one of his victims. He told police the remains were those of Shirley Bridgeford*

the two of them rolled out of the car a highway patrolman arrived; Miss Vigil actually had the gun pointing at Glatman when she was rescued.

When Glatman's home was searched police found the walls covered with his perverse photos of his tied-up victims, both dead and alive. Glatman almost boasted of his actions. 'I kept a five-foot length of sash cord in the car with the gun. I made them lie on their stomachs, then I tied their ankles together, looped the end of the cord about their necks and pulled until they were dead,' he said.

Glatman's greatest concern was that his 69-year-old mother should be kept from the trial. He was convicted and sentenced to death. He refused to appeal against the sentence, announcing that he wanted to die. 'I knew this is the way it would be,' he said.

Glatman was killed in the gas chamber on 18 August 1959. While he awaited execution, there were many bids from periodicals to publish his photographs of his deeds.

# Joachim Kroll

IN 1976 the police of Laar, in the Ruhr district of Germany, were engaged in house-to-house questioning following the disappearance of four-year-old Marion Ketter, who had been abducted from a playground. From a tenant in one of the blocks of flats they heard an extraordinary story: a neighbour, Joachim Kroll, had warned him not to use the lavatory on the upper floor because it was 'clogged with guts'. When a plumber was sent up to investigate, he fished out the organs of a young child, including the lungs.

When the police entered Kroll's flat, they found a stew cooking on the stove: it contained carrots, potatoes and a child's hand. In the deep freeze were a stack of plastic bags containing chunks of human flesh. Though Kroll was a small, balding middle-aged man with a gentle manner, the officers soon decided that they had found the 'Ruhr hunter', a sex-killer who carved slices of flesh from the bodies of his victims.

Kroll took a simple-minded delight in recalling the details of his murderous activities – the only problem was, he had committed so many murders that he could not remember all of them. Though he filled his flat with electronic sex gadgets and inflatable dolls, which he habitually strangled while he achieved orgasm, this was not sufficient to satisfy his sexual urges. He had always been too shy and diffident to approach a woman in a normal manner and had begun his career of rape at the age of 22. He would mark out a victim and then often stalk her for days, waiting for the right opportunity.

The first murder that he could remember was in February 1955 when he had raped and killed 19-year-old Irmgard Strehl in a barn near the village of Walstedde. Next came 12-year-old Erika

Schuletter, whom he had raped and then strangled in Kirchhellen a year later. The naked body of Klara Tesmer was found in the woods near Rheinhausen in 1959; she had been raped while unconscious and then murdered. One reason that Kroll evaded capture for so long was that he usually chose a different area for each killing so that the police had no reason to connect the first few murders – and even after he developed his horrifying trademark it was difficult for them to coordinate their enquiries.

In July 1959 he raped a 16-year-old girl, Manuela Knodt, at Bredeney, near Essen. After he had strangled her, it occurred to him that if he took some slices from her chubby buttocks and thighs it might save some money on his housekeeping bills. He took the slices of flesh home, cooked them and enjoyed his meal. After the discovery of this body the newspapers began calling him 'The Cannibal Killer'.

Thirteen-year-old Petra Giese went missing after visiting a fair near Walsum with a friend and her body was found in a nearby wood next day. Her clothes had been forcibly torn from her and both buttocks, as well as one of her forearms and hands, had been sliced off. Steaks were carved from the buttocks and thighs of 13-year-old Monica Tafel, who disappeared on her way home from school, and five-year-old Ilona Harke, who was abducted from a park playground. Kroll was choosy about the meat he collected; if his victims were skinny and he considered that their flesh might not be sufficiently tender, he left their bodies uncut.

In two cases, other young men came near to paying the price for Kroll's crimes. Ursula Roling's body was found in a park in Marl, naked from the waist down, with her legs spread wide. She had disappeared on the way from the flat she shared with her boyfriend to her parents' home. Her boyfriend was the chief suspect and spent three weeks in custody; as there was no evidence that Ursula had fought against the rape, police suspected that she had been killed during a quarrel and her boyfriend had then taken her body to the park to make her death look like a sex murder. In fact, the assault on

Ursula conformed to Kroll's usual pattern, as he was in the habit of strangling girls into unconsciousness before he raped them.

When 13-year-old Jutta Rahn was raped and strangled in Breitscheid, having been waylaid as she hurried through a rainstorm to catch the train to school, a young man from the village was arrested because his blood type matched that of the murderer. The police finally accepted his innocence but many of the villagers continued to believe him guilty for the next six years, until he was finally cleared by Kroll's confession.

When Kroll's murderous career hit the headlines, one young woman in Grafenhausen realized how close she had come to death nine years earlier. At the time Kroll had been living in the town and was very popular with the local children, who called him 'Uncle' and had no reason to fear him. One day he had invited a 10-year-old girl to walk through a field with him so that he could show her a rabbit. Instead of a rabbit he produced a set of obscene photographs and then made a grab for the terrified child as she ran away. She told no one of her experience until she eventually heard the full facts about Kroll.

Joachim Kroll was able to give police details of 14 murders but he admitted that this might not be the final count, for his memory was poor. As capital punishment no longer existed in Germany, he was sentenced to life imprisonment.

# Peter Manuel

PETER MANUEL was a known troublemaker from the age of 11, but when he went on a murder spree in 1956 it took two years to catch him, and an innocent man was charged with some of his crimes.

He was born in Manhattan, New York, on 15 March 1927, of a Scottish Roman Catholic family who had gone to the United States to seek a better life. They all returned to Scotland in 1932 but, five years later, moved to Coventry. When he was 11 Manuel was convicted of crimes that included shopbreaking, and spent much of his time thereafter in approved schools and in borstal. His parents moved close to Glasgow in 1941 when their house in Coventry was bombed, and Manuel, having assaulted a woman with a hammer in 1942, when he was 15, joined them on his release from borstal in 1946.

Manuel was shorter than average, but strong. He had dark hair and dark, piercing eyes. He liked to draw and to write stories, fantasized about his life and was an impressive talker and convincing liar – although an attempt to establish American citizenship in 1954 at the US Consul in Glasgow with stories of being a member of the British security services was soon shown to be untrue.

No sooner was Manuel back in Scotland than he was caught housebreaking and, while awaiting trial, he raped an expectant mother and indecently assaulted two other women. At his trial for these offences he ably conducted his own defence but was sentenced to eight years' imprisonment. He was released, with remission, in 1953.

Manuel returned to crime and began courting a girl in 1953. However, after fixing the date for the wedding as 30 July 1955, his fiancée broke the engagement, having discovered his life of crime. On what would have been his wedding night Manuel attacked a woman in a field. Her screams were heard, and police unsuccessfully searched the area, while Manuel kept the girl quiet at knife-point. By acting sympathetically, the girl kept Manuel talking much of the night, until he threw away the knife and let her go. Manuel was arrested and charged with sexual assault but acquitted.

Manuel's first murder was committed on 2 January 1956. The body of 17-year-old Anne Knielands was not discovered until two days later, when a man found her on a golf course at East Kilbride, just outside Glasgow. She had not been sexually assaulted, but semen stains showed that her killer had achieved sexual satisfaction through violence. Her head had been savagely beaten. While running to report his find, the man who was unfortunate enough to come across the body met some gas board engineers and told them his story. One of them was Peter Manuel, who was thus interviewed by the police. They were immediately suspicious of him, as he had scratches on his face and clothing he was known to possess two months earlier was missing, but Manuel's father confirmed his son was indoors on the evening in question and no real evidence was forthcoming.

In March, Manuel was arrested attempting a burglary after police had received a tip-off. While he was awaiting trial, there were local burglaries on successive nights in September 1956, both bearing Manuel's hallmark: footprints on bedding and tins of food and ashtrays emptied on to carpets. The morning after the second burglary, a daily help found three bodies at a bungalow a few doors away; her employer, Mrs Marion Watt, and Mrs Watt's daughter Vivienne and sister Margaret Brown had all been shot at close range, the older ladies dying in their beds.

Manuel was interviewed and his home searched, but without any evidence being found. Police interest switched to the other occupant of the house, Marion's husband William Watt, who had gone away on a fishing holiday to Argyll, staying at the Cairnbaan Hotel. He had been seen there at 1.00 am and 8 am but police formed the theory that he could have driven home between these hours, killed the three women

*Peter Manuel*

and driven back. He was charged and held in Barlinnie Prison outside Glasgow, where Manuel was sent on 2 October after being sentenced to 18 months' imprisonment for the attempted robbery in March.

From his cell, Manuel wrote to Watt's solicitor asking him to represent him in an appeal against his sentence for burglary and hinting that he would tell him something that would help him in his defence of Watt. He also related details which convinced the solicitor that Manuel had been present at the murder. An informer then told police that Manuel had bought a gun a week before the murders. After 67 days police released Watt, now sure they had arrested the wrong man. Four days after Manuel's release on 30 November 1957, Watt agreed to meet Manuel, hoping to discover more about his family's murder, but Manuel merely pointed the finger at a criminal he knew and admitted nothing.

On 29 December, less than a month after Manuel's release, 17-year-old Isabelle Cooke was reported missing. A shoe and handbag were found in a water-filled colliery shaft. While police were still searching for her, news came on 6 January of the discoveries of three bodies in a bungalow in Uddingston, only 10 minutes' walk from Manuel's house. Peter Smart, a 45-year-old manager of an engineering firm in Glasgow, his wife Doris and 11-year-old son Michael had been shot through the head at close range while in their bedrooms. They had been killed on 1 January, and neighbours reported that between then and the date of their discovery lights had been switched on and off, so the killer had either stayed there or returned to the scene of the crime. On 4 January, another local couple, Mr and Mrs McMunn, had woke at 5.45 am to see a man at the door of the bedroom. He had fled when quick-thinking McMunn had pretended he had a gun.

Police arrested Manuel on 14 January 1958 and charged him with the murder of the Smarts and the break-in at the McMunns. They also arrested his father for receiving stolen goods. A camera and gloves had been taken from a house near Isabelle Cooke's home, and

Manuel's father, in an attempt to protect his son, had claimed to have bought them in a market.

As the police hoped he would, Manuel now showed feelings for his father. He offered a deal – a confession in exchange for his father's release. He duly wrote a full confession of all the murders and led police to the ploughed field where he had buried the body of Isabelle Cooke, identifying the exact spot. He also showed them where he had thrown the two guns into the river.

Manuel's trial on eight murder charges began on 12 May 1958. Ten days later he sacked his counsel and conducted a brilliant defence himself. He had renounced his confession and part of his defence was that William Watt had murdered his own family, so Watt had to face cross-examination by the killer of his loved ones.

Manuel was found guilty of seven murders, being acquitted of that of Anne Knielands on lack of evidence. He was hanged on 11 July 1958. Seventeen days later, a coroner's jury in Newcastle decided that taxi-driver Sydney Dunn, who had been shot on 8 December 1957, was another of his victims, for Manuel had gone to the city for a job interview.

# Jerry Brudos

THOSE who ponder the question of how much of a person's character is inherited and how much is shaped by his or her experiences would find Jerry Brudos an interesting study.

Even at the age of five Brudos had a fixation for women's shoes, which he would play with. As an adolescent, he was excited by women wearing black stiletto heels. At 17 he forced a woman at knife-point to pose nude while he took photographs of her. He was confined to a mental hospital for nine months with a personality disorder, then, when he was released, began to steal women's underwear and shoes. First the underwear came off clotheslines, then he stole from apartments while the owners slept, and if the women woke he would rape them. By the time he committed his first murder, he had a large collection of women's clothes.

Brudos, tall, very strong and freckle-faced, was 28 by this time, married and the father of a child. He had the strange foible of insisting that his wife should walk about the house in the nude.

In January 1968 a 19-year-old encyclopaedia saleswoman called Linda Slawson had the bad luck to walk down Brudos's street in Portland, Oregon, while he was outside his house. She asked Brudos if his was the house where she was expected, and he asked her in. Brudos's mother and child were upstairs, so he took Miss Slawson into the basement, where he knocked her unconscious with a piece of wood then strangled her. He sent his mother out on an errand and then enjoyed himself with the corpse, dressing it in his collection of underwear and photographing it. Then he chopped off her left foot, fitted her shoe on, and stored it in the refrigerator. Finally, he tied a piece of car engine to the body, took it to a bridge over the Willamette River and dropped it in.

On 26 November 1968, Jan Whitney was driving home when her car broke down. Jerry Brudos stopped to help. She wasn't seen again, but a photograph of her hanging by the neck in Brudos's garage was found later. Brudos repeated his sexual games with the corpse and this time kept the right breast. He was later to say that he made paper-weights from the breasts of some of his victims.

A highly intelligent, beautiful 19-year-old student was the next girl to disappear. Karen Sprinker failed to show up for lunch with her mother at a department store and was reported missing. After waiting 24 hours the police found her car on the top floor of the store's car park. Brudos had abducted her, subjected her to various sexual acts before and after killing her, photographed her, cut off and kept her breasts, and dropped the rest of her body in the river.

That was in March 1969, and in April Linda Salee disappeared on the way to a date with her boyfriend. Her car was found on the top floor of a supermarket car park, where Brudos had picked her up by posing as a store detective. He had strangled her and then wired her up to the electricity so that he could photograph her while passing electric shocks through her corpse.

Soon Linda Salee's body was found by a fisherman in the Big Tom River with part of an engine tied to it. Then the corpse of Karen Sprinker was similarly discovered. The police realized that a sick killer was at large and would strike again. A huge operation was mounted, which included asking all Karen Sprinker's fellow students at the Oregon State University if they had seen or heard anything unusual.

At last police found a possible lead. Three girls had received calls from a man claiming to be a Vietnam veteran and asking if they were interested in 'Coke and conversation'. One had actually met him, a tall red-haired man with freckles. The girl was told to stall and get in touch with the police if there were further telephone calls. A fortnight later the man rang again, and the girl arranged to meet him in an hour then warned the police. The police met him instead, learned his name and later, when checking, discovered his conviction and mental history. They decided to watch his house.

One day in May Brudos began to load up his car as if going away. The police quickly got a search warrant and arrested him. Slowly Brudos began to talk, and soon the police had all the gory details of his murders. At his trial Brudos pleaded insanity but psychiatrists pronounced him sane; he was sentenced to life imprisonment in the maximum security Oregon State Penitentiary, where he is a model prisoner.

# Albert DeSalvo

ON A WARM June night in Boston, Juris Slesers arrived at his mother's third-floor apartment to take her to a service at the nearby Latvian church. He received no answer to his knock and when, after half an hour, there was still no answer, he was worried enough to force open the door. He found his mother, a 55-year-old divorcee, lying on the floor, naked except for her housecoat, which was flung open. Her legs were spread wide apart and the blue cord of the housecoat was knotted tightly round her neck and finished with a bow under the chin.

At first Slesers thought that his mother had hanged herself on the bathroom door and fallen, but the police decided otherwise, for Anna Slesers had been sexually assaulted, probably with a bottle. The bath was half-full of water, so it looked as though she had been preparing to take a bath when she had answered the door to her murderer. Various drawers had been opened and the contents scattered around, but nothing valuable was missing. It seemed that Mrs Sleser's assailant had merely rifled through her possessions out of interest.

It seemed at the time like a random sex killing, but in fact it was the first of a series of Boston murders bearing the same trademark: the bow tied under the chin of a woman who had been sexually assaulted and strangled in her own home. The 'Boston Strangler' was to remain at large for the next two years, from 1962 to 1964, sending a wave of fear through the city as lone women bolted and barred their doors and slept with knives or guns beside their beds.

Two weeks after Anna Sleser's murder, 63-year-old Mrs Nina Nichols was in the middle of a telephone conversation with her sister when the doorbell rang. She broke off, saying she would ring back when the caller had gone. She never did and when her sister failed to get an answer later in the evening, she asked the janitor to check the apartment. He found Mrs Nichols lying on her back, her legs spread wide and her housecoat and slip pulled up above her waist to expose her body. She had been assaulted with a foreign object – later shown to be a wine bottle – and strangled with her own stockings, which were knotted into a bow. The apartment had been ransacked but apparently there had been no theft.

Panic truly took hold in the city with the discovery of the body of Helen Blake, a 65-year-old retired nurse. Though she was not found until 2 July, when neighbours became concerned that she had not been seen for some time, she had been killed on the same day as Nina Nichols. The next two murders also came as a pair: 75-year-old Mrs Ida Irga and 67-year-old Jane Sullivan, who lived on the other side of the city, were both strangled on 20 August. Mrs Irga's body was arranged on the bed with a pillow under her buttocks, the legs spread and propped up on the rungs of two chairs as though she had been prepared for a gynaecological operation. It had been positioned so that it was the first thing seen by anyone entering the room. Jane Sullivan, a strong, heavy ex-nurse, had put up quite a fight, She was found in the bath in a half-kneeling position, her face in 15 cm (6 inches) of water. Her clothes had been pulled up to expose her buttocks and she had been sexually assaulted with a broom handle.

A special 'Strangler Squad' was formed at police headquarters, patrols were increased to unprecedented levels and hundreds of suspects were rounded up but without result. The search became even more difficult when the killer suddenly departed from his normal *modus operandi*: the next three victims – Sophie Clark, Patricia Bissette and Beverly Samans – were young women and, unlike the earlier victims, they had been raped. Beverly Samans had been stabbed to death, though stockings were tied around her neck in the familiar pattern. Police began to wonder if they were looking for more than one murderer.

Two more strangled victims were found in 1963: 58-year-old Evelyn

Corbin and 23-year-old Joann Graff, who was killed on 23 November, a day of national mourning after the assassination of President Kennedy. In January 1964 the final strangling took place: the victim was the youngest so far, 19-year-old Mary Sullivan, a secretary who was found strangled in the shared apartment she had moved into three days before. Along with the stockings, two brightly coloured scarves were round her neck and between the toes of her right foot was slotted a card reading 'Happy New Year'. Semen was running from her mouth and a broom handle had been rammed into her vagina.

The killing stopped but the investigation went on at full strength. A committee of psychiatrists was set up to build up a profile of the Boston Strangler and many of them inclined to the view that there were two stranglers, one favouring elderly victims, the other out to rape young women. Dr James Brussel was convinced that it was one man, whose personality had changed over the time period of the murders: at first he had been obsessed with his mother and had assaulted the elderly women in childish ways but later, when he felt he had revenged himself on her and grown up emotionally, he had turned his attention to younger women. The murders had stopped because he had finally worked through the need to kill. Dr Brussel suggested that the killer would be physically strong, possibly Italian or Spanish, around 30 years old and a neat dresser with a good head of hair; he thought that he would be caught because, rejoicing in his new-found 'maturity', he would need to talk about his crimes.

He was proved right on most counts when, in February 1965, the police received information from a young lawyer about the confession of an inmate of Bridgewater State Hospital. Albert DeSalvo had been arrested for a series of sex crimes and while under observation at the hospital had boasted of being the Boston Strangler to his cellmate, murderer George Nassar. Of course the police were used to dealing with false confessions but this sounded authentic: DeSalvo was able to supply unpublished details about the crimes and the apartments where they had taken place.

DeSalvo came from an unsavoury background: his father had battered his wife and children regularly and taught them to steal from an
early age. He brought prostitutes home and had sex with them in front
of the children. Albert's mother was too centred on her own problems
to spare any love or attention for the children. He joined the army
immediately after leaving school and married a girl he met in Germany, though she divorced him later, complaining of his unreasonable
sexual demands; from an early age he had been obsessed with sex and
needed intercourse four or five times a day.

In 1960 he had been arrested as the 'Measuring Man'. He had been
gaining entry to the apartments of young women on the pretext of
being the representative of a model agency. Often he would simply
take the girl's measurements, thank her politely and leave: other times
he would manage to seduce her, but there were no complaints of
assault.

When detectives investigating a series of rapes covering a wide
area of New England saw a sketch of the rapist, made with the help of
one of the victims, they immediately saw the likeness to the 'Measuring Man' and DeSalvo was arrested again. During 1964 he had carried
out some 300 assaults and had also become known as the 'Green Man'
because he always wore green work trousers. He would break into the
homes of young women, force them to strip at knife-point then kiss
and caress them all over, often raping them, but usually apologizing
before he left. Several of the victims were able to identify DeSalvo.

Once DeSalvo had begun confessing to the 'Strangler' murders,
there was no stopping him. He included two other murders where he
had failed to leave his trademark, so they had never been linked by
the authorities. One was 69-year-old Mary Brown, stabbed and beaten
in her apartment in March 1963, and the other was 85-year-old Mary
Mullen, who had collapsed and died of a heart attack when he grabbed her round the neck so he had left her body undisturbed on the
couch. As the strangler, his method had been to knock on apartment
doors and, when a woman opened the door, he would pretend that he

*Albert DeSalvo*

had been sent to do some maintenance work. No one who met him doubted his ability to convince the women that he was genuine; he gave the impression of being a very pleasant young man. He had chosen his victims at random whenever he felt the urge and the bow he always tied around the neck was the type he used when tying removable casts on his daughter Judy's crippled hip.

DeSalvo maintained that he had no idea why he killed and that he often felt deep shame. Before the murder of Anna Slesers he had been tempted to rape and kill another woman but had pulled back at the last moment in the face of her fear. He had gone down on his knees, sobbing, 'Oh God, what was I doing? I am a good Catholic man with a wife and children. I don't know what to do.' Instead of calling the police she had told him to go home, but now he wished desperately that she had turned him over to the law immediately. The last and youngest victim, Mary Sullivan, had tried to persuade him not to rape her. 'I recall thinking at the time, yes, she's right. I don't have to do these things any more now.' Afterwards he thought: 'Why? I say to myself, it could have been my daughter, too.'

Most of those who heard the 50 hours of tapes produced by DeSalvo were convinced that he was the Boston Strangler but there was no hard evidence. Witnesses who had seen the killer leaving his victims' apartments failed to identity him and there were no fingerprints to tie him to the scene. In a remarkable piece of plea-bargaining DeSalvo's lawyer Lee Bailey managed to agree that his client would receive a life sentence for the other sexual offences. He hoped that DeSalvo would be committed to a mental hospital for treatment but instead he was eventually sent to a maximum-security prison. Six years later he was found dead in his cell, stabbed through the heart by an unknown assailant.

# Ian Brady and Myra Hindley

WHEN the trial of the 'Moors Murderers' took place at Chester Assizes in 1966, the whole of Britain was rocked by the horrific revelations of the century's most cold-blooded killings. Day after day newspapers carried the sombre details of the terrible crimes committed by a 27-year-old stock clerk and a 22-year-old typist who had enticed young children to their home, tortured them for their sadistic gratification, then killed them and buried the small bodies on a desolate stretch of the Pennine moors.

Ian Brady was an illegitimate child brought up by foster parents. He grew up with a taste for torturing animals and in his teens began collecting a list of convictions for theft. At the time he met Myra Hindley in 1961, when they both worked for a chemical supply company in Manchester, she was still a virgin, a homely girl who had converted to Roman Catholicism and was keenly religious. Brady introduced her to sex and to sadism: she posed for obscene photographs and together they gloated over accounts of Hitler's atrocities in Nazi Germany. Eventually this was not sufficiently exciting and they turned to kidnapping and murdering children.

Though several children disappeared from the area, the authorities might never have connected this with the unremarkable young couple if the latter had not tried to recruit Myra's brother-in-law, Dave Smith, to their murderous activities. One night in October 1965 they asked him round on a pretext and while he was waiting in the kitchen he heard 'a hell of a scream', then Myra calling for help. He rushed into the living room, where he saw Brady attacking what he first took to be a rag doll – then realized was a young man. At the trial he was to describe the scene: 'The lad was laid out on his front and Ian stood

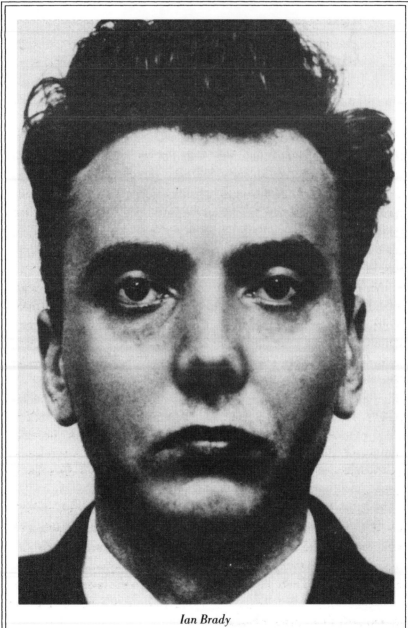

*Ian Brady*

over him with his legs apart with an axe in his right hand. The lad groaned and Ian just lifted the axe over his head and brought it down on the lad's head . . . The lad stopped groaning then. He was making a gurgling noise like when you brush your teeth and gargle with water. Ian had a piece of wire and he wrapped it round the lad's neck and began to pull it.'

The young man on the floor was 17-year-old Edward Evans, a homosexual who had been picked up by Brady on Manchester Central station and attacked 14 times with a hatchet before being strangled. Once Brady and Hindley were sure that he was dead, they moved the body to the back bedroom and mopped up the blood before sitting down to a cup of tea.

Dave Smith, horrified by his experience, contacted the police early next morning and when officers called at the house they found Brady in the middle of writing a note for the office, explaining that he was sick. He had been planning to spend the day disposing of the remains of Edward Evans on the moor. The police found not only the body and the bloody hatchet but other items that set them on the trail of two missing children, 12-year-old John Kilbride, who had disappeared in November 1963, and 10-year-old Lesley Ann Downey, reported missing in December 1964. Seemingly innocent photographs of Myra posing in isolated spots on Saddleworth Moor pinpointed the areas for the search and on 16 October the naked body of Lesley Ann Downey was found, buried in a shallow grave along with clothes identified by her mother. Five days later John Kilbride's body was discovered nearby.

At the trial, a stunned courtroom heard the tape the defendants had made of the torture of Lesley Ann Downey, during which the little girl had screamed, sobbed and pleaded: 'I want to see my mummy . . . Please God, help me . . . I can't breathe . . . It hurts me.' The all-male jurors lowered their heads as the horrific tape was played. People in the court swayed with disgust and onlookers in the public gallery buried their faces in their hands.

Brady admitted to killing Evans, though he said that the murder was not premeditated. He maintained that he and Smith had planned to 'roll the queer' but he had fought back so hard that he had had to be kept quiet. He denied all knowledge of John Kilbride and claimed that he had paid Lesley Ann Downey 10 shillings to pose in the nude for photographs, but that she had become distressed and had left with Smith. When he was asked how he felt when he heard the tape he said he was 'embarrassed'. Hindley, who denied involvement in any murder, admitted: 'I am ashamed.'

In his summing up, Mr Justice Atkinson said: 'I suppose that hearing and reading about these allegations, the first reaction of kindly, charitable people is to say this is so terrible that anyone doing anything like that might be mentally afflicted . . . There has not been the smallest suggestion that either of these two are mentally abnormal or not fully and completely responsible for their actions. If, and I underline if, the prosecution is right, you are dealing with two sadistic killers of the utmost depravity.'

It took the jury only two hours and 20 minutes to decide that Brady was guilty of all three murders and Hindley was guilty of murdering Evans and Lesley Ann Downey and of harbouring and assisting Brady, knowing that he had murdered John Kilbride. Brady received three concurrent life sentences and Hindley two life sentences plus seven years in the Kilbride case.

In 1985 Brady confessed in a newspaper interview to two more murders, that of 12-year-old Keith Bennett, missing since 1964, and 16-year-old Pauline Reade, who disappeared in 1963. Later Myra Hindley was allowed out of prison to take police to Pauline's grave on the moors, but Keith Bennett's body was never found. In August 1987 Brady wrote a letter to the BBC in which he talked about five other murders, but the victims have not been identified.

# Richard Speck

WHEN a pretty young Filipino student nurse, Corazon Amurao, opened the door of a Chicago nurses' home on the night of 13 July 1966 she found herself facing a tall, blond man smelling strongly of alcohol. He had a gun in one hand and a knife in the other but his words were, comparatively speaking, reassuring. 'I'm not going to hurt you,' he said as he shepherded Corazon and two other nurses upstairs. 'I'm only going to tie you up. I need your money to get to New Orleans.'

In the back bedroom were three other nurses and the gunman tied them all with strips torn from the bedsheets. Over the next half hour, while he collected all the money he could find, three more student nurses arrived home and they were trussed up alongside their colleagues. Then the intruder began taking them out, one by one. The remaining girls, panic-stricken, tried to roll themselves under the beds but only Corazon Amurao, who was small and slight, managed to hide herself well enough to fool their attacker. When only Gloria Davy was left in the room, apart from Corazon, the man returned and spent 25 minutes raping her before he led her from the room.

Corazon lay were she was for hours before daring to roll out from under the bed and scream from the window for help. When the police arrived they found a scene of carnage. The first girl to die had been Pamela Wilkening, who had been stabbed and then strangled. This first murder seemed to have roused the killer to a pitch of sexual excitement and after that he killed every 20 minutes or so. The girls had been stabbed or strangled or both; one of them, 20-year-old Suzanne Farris, had been stabbed 18 times and her underclothes had been ripped to shreds.

The sole survivor was able to give the police an accurate description of the killer, down to his southern drawl and the tattoo 'Born to raise hell' on his arm. Another important clue was that the knots in the girls' bonds were of a kind used by seamen, so police made enquiries at the office of the Seaman's Union near the nurses' hostel and, sure enough, staff there remembered a man matching the police description enquiring about a ship to New Orleans. He had filled out an application form in the name of Richard Franklin Speck and the fingerprints on the form corresponded with those found at the murder scene.

Speck was 25 and had a long record of burglary and drunk and disorderly offences. He had married at the age of 20 but his wife's infidelities had enraged him to the point where he once attacked a complete stranger, holding a carving knife to her throat, because she reminded him of his wife. Later they separated but he was often heard to say that he would kill her if it was the last thing he did. On the night he went to the nurses' hostel he was under the influence of both drink and drugs and it may be that he intended only robbery, not murder. Corazon Amurao remembered him gazing at Gloria Davy all the time he was talking about money, as though fascinated by her, and his family later confirmed that she looked very much like his wife. It may be that the sight of her triggered some deep desire for revenge and he went berserk; it is significant that he left Gloria until last (or so he thought) and that she was the only girl to be raped.

After his frenzy of killing, Speck began a further round of hard drinking, drug-taking and visiting prostitutes. Having spent all the money he had taken from his victims, he registered in a seedy backstreet hotel where he annoyed his neighbours by begging for dollars or drink. Then, on the night of 16 July, he staggered out of his room with blood streaming from his slashed wrists. He was taken to hospital, where the doctor recognized him by his tattoo. As the doctor told the nurse to ring the police, Speck whispered: 'Do you collect the $10,000 reward, doc?'

Speck's trial lasted for eight weeks but it took the jury less than an hour to convict him of multiple murder. He was sentenced to death but was saved when the US Supreme Court ruled that capital punishment was unconstitutional – a decision that was later reversed. Instead he received eight consecutive life sentences and though he did come up for parole several times this was always refused. A difficult prisoner at first, he eventually settled down to life in gaol and was put to good use painting the prison walls. He died of a heart attack in 1991 at the age of 49.

# Norman Collins

In 1967, some teenage boys exploring a ruined farmhouse near the town of Ypsilanti in Michigan, USA, stumbled across a decomposing body thrown on a rubbish heap. The remains were identified as those of Mary Fleszar, who had been missing for a month; she had been stabbed and her hands and feet had been hacked off. As her body lay in the funeral parlour a young man claiming to be a friend of the family arrived and wanted to take photographs.

A year later Joan Schell, like Mary Fleszar a student at Eastern Michigan University, went missing five days before her body was found with 47 stab wounds. Her clothes were bunched up around her neck and she had been raped. Friends reported that she had been seen with a fellow student, 21-year-old Norman Collins, on the night of her disappearance. Collins was a good-looking young man with plenty of charm and when he explained that he had been at home with his family on the day in question, the police had no reason to disbelieve him.

In March 1969 the body of a third university student, Jan Mixer, was found in a cemetery, shot and strangled. Fellow students knew that she had advertised on the noticeboard for someone to give her a lift to her home in Muskegon, so it seemed possible that she had been killed by the driver who had offered a ride. In the next three weeks two more bodies were found: 16-year-old Maralynn Skelton, who had been flogged with a belt before she was bludgeoned to death, and 13-year-old Dawn Basom, who was found half-naked, with the black electric cord used to strangle her still wound round her neck.

The 'Michigan Murderer' struck again in June, this time apparently in a frenzy of rage and excitement, for he stabbed Alice Kalom over and over again, cut her throat, then shot her through the head. She was found lying in a field covered in blood; she was naked from the waist down and had been raped.

So far the police had no major clues, but in July the case began to break. The last victim was 18-year-old Karen Bieneman, who had been savagely beaten, sexually assaulted and strangled. Her breasts and stomach had been scalded by some corrosive liquid and her briefs had been stuffed into her vagina. On the day she disappeared she had been shopping in town and the manageress of one of the shops remembered that a dark-haired young man had been waiting outside on a motorbike – Karen had even mentioned that she had accepted a lift from a stranger. The description given by the manageress sounded remarkably like Norman Collins.

Meanwhile Collins's uncle, State Police Corporal David Leik, returned home to Ypsilanti after a holiday to find splashes of black paint on his basement floor, which he could only assume had been left by his nephew, who had a key to the house so that he could feed the family dog. When he scraped up some of the paint, he uncovered suspicious brown stains underneath and notified the police. Tests showed that the stains were nothing more gruesome than varnish, but in the course of their investigations the forensic team gathered hair clippings (Mrs Leik had trimmed her son's hair before the holiday) which matched those found on Karen Bieneman's briefs. It seemed that Collins might well have taken Karen back to his uncle's basement to torture and kill her, then, thinking that the varnish stains were blood, he had attempted to cover them with paint, inadvertently leading the police to evidence that would incriminate him.

Collins's alibi for the day that Karen Bieneman disappeared did not stand up and, according to his roommate, he had carried a cardboard box containing various items of women's clothing out to his car on the day in question and had returned without it. The description the roommate gave of some of the items he had seen sounded like clothes belonging to the murder victims.

Collins was an attractive young man who always had plenty of girlfriends, but those who knew him reported that he was oversexed and subject to violent rages if he could not get what he wanted from a girl. He had been seen to chase a girl fitting the description of Alice Kalom down the stairs, angrily accusing her of being a tease. He was interested in bondage and found any contact with menstruation revolting. This was interesting to the police, because several of the girls had been menstruating at the time they were killed and they had been assaulted but not raped. Yet another interesting fact was that Collins had used a dud cheque to rent a trailer from a local firm in June 1969 and had never returned it. The trailer had eventually been found in California, near the site of another unsolved rape and murder, that of 17-year-old Roxie Phillips, who had disappeared while Collins was on holiday in California. However, Collins denied all knowledge of the girl and nothing could be proved.

Collins was tried only for the murder of Karen Bieneman and, apart from the identification by the shop manageress, most of the evidence was forensic. It was enough to result in conviction and Collins was sentenced to 20 years in gaol.

# Wayne Boden

THEY called him the 'Vampire Rapist', the weird sadistic killer who murdered one girl after another, leaving deep bite marks all over the breasts of each victim. The first warning that there was a killer with an obsession with breasts on the loose was when a 21-year-old teacher, Norma Vaillancourt, was found strangled in her apartment in Montreal, Canada, on 23 July 1968. She was naked and her breasts were covered with human bite marks but, surprisingly enough, there were no signs of a struggle and the girl's face, far from displaying fright, bore the signs of a faint smile.

Almost a year later the body of Shirley Audette was found dumped in the yard behind her apartment block in West Montreal. She was fully clothed but had been raped and strangled and there were vicious bite marks all over her breasts. Once again there had been no apparent struggle so it seemed likely that she had known her killer and had been willing to indulge in some rough foreplay before he lost control. She had told friends that she was scared that she was 'getting into something dangerous with a new boyfriend' but no one knew who she was dating at the time.

When the jewellery store where Marielle Archambault worked as a clerk closed on 23 November 1969 she left on the arm of a young man she called 'Bill', smiling happily and obviously looking forward to her date. The next day when she failed to report for work the manager phoned her landlady to find out if she was sick. The landlady entered Marielle's apartment to find her naked body lying on the floor, partly covered by a blanket. This time there had been a violent struggle and the killer had ripped her clothes in order to rape her and savage her breasts. A crumpled photograph found on the floor of the flat was identified by Marielle's workmates as the man named Bill but though sketches appeared on the front page of the city's newspaper under the headline 'Montreal Vampire', the identity of the killer remained a mystery.

He struck again two months later, when 24-year-old Jean Way died in her Montreal apartment. On 16 January she had a date with her boyfriend but he turned up early and received no answer to his knock. He went away and returned later, this time finding the door unlocked and his girlfriend dead, her breasts bloody and covered with teeth marks. The police thought that the murderer had probably been with Jean when her boyfriend knocked the first time. In spite of the violence her body had suffered, her expression was tranquil.

Perhaps the Vampire Rapist felt that the police were getting too close, for he moved his scene of operations to Calgary, 4000 km (2500 miles) away, where schoolteacher Elizabeth Porteous failed to arrive for work on 18 May 1971 and was later found dead on her bedroom floor. She had struggled hard against her attacker, her clothes were torn, she had been raped and strangled and her breasts showed the all-too-familiar bite marks. A broken cufflink lay on the floor near the body. Friends from school said that she had a new boyfriend called Bill and they had seen her riding with a young man in a blue Mercedes on the night of the murder. They recalled that the car had a sticker advertising beef in the window. The description of Elizabeth's companion – the neat hairstyle and trendy clothes – matched that given by Marielle Archambault's colleagues.

The following day police found a blue Mercedes with a beef advertisement sticker parked near Elizabeth Porteous's home and they kept a watch on it until the driver returned. He was obviously the man in the photograph from Marielle's apartment and when police approached him he put up no resistance and went quietly with them to the station. He identified himself as Wayne Clifford Boden and said he had lived in Calgary for a year since moving from Montreal; he admitted that he had been with Elizabeth Porteous in her apartment the previous night, and that the cufflink belonged to him, but he insisted that Elizabeth had been alive and unharmed when he left her.

However, his account did not hold up against the evidence of the dental expert who compared a cast of Boden's teeth with the bite marks on the body and found 29 points of similarity. Boden was sentenced to life imprisonment for the murder of Elizabeth Porteous, then sent to Montreal for trial on three other murders, for which he received three more life sentences. Oddly enough, he always denied killing Norma Vaillancourt and was never charged with this early murder.

Boden was obviously attractive to women and able to convince them to go along with some of his strange inclinations. Perhaps he sought out girls with a masochistic streak who would submit to a certain amount of painful 'experiments' in lovemaking, little knowing that his overpowering sexual urges would lead to death. In two cases he may have misjudged his target, for both Marielle Archambault and Elizabeth Porteous tried to fight him off, but in the other cases, where girls were found with serene faces, he may well have strangled them into unconsciousness before they realized what was happening to them, then indulged his overwhelming need to rape them and worry their breasts with his teeth like a wild animal.

# George Putt

LONG before George Putt committed his first murder, he was entangled with violence and criminality. At the beginning the violence was directed against him; when he was only three months old his father was arrested for child cruelty after he had thrashed his baby with a strap. By the time he was eight both his parents were in prison and George and his brothers were living with their grandparents in Virginia, USA. When George and one of his brothers got into trouble with the police after stealing an air rifle and shooting at a neighbour's windows, his grandparents sent him to an orphanage where every misdeed was punished by a beating.

At the age of 15 he attacked two young girls, forcing one of them to practise oral sex, and was considered for committal to a mental institution. While awaiting trial for sodomy later the same year he escaped from custody. Once on the run he robbed and raped a 30-year-old Richmond woman at knife-point, then fled to Texas where he broke into an apartment in Laredo and forced a woman to drive him out of town by threatening the lives of her children. After a police chase he crashed the car and escaped on foot, only to be arrested the next day.

He spent some time in secure schools and was entered into various assessment and treatment programmes. By 1965, when he was 19, doctors had described him as psychotic and referred to the 'almost unbelievable physical and emotional deprivation' he had suffered. Nevertheless, he was automatically released from custody on his twenty-first birthday in 1967 and drifted from place to place, usually moving on when he was caught stealing.

By 1969 he was married and living in Memphis. Soon after he arrived in the city a middle-aged couple, Roy and Bernalyn Dumas, were found beaten and strangled. Mrs Dumas was spread out on the bed, her wrists and ankles tied to the bedposts. She had been raped and her sex organs had been mutilated with knife cuts. Later he was to claim that all he had planned was a robbery, but that he had been carried away by a wave of sadistic violence.

Only 11 days later, on 25 August, an 80-year-old widow, Leila Jackson, was found dead in her apartment; she had been strangled with a stocking and her genitals had been mutilated with a kitchen knife. It seemed that once Putt had tasted the thrill of murder he was unable to stop, for he claimed another victim four days after Mrs Jackson. This time the dead woman was 21-year-old Glenda Harden, whose body was found in a park; she had been tied up, then stabbed 14 times.

Putt's wife was pregnant at this time and on the night of 10 August he had a nightmare and woke her with his cries. The following day tenants in an apartment block heard screams from 59-year-old Mary Pickens and saw a young man running away, a bloody knife in his hand. Police officers found Mary Pickens lying dead with 19 stab wounds. They radioed ahead to squad-car colleagues and after a chase, Putt was caught breathless and bloodstained. When questioned at the station, he admitted, 'I killed them all.'

Putt was found guilty of murdering Mary Pickens in October 1970 and sentenced to death, but his appeals were still continuing when a US Supreme Court ruling set aside the death penalty. It was not until 1973 that he was tried and convicted for the murders of Mr and Mrs Dumas. His sentences added up to a total of 497 years.

# Dean Corll

ON THE morning of 8 August 1973, Pasadena police received a call from 18-year-old Wayne Henley, claiming he had just shot a man. When officers arrived the young man led them to the body of 33-year-old electrician Dean Corll, who was lying face down in the hallway of his house with six bullets from a .22 calibre pistol in his body.

Corll was known locally as a 'good neighbour and a real good guy', a lover of children who generously handed out candy and gave neighbourhood youngsters rides in his van. Meanwhile, he was paying Henley and another young man, David Brooks, to procure boys for him to torture and kill. Henley took the officers to a boatshed where Corll had rented a stall and they had only dug down about 15 cm (6 inches) when they unearthed a large parcel wrapped in clear plastic and saw a boy's dead face looking up at them. There was no doubt about the way he had died; the rope was still embedded deep in his neck. After that they made a thorough search of the shed and dug up 16 more bodies. Henley then directed them to two other sites where bodies had been buried and in all 27 were recovered, though Henley insisted there were at least four others that were never found.

Henley had been introduced to Corll by David Brooks two years before. Corll and Brooks had known one another since their school-days and had been roommates from time to time, when Corll would pay Brooks for sex acts. The latter told how he had once surprised Corll in his apartment molesting two naked boys who were tied to boards; Corll had bought his silence with the gift of a car.

Corll was, on the face of it, an ordinary young man, with nothing in his background to suggest that he was a sadistic killer. As a child he was oversensitive and sickly, tied to his mother's apron-strings. Later he had two serious relationships with women and considered marriage; it was only when he joined the army at the age of 25 that he realized he was a homosexual and became more introverted and touchy, imagining slights where none were intended. According to Brooks he committed his first murder in 1970, killing a student hitchhiker named Jeffrey Konen.

With his two young accomplices he organized glue-sniffing parties to pick out potential victims, then the boy selected would be asked round alone and plied with drinks and drugs until he lost consciousness. Then Corll would take him to his 'torture room', strip him and handcuff him to a plank of wood. Sodomy was routine and Corll had plenty more sadistic games to play, such as plucking out his victim's body hairs one by one and sexually assaulting him with various objects. One of the boys found in the boatshed had had his sex organs removed and buried in a separate plastic bag and another had bite marks on his genitals. Sometimes Corll would amuse himself with the boys for several days before he shot or strangled them. Most of the boys were aged between 13 and 17, with the youngest – the son of a shopkeeper living opposite Corll's home – only 9, and on at least three occasions he killed two youngsters in one day.

Eventually, Corll pushed his luck too far. In the early hours of the morning of 8 August Henley brought 16-year-old Timothy Kerley and 15-year-old Rhonda Williams round to Corll's apartment for a glue-sniffing session and within an hour all three teenagers had passed out. When Henley came round he found that Corll, angry because he had ruined his plans by bringing a girl along, was threatening to shoot him. He had to beg and plead for his life, only persuading Corll to free him by promising to rape and kill Rhonda while Corll did the same to Timothy. Both youngsters were stripped and handcuffed to the 'torture boards'. Henley then attempted to rape Rhonda but was unable to perform and a heated argument broke out between the two men. Somewhere in the midst of the shouting, Henley seized the gun and threatened Corll, who mocked him, saying, 'Go on, kill me if you dare.' At the end of his tether, Henley pumped six bullets into him. He then released Rhonda and Timothy, who were still only half-conscious, and called the police.

At first Henley maintained that he had not been directly involved in the murders but Brooks had. Brooks, on the other hand, said that he knew nothing about murder but that Henley, who enjoyed inflicting pain, had been closely involved. Both were tried for murder: Brooks was sentenced to life imprisonment and Henley was given six 99-year terms.

# John Wayne Gacy

JOHN WAYNE GACY'S parents called their son after their screen idol in the hope that he might one day make his mark on the world, but they could never have envisaged that the name would be remembered with horror by millions of Americans as one of the country's most sadistic mass murderers, the 'Killer Clown'.

Young John's father was disappointed in his son, who was overweight and frequently ill. Gacy senior was a natural bully who drank too much and beat his son at the slightest excuse, calling him 'sissy' and 'stupid'. The boy never came to terms with his father's rejection and grew up longing to win his love and respect. He had various careers; during his first marriage he was a successful restaurant manager, showing himself adept at building up the business, and later he did well as a building contractor.

In the late 1970s he was a resident of a prosperous suburb of Chicago and was active in Democratic politics. Every year he organized the town's political summer fête, which was attended by all the local dignitaries and raised funds for President Jimmy Carter's re-election fund. Gacy treasured the photograph in which he was seen shaking hands with the President's wife. He desperately needed to be liked and to that end he became 'Pogo the Clown', designing his costumes himself and performing in full make-up at children's parties, hospitals and benefits.

Gacy was now 36 but, unknown to his fellow townsfolk in Chicago, he had a record for sex crimes dating back ten years. At the time of the first incident, in 1968, he was running a fried-chicken restaurant in Iowa, was active in the Junior Chamber of Commerce and was hotly tipped as a future mayor. He was charged with coercing two boys,

*John Wayne Gacy in full clown costume outside his home*

aged 16 and 15, into homosexual acts and then with hiring a young thug to beat up one of the prosecution witnesses. The judge rejected the defence submission that Gacy was simply experimenting with homosexuality and needed no more than parole supervision. Recognizing a sadistic streak in the defendant, he sentenced him to 10 years' imprisonment. Gacy's first wife, the mother of two children, divorced him while he was in prison, though he protested his innocence so vigorously that many of his friends believed that he had been framed by political opponents. He was such a model prisoner that he was freed in 18 months.

He moved to Chicago, started his construction business and began courting a young divorcee with two children, Carole Hoff. In 1971 a homosexual youth complained to the police that Gacy had picked him up at the Greyhound bus terminal and attempted to rape him. The boy failed to attend court for the hearing and the charges were dropped. The following year Gacy married Carole Hoff but the marriage was not a success: Gacy was little interested in sex with his bride and she soon realized that, though he assured her that he was bisexual not homosexual, he preferred boys. There was his violent temper, too – not to mention the bad smell that always seemed to hang about the house and which he said was all in her imagination.

In January 1978 Gacy came to the attention of the police again when a 26-year-old homosexual, Jeffrey Rignall, told them that he had been brutally assaulted. He had accepted an invitation to smoke a joint in Gacy's car, but Gacy had suddenly clapped a chloroform-soaked pad over his face and when he woke up he was confined in a basement room, where Gacy had alternately raped and chloroformed him. The next morning he regained consciousness in Lincoln Park in the snow. Though Rignall, who suffered permanent liver damage from the effects of the chloroform, spent weeks watching the major roads of the city until he spotted Gacy's car and identified him to the police, they decided there was too little evidence for an arrest.

Then, in December, 15-year-old Robert Piest went missing. Robert, who worked after school at a pharmacy because he was saving to buy a car, had said that he might be a bit late home because he had to talk to a local contractor about a summer job. It was his mother's birthday and the family were waiting for Robert's return to start her party, but Robert never did come home. At 11.30 pm the Piests reported his disappearance to the police, who discovered that the interior of the pharmacy where Robert worked had been remodelled recently by Gacy's firm, so it seemed likely that he might be the contractor the boy had mentioned.

When the police, now aware of Gacy's previous record, called at his bungalow to interview him, they immediately noticed a pungent odour and recognized it as the smell of decaying flesh. They opened a trapdoor leading to the crawl space under the house and found themselves gazing at the rotting remains of a number of bodies. Under the appalled gaze of the neighbours seven bodies were found under the house, all in various stages of decomposition, and eight more in lime pits about the house – there seemed no end to the horror as body after body was carried out. The investigating officers wore disposable overalls and gas masks and bathed in disinfectant at the end of each shift.

Gacy, meanwhile, was confessing to 32 murders of teenage boys in seven years – though in fact he had miscounted and there were 33. When he ran out of space to bury the bodies around the house he began throwing them into the Des Plaines River, and this had been the fate of Robert Piest. His favourite method was to lure the young man to his home then produce a pair of handcuffs and offer to show his guest a 'handcuff trick'. Once he had his victim firmly cuffed, Gacy would subject him to savage homosexual rape. 'The real trick in getting out of the handcuffs is to have the key,' he would taunt him. When he had finished, Gacy would throw a piece of cord around the young man's neck and tie two knots in it. Then he would push a piece of wood through the loop and slowly turn. Within seconds the victim was unconscious, a few seconds more and he was dead.

It was early in 1972, a few months before he married Carole Hoff, that Gacy committed his first murder, though he insisted that he was acting in self-defence. He had taken home an 18-year-old youth he had met at the Greyhound bus station and they had enjoyed oral sex together, but in the early hours of the morning he awoke to find his guest standing over him with a knife. They fought and the young man fell on the knife but Gacy was afraid that in view of his past record the police would not believe his version of events, so he buried the body in the crawl space.

Some of his victims were homosexual, others were not. Occasionally a male prostitute was well paid for sex and allowed to go free. Gacy used the construction business to contact teenagers. One of them was John Butkovich, who had argued with him over wages and was assumed to be a runaway when he disappeared in 1975. After his divorce from Carole the following year, Gacy was able to speed up his activities: Darrell Samson disappeared in April 1976 and a month later Randall Reffett and Samuel Stapleton were killed on the same day. In June, Billy Carroll joined the others in the crawl space, and so the killings continued.

Under questioning, Gacy denied being a homosexual and insisted that he hated homosexuals, which perhaps went some way towards explaining why he wanted to kill those with whom he had participated in homosexual acts. He claimed that the killings were performed by a wicked alter ego called Jack, who took over his personality when he had been drinking. It was Jack who drove him out to search for boys, then later in the night he would come to his senses to find a corpse stretched in front of him and know that Jack had been at work again. His defence lawyers argued that Gacy was insane; University of Chicago psychiatrist Lawrence Freedman decided that he was psychotic and reported that he was one of the most complex personalities he had ever encountered. However, the prosecution considered that it was incredible that a man could have committed all of 33 murders over so many years in periods of temporary insanity. Two psychiatrists testified that Gacy's insanity was feigned and that he had known quite well what he was doing. The jury accepted their opinion and in March 1980 they convicted him on all counts of murder and he was sentenced to death.

# David Carpenter

THE BODY of 44-year-old Edda Kane was found on a hiking trail in Mount Tamalpais State Park near San Francisco, USA, in August 1979. She was naked and had been raped and then shot through the head while kneeling, as though she had been begging for her life. Seven months later another hiker, 23-year-old Barbara Swartz, was murdered in the park, stabbed in the chest while on her knees. The third victim of the 'Trailside Killer' was Anne Alderson, who had been jogging in the park and was found with three bullets in her head. She, too, had been kneeling.

In November 1980, 25-year-old Shauna May went missing in Point Reyes Park, near the same city, where she had gone to meet a boyfriend. After a two-day search her body was found in a shallow grave alongside that of 22-year-old Diane O'Connell, who had been missing for several weeks. Both had been killed by bullets in the head. The decomposing bodies of two missing teenagers, who had been killed in the same manner were also discovered.

On 29 March 1981, hikers Gene Blake and Ellen Hansen were accosted by a gunman who threatened Ellen with rape, then shot her when she resisted, killing her instantly. Her companion was also shot but, bleeding from wounds on his face and neck, he was able to drag himself back along the path, leaving a trail of blood. He was able to provide police with a full description of his assailant, right down to his yellow, crooked teeth. When sketches were made, they bore a distinct resemblance to an ex-convict named David Carpenter who was now living and working in San Francisco.

Carpenter had served a 14-year sentence for attacking a woman with a hammer and was later imprisoned for robbing and kidnapping. With four other convicts, he staged a violent gaol-break but was recaptured by the FBI. In the 1970s he had been a suspect in the Zodiac killings, when five people had been shot by a gunman who bragged about the murders in letters to the newspapers (see page 361). Carpenter was cleared when fingerprint and handwriting checks proved negative.

Police questioned 53-year-old Carpenter and searched his home but found no weaponry. However, Gene Blake identified him from police photographs as his attacker in the park and while investigations were under way, reports of another missing girl threw further suspicion on Carpenter. Heather Scaggs, a 22-year-old colleague from the print shop where Carpenter worked, had disappeared after setting off to see him about a car sale. Over three weeks later, her body was found by a party of hikers in Big Basin Redwood State Park, near San Francisco. The bullets found in her body matched those used to shoot Gene Blake and Ellen Hansen. Soon afterwards, a remand prisoner gave evidence that Carpenter had recently sold him a .38 revolver and when the gun was examined it was found to be the weapon from the three shootings.

Now that Carpenter had emerged as the likely killer, police were able to link yet another murder with the 'Trailside Killings' – that of Anna Menjivas, whose body had been found in Tamalpais State Park in June 1980. She had known Carpenter well and he had often taken her home after work.

Carpenter was tried for the murders of Heather Scaggs and Ellen Hansen in Los Angeles, after his lawyers had protested that it would be impossible for him to obtain a fair trial in San Francisco. All the same he was found guilty of first-degree murder, with the judge saying that Carpenter's whole life had been 'a continuous expression of violence and force almost beyond exception. I must conclude with the prosecution that if ever there was a case appropriate for the death penalty, this is it.' He sentenced him to death in the gas chamber of San Quentin.

At a second trial, in San Diego, he was convicted of five more murders as well as two rapes and again sentenced to death. On a later appeal it was decided that, because of a legal technicality, Carpenter must be granted a new trial for the second set of murders, so there may yet be more developments in the case.

# Pedro Lopez

ONE DAY in April 1980 Carvina Poveda, who worked in the Plaza Rosa marketplace in Ecuador, realized that her 12-year-old daughter Maria, who had been playing nearby, was missing. Frantically she ran through the market, calling for her daughter, before she saw her walking away holding the hand of a tall stranger. She hurried after them, shouting for help, and a dozen local Indians jumped on the man and held him down until the police arrived.

He was 31-year-old Pedro Lopez, who, once in custody, was to admit to the rape and murder of 300 girls, averaging two victims a week over the past three years. The story that unfolded was so revolting that Lopez had to be segregated in a cell in the women's section of the prison as other prisoners threatened to castrate him and then burn him alive. The women prisoners were held to be in no danger from Lopez as 'his sex drive was geared only to young children'.

The 'Monster of the Andes' was born in a small Colombian village, the seventh son of a prostitute with 13 children in all. At the age of eight his mother turned him out for sexually fondling one of his younger sisters. When he went back home, his mother took him to another town on a bus and abandoned him there. He was sitting crying in the gutter when a man approached, treated him kindly and promised to look after him. Instead he took him to a deserted building and raped him. After that, Lopez refused to sleep indoors. 'I slept on the stairs of marketplaces and plazas,' he said. 'I would look up and if I could see a star, I knew I was under the protection of God.' For some time he lived on the streets, then an American family in Bogotá took him in and sent him to a school for orphans. He repaid them by stealing money from the school and running away.

At 18 he was gaoled in Colombia for car theft and on his second day behind bars he was gang-raped by four other prisoners. He was determined to take revenge and spent two weeks making a knife. Then he lured the men into a quiet corner, one by one, and killed the first three, though the fourth man managed to escape and ran screaming through the prison. Lopez claimed that the killings were self-defence and two years were added to his sentence.

Once released from prison, he began his future pattern of stalking young girls. 'I lost my innocence at the age of eight,' he said later. 'So I decided to do the same to as many young girls as I could.' He concentrated mainly on Indian girls, as the authorities were not much concerned about their disappearance. His crimes first came to light when he was caught by a group of Ayachucos Indians in northern Peru as he attempted to abduct a nine-year-old girl. They stripped and beat him, then put him in a hole and prepared to bury him alive. He was saved by an American missionary, who persuaded them that they should turn him over to the police. She took him to the nearest police outpost herself, but instead of mounting a thorough investigation the police solved their problem by deporting him.

He then travelled through Colombia and Ecuador, where the killing spree began in earnest. 'I liked the girls in Ecuador,' he told police. 'They are more gentle and trusting, and more innocent. They are not as suspicious of strangers as Colombian girls.' He would prowl the markets until he found the right girl 'with a certain look of innocence and beauty'. If necessary he would watch the child for days until she was alone and unprotected. He would then pretend to be a friend of her mother's and lead her off to a quiet spot where he could rape and kill.

'I would become very excited watching them die,' he remembered. 'I would stare into their eyes until I saw the light in them go out. The girls never really struggled – they didn't have time. I would bury a girl, then go out immediately and look for another one. I never killed any of them at night, because I wanted to watch them die by daylight.'

Police in three countries had been concerned about the number of young girls who were disappearing but they thought that they were looking for white-slavers, kidnapping girls to serve as prostitutes in the cities. Then in April 1980, a flash flood near the town of Ambato in Ecuador washed away the river bank and exposed the remains of four of the missing girls. It was just a few days later that Pedro Lopez was brought in after the incident in the Plaza Rosa.

At first Lopez denied everything but he was tricked into revealing the truth. A priest, Pastor Córdoba Gudino, spent a month masquerading as a prisoner, sharing a cell with Lopez and exchanging stories of past crimes. Gudino passed on the information to the police, who were then able to extract a full confession from Lopez. Once he began giving details the police were inclined to think that he was exaggerating, for he admitted to raping and killing 110 girls in Ecuador, 100 in Colombia and 'many more than 100' in Peru. Their doubts soon evaporated when he took them to the graves of dozens of girls. At Ambato, 3000 m (10,000 ft) up in the Andes, he directed them to the remains of 53 girls, all aged between 8 and 12. At 28 other sites the bodies could not be found because prowling animals had reached them first; other corpses had been buried at roadworks and construction sites so that they were now encased in concrete.

'We may never know exactly how many young girls Lopez killed. I believe his estimate of 300 is very low, because in the beginning he cooperated and took us each day to three or four hidden corpses. But then he tired, changed his mind and stopped helping,' Major Victor Lascano, director of Ambato prison, told reporters.

Convicted of multiple murders, Lopez received a life sentence, which in Ecuador meant a maximum of 16 years. He was lucky; if he had been tried in Colombia he would have faced death by firing squad.

# Gerald Gallego
# and Charlene Williams

WHEN Gerald Gallego was convicted of murder and sentenced to death he was following in his father's footsteps, for Gallego senior was executed in Mississippi's gas chamber for the murder of two police officers. His son was only eight years old at the time and was told by his mother that his father had died in an accident. He only learned the truth at the age of 17, by which time he already had a criminal record himself: he was sentenced to juvenile detention at the age of 13 for having sex with a six-year-old girl, and at 16 he was convicted of armed robbery and sent to a reform school.

He married his first wife at 18 and by the time he was 32, in 1978, he was preparing for his seventh wedding. However, his 14-year-old daughter Sally Jo went to the police to report that he had sexually abused her since she was eight and on his thirty-second birthday had given himself a special treat by raping and sodomizing both Sally Jo and a teenage schoolfriend. A warrant was issued for his arrest and he was forced to flee. With him went his wife-to-be, Charlene Williams, who was besotted by the dominating, egotistical Gallego.

Charlene came from a very different background: her home in Sacramento was solidly middle class, and her father was a well-to-do businessman who had given her every chance in life. She was a shy, intelligent child who did well at school, but when she went to college she became involved in drug-taking; her academic career was ruined and by the age of 21 she had been married and divorced twice. She met Gallego on a blind date and found him an exciting and fascinating lover. They married in 1978, though the marriage was bigamous, as

Gallego was still married to his previous wife. He shared with her his sexual fantasies about finding the perfect 'sex slave' who could be forced to do anything he demanded.

Gallego was determined to translate fantasy into reality and Charlene was to play a vital part in helping him. On 11 September 1978 she got talking to two young girls – 17-year-old Rhonda Scheffler and 16-year-old Kippi Vaught – and asked them back to her van to share a joint. Once inside, they were forced into the back by Gallego, who raped and battered them. Afterwards they were driven to a quiet spot outside Sacramento and shot through the head.

Nine months later 14-year-old Brenda Judd and 13-year-old Sandra Colley disappeared from a fairground in Reno, Nevada. Their bodies were never found but, according to the account given by Charlene Williams after her arrest, they suffered the same fate as the first two girls and were buried in a shallow grave near the town of Lovelock. On 24 April 1980 Stacy Ann Redican and Karen Chipman-Twiggs, two 17-year-olds on a shopping trip in Sacramento, were lured into the van for Gallego's pleasure and later battered to death with a hammer.

On 8 June 1980 Charlene stopped the van at Port Orford, Oregon, and offered 21-year-old Linda Aguilar a lift. Linda was four months pregnant and glad of the ride, never dreaming that she had anything to fear from a woman driver. When her body was found two days later, in a grave to the south of Gold Beach, her skull was shattered and her wrists and ankles tied with nylon rope. Sand in her nose, mouth and windpipe showed that she had been buried alive. Only five weeks later Virginia Mochel disappeared from the car park of the tavern where she worked as a barmaid, shortly after she had been seen talking to a young couple: a quiet, attractive girl and a loud, extrovert man. Her naked body was found in the autumn, her hands tied behind her with fishing line and a cord tight round her neck, indicating strangulation.

Craig Miller and Beth Sowers left a restaurant in Sacramento, where they had been attending a fraternity dance, shortly after midnight on 2 November 1980. As they went towards their car a respectable-looking young woman approached them and, as they paused to see what she wanted, she produced a gun and told them to get into the back of the van. Andy Beal, a friend of Craig's, had followed the couple from the dance and now tried to get into the van after them, chatting merrily. He only realized that something was wrong when Charlene Williams slapped his face and screamed at him to get out. As the van sped away, Andy Beal noted the licence number and phoned the police to report a suspected kidnapping.

Ownership of the vehicle was traced to Charlene Williams, but when the police called to interview her at her address in Sacramento she maintained that she had been at home the previous evening and had not used the van. Later in the day Craig Miller's body was found in a field in the next county; he had three bullets in the back of his head. When detectives returned to interview Charlene Williams further she had left with Gallego. The couple fled to Omaha, Nebraska, and Charlene appealed to her parents to wire $500. They did so, but they also informed the police, who were waiting when the money was collected. A few days after the arrest Beth Sowers' body was found; she had been raped and shot, then dumped unceremoniously in a field.

At first neither partner would admit anything but when she realized that she was facing the death penalty Charlene turned state's evidence, saying that she had been totally dominated by Gallego, willing to do anything he wanted, but that her love had gradually turned to fear and she had wanted to escape from him. In return for her testimony, Charlene received a sentence of a maximum of 16 years in gaol. After a four-month trial, Gallego was found guilty on two counts of first-degree murder for the killing of Craig Miller and Beth Sowers and sentenced to die in the gas chamber. He was then sent to Nevada, where he was tried for the murders of Stacy Ann Redican and Karen Chipman-Twiggs and received a second death sentence. At both trials, Charlene was the chief prosecution witness.

Gallego was an obstreperous, uncooperative prisoner. At one of his court appearances he tried to leap across the table to attack reporters, yelling, 'Get the hell out of here! We're not funny people! We're not animals!' After conviction, he was considered too disruptive to be kept on Death Row and was confined in a special section of the prison while he awaited his execution.

# Bobbie Joe Long

BOBBIE JOE LONG, from West Virginia, USA, seems to have been accident-prone from an early age. When he was five he fell from a swing, banging his head and losing consciousness. Later he suffered concussion after he crashed into a parked car on his bicycle. It wasn't long before he was then thrown from a pony and suffered dizzy spells for some time afterwards. His most significant accident was when, as a young man, he sustained head injuries in a serious motorcycle crash. At his trial for multiple sex murders in 1985 his lawyers argued that his personality changed after the crash, so that he experienced violent rages and an overwhelming sex urge.

Long also grew up with a confused attitude towards women. A glandular disturbance meant that he developed breasts as a teenager and only surgery could return his body to normal. He was an only child, brought up by his divorced mother, and, as her wage as a waitress was insufficient to rent more than a single room, Long shared her bed up to the age of 13. Later he was to claim that he watched her making love to a number of boyfriends in their cramped accommodation but his mother denied that this had ever happened. Nothing improper had ever taken place, she insisted, and her son had never seen her unclothed.

He certainly seems to have been dominated by women all his life: first his mother and then the girl he married, his teenage sweetheart Cindy Jean. From the time of his motorcycle accident his sexual demands on his wife became more frequent, and in addition to making love to her two or three times a day he also needed to masturbate several times. Soon he started looking for outside satisfaction.

In the three years from 1980 he raped more than 50 women in the Miami, Fort Lauderdale and Ocala areas of Florida. He became known as the 'Classified Ad Rapist' because he would scour the local newspaper columns for household items offered for sale then pose as a prospective purchaser and arrange to call round when the woman of the house was likely to be alone. He would then threaten the woman with a knife, tie and gag her, and commit violent rape. Though he was identified by a victim and convicted in 1981, the conviction was overturned on appeal and he was left free to continue.

It was after his divorce that rape no longer satisfied Long and he committed his first murder, on a Vietnamese woman called Ngeon Thi Long who had, he said, picked him up one evening. He had driven her to a secluded spot then tied her up, raped and murdered her, and pushed her body out of the car on to the roadside. After that Long haunted backstreet bars and striptease clubs, looking for victims. He would always wait for a woman to approach him, because this convinced him that she was a whore and deserved to die. He adjusted the front passenger seat in his car so that, once a potential victim was sitting there and he had tied her up, he could push the seat flat. Then, as he drove to a suitably lonely spot, no one would see that he had a passenger.

During 1984 he killed nine women, either strangling them or slitting their throats. In November he abducted a 17-year-old girl and kept her in his apartment for 24 hours. He raped her but spared her life when he discovered that she had been forced to leave home because her father abused her sexually. She did not fit his stereotype of a whore so when he had finished with her he drove her back to where they had met and released her, even though she was capable of identifying him.

Two days later he murdered Kim Sann in Tampa, but not without a struggle. She fought and screamed and, even though she passed out twice as Long attempted to strangle her, she each time came round fighting. Finally Long overcame her and choked her to death, but the excitement of the struggle had left him without the need to rape. Only a few days afterwards, when he was picked up on the evidence of his 17-year-old victim, Long said that he had expected the arrest and was glad to be caught. Perhaps he had become sickened by the killing and this explained his apparent carelessness in freeing a girl who could give enough first-hand evidence to convict him.

Long's defence lawyers tried to blame his actions on the brain damage caused by his head injury, but the jury did not accept their representations and found him guilty on nine counts of first-degree murder. He was sentenced to die in the electric chair.

# Randall Woodfield

FROM December 1980 the police found themselves investigating a series of robberies, often coupled with sexual assaults, in the vicinity of the Interstate 5 highway in Oregon and Washington, USA. A gunman, often wearing an obviously fake beard as a disguise, was holding up restaurants, ice-cream parlours, petrol stations and grocery stores, some of them more than once. At a garage he forced a female member of staff to bare her breasts before making off with the money; at a fast-food restaurant he made a waitress masturbate him and during other robberies he committed minor sexual assaults on staff and customers alike.

In mid-January 1981, in Corvallis, Oregon, two girls aged eight and ten were stripped and made to perform oral sex in their own bedroom by an intruder whose description fitted that of the bandit down to the false beard. Only a few days later the 'I-5 bandit' became the 'I-5 killer' when two Salem office workers, Shari Hull and Lisa Garcia, were held at gunpoint, stripped and sexually assaulted, then shot in the head as they were lying on the floor. Neither was killed and Lisa managed to struggle to the telephone and call for help. When she described her assailant, police realized that their robber was ruthless and dangerous. Shari Hull died in hospital and the enquiry turned into a murder hunt.

The bandit's sexual appetite seemed to be increasing, for on 3 February 1981 a young woman was raped and sodomized after a robbery in Redding, California, and on the same day, in the same town, a 37-year-old woman and her young teenage daughter were sodomized and shot dead in their own home. There was another rape the following day and several more robberies and assaults over the next week.

Then came the shooting of a teenage girl, Julie Reitz, in her home in Portland, Oregon. A routine check on all Julie's friends led the police to Randall Woodfield, a 30-year-old bartender who had a record for robbery and sex offences. Woodfield had been a promising student at high school and had shown great promise as a footballer, with hopes of a successful professional career. He was given a tryout with a well-known team but was turned out because of his hobby of exposing himself, which had already earned him two suspended sentences. In 1975 he had been imprisoned for robbing women at knife-point and forcing his victims to perform oral sex before he would release them. He was released shortly before the spate of I-5 robberies began.

Lisa Garcia identified Woodfield as her attacker and Shari Hull's murderer and several other witnesses picked him out of identification parades as the bandit. Further investigations suggested that Woodfield might be linked to more than a dozen murders, but most of them never came to trial. In June 1981 he was tried for the murder of Shari Hull and the attempted murder of her friend and was sentenced to life imprisonment plus 90 years. Later he was to collect a further 35 years for rape and sodomy.

# Andrei Chikatilo

IN 1992 the West was shocked by the trial of Andrei Romanovich Chikatilo, a man who was charged with 53 murders plus numerous sexual assaults over a 12-year period. He was nicknamed the 'Rostov Ripper', and admitted to a liking for chewing parts of his victims' bodies.

Chikatilo was born on 16 October 1936 in Yablochnoye, in the Ukraine. When he was five his mother told him the story of his cousin, who had disappeared from the village two years before Chikatilo's birth. The rumour in the village was that the boy had been kidnapped, killed and eaten, such was the level of hunger at the time. After his eventual arrest, Chikatilo was to say that the story both repelled and fascinated him, and may have been the seed of what became an obsession with death and cannibalism.

Chikatilo was a weakly boy who was bullied at school. He was so shortsighted that he could not read the blackboard, yet he was not to own a pair of spectacles until he was 30. Nevertheless, he qualified in communications engineering at a technical college, did his military service and, in 1960, began work as a telephone engineer in a little town 32 km (20 miles) north of Rostov, where his parents and sister joined him. In 1963 he married and, although his pathological shyness made sexual relations between him and his wife difficult, they had first a daughter and then a son. In 1971 he gained a degree in philosophy and literature and began teaching in Novoshakhtinsk, a few kilometres further north.

Chikatilo's new job placed him in an authoritative position over young girls, and he soon began to fantasize about his students. However, his shyness made it impossible for him to control his classes, and he was a poor teacher who was disliked by his pupils. This fed a desire to dominate, which increased as his sex life with his wife diminished. He became a peeping tom hanging around the dormitories and, in 1973, he molested a 15-year-old girl while they swam in a river on a school outing. He was once aroused to sexual excitement by beating a girl with a ruler.

Outside school, Chikatilo was in the habit of brushing against young women in buses and public places. He also molested his wife's six-year-old niece. Finally, in 1974, when his activities at school could no longer be ignored, he was asked to resign. He worked at two more schools, and it was while teaching at the nearby town of Shakhti that he committed his first murder in December 1978.

On that day Chikatilo met a pretty nine-year-old, Lina Zakotnova, hurrying home after playing with a friend after school. He fell in step and chatted, and she told him she needed to go to the toilet. They were near a lane called Mezhevoi Pereulok, where unbeknown to his wife he had bought a little house to use for his sexual escapades, and he said Lina could use his facilities. As they approached the house, Chikatilo became more and more excited and, as soon as they were indoors, he literally threw himself upon her. Stopping her screams with his large hand, he ripped off her clothes and attempted to rape her.

Chikatilo's frustrations persisted, however. He was unable to get an erection. Nevertheless, he made the little girl bleed, and the sight of the blood gave him the greatest thrill of his life. He reached for a knife he carried and began stabbing and tearing at her. In a moment his life was changed.

Afterwards he carried the dead girl, her clothes and bag to the nearby Grushevka River and threw them in. He threw the bag too hard; it landed on the opposite bank and was to pinpoint the place. Then he went back to his room in the school and cleaned himself up before his wife arrived home.

When the body was found two days later, the Shakhti police made enquiries in Mezhevoi Pereulok. A neighbour, already suspicious of him, told them that on the night of Lina's disappearance his light had been on all night (a simple mistake on his part in the excitement of the killing) although he rarely slept there.

When the police noticed a bloodstain in the snow outside his door they questioned him and discovered his record. They suspected him of the murder, but his wife gave him an alibi, innocently believing he had been indoors all evening. With incredible luck for Chikatilo, another man living in the street had a previous conviction for such a killing and had dodged the death penalty because he was only 17 at the time. The man's wife, for reasons of her own, told police he had confessed to her. He was convicted and shot, and Chikatilo had escaped.

Despite the horror of his situation Chikatilo realized that, given the chance, he would kill again. In 1981 his continuing misdemeanours forced the school to dispense with his services and he took a menial job as a clerk in the offices of a factory. This entailed travelling to suppliers and signing for components, which gave him the maximum opportunity to kill and get away.

Chikatilo acted like a madman on his second killing, that of a 17-year-old girl. For several minutes he ran round and round the body in ecstasy, throwing her clothes as far as he could. Only later did the need for concealment and escape impress itself on him.

In the next few months the rate of killings increased. In 1982 there were seven victims; in 1983 eight died; and in 1984 he killed no fewer than 18 people. He usually chose poor young women who would go with him on the promise of a meal, or naive girls or boys; as the killings increased, the proportion of boys grew larger. Often he would find the victims near railway stations, or on trains. They would alight at unmanned stations with woods nearby, where Chikatilo would attack them – on one occasion killing a mother and daughter. He became more expert at carving up the bodies, and would remove nipples or genitals. Sometimes they would be bitten off and chewed, although he was not strictly a cannibal. His main obsession was with uteruses, and he described the sensation of chewing them. There was one distinctive trademark, which was that victims were always cut around the eyes, as if he could not bear them looking at him. Often the attacks would come after an attempt at intercourse had been followed by scorn on the part of the victim.

The best minds in the police concentrated on the problem as his killings spread over a wider area, reflecting the distances he travelled by rail or air in his job. Several suspects were held by local police – usually subnormal men who confessed – but the killings continued. The clothing of several victims was examined minutely and the traces of semen found in nine murders was analysed. This revealed the killer's blood type to be AB. Apart from that and his shoe size – discovered from a footprint – not much was known of him.

In September 1984 Chikatilo was detained after an inspector had followed him all night for nine hours as he crossed and recrossed Rostov trying to pick up a victim. In his bag were knives and a length of rope. His shoe size fitted. The card index which now ran to thousands of entries revealed he had been questioned back in 1978 for the very first killing. He fitted rough descriptions, and the police were sure they had their man. A blood sample was taken; it was type A, so he was released. Only four years later did scientists discover that in rare cases – one in thousands – a man's sperm could be of a different group to his blood. Chikatilo had escaped again.

The narrow escape sobered Chikatilo and the number of killings was reduced – only five in the next three years, and those in far-flung regions. This control of his emotions was a powerful argument against his plea of insanity at his trial. However, in 1989 the rate of killing began to return to its previous level.

Police had now identified the role of the railway in the killings and hundreds of men were deployed on usually unmanned stations to check all passengers. On 17 October 1990 Chikatilo killed a boy near Donleshkov station without being noticed. On 6 November he murdered a woman there, but this time a sergeant saw him emerge

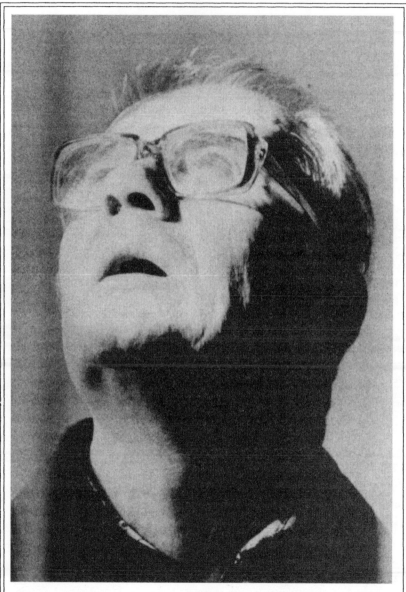

*Andrei Chikatilo looks at the sun through a window in court, while the judge delivers his verdict*

from the woods at 4 pm and wash his hands at a water hydrant. He had a red mark on his cheek which might have been blood, and a bandaged finger. The sergeant examined his passport, and put his name into a report.

A few days later a senior policeman came to Donleshkov to inspect the site where the boy's body had been found. A piece of blue nylon fabric was hanging from a tree. One of the local prosecutors swore it was new, saying he had been there when all the clothing from the murder was removed. The only explanation, if he was right, was that the murderer had returned and killed again. An army of men and dogs began a search, and soon the body of the woman was found. The sergeant's report was read and its contents noted. The head of the regional crime squad, who was about to attend a funeral nearby, instead called in at the local police station on hearing of the latest body; he read the report and remembered Chikatilo's name from 1984. Once more Chikatilo's card was produced from the 20,000 or so now on file. Everything except his blood group pointed in his direction, and it was decided to put him under constant surveillance, in the hope of catching him with his next victim.

Over the next few days his method of operating became clear as the police watched him try to pick up several potential victims. If there was any resistance he would give up and patiently try another, a precaution which had made him so difficult to catch. Finally, aware of the terrible risk they were running of another murder being committed, the police stepped in and quietly arrested him as he stood outside a café. His bag contained a mirror, rope and knife.

This time tests were taken on other bodily samples as well as blood. The sperm group was AB. However, several days of police questioning failed to draw any admissions from Chikatilo. It was only when he was interviewed by a Rostov psychiatrist that he began to confess to the killings.

He was charged at first with 36 murders and various rapes and assaults. As he detailed others of which the police had no knowledge, the number rose to 53. He took the police to sites where bodies were found and demonstrated with dummies what he had done to the victims. For the first time the police discovered that they had shot the wrong man for Chikatilo's first murder in 1978.

None of Chikatilo's associates during his life had suspected he was other than ordinary. His wife, who knew of his sexual problems, was hardly able to believe he was a murderer; he had been a loving father and grandfather. The knives he had used to mutilate his victims were in many cases from her kitchen drawer. She and her daughter were sent to another part of the country so they could begin a new life and escape any reprisals.

Chikatilo was judged sane, and his trial began on 14 April 1992. It took three days to read the charges, and doctors had to stand by to treat the relatives of the victims as the terrible story was told. As the trial wore on Chikatilo himself behaved outrageously, shouting, arguing and, on one occasion, stripping to wave his penis which be described as the useless cause of his problem. As the trial descended to near farce, the judge, the counsel, the police, the psychiatrists all argued with each other. The judge took weeks to write his verdict and days to read it. Finally, on 15 October 1992, while Chikatilo screamed from the cage which was necessary to protect him from witnesses, he was found guilty of 52 murders and sentenced to death. The hundreds of spectators applauded.

# Chapter Six

# UNBALANCE
# OF MIND

# Introduction

THERE is an argument that all serial killers must be mad, that no sane human being could plan one murder after another, often torturing the victim beforehand or mutilating the body afterwards. Certainly insanity is the first line of defence for multiple murderers but quite often courts consider that a killer who is obviously unbalanced is still capable of telling the difference between right and wrong and must therefore take responsibility for his actions. In some cases juries are so revolted by the nature of the crime that they feel the murderer deserves tough punishment whether he or she is sane or not, and killers sick in mind are imprisoned for life instead of receiving specialist psychiatric care.

Some of the killers in this section had already slipped through the net of psychiatric care by the time they launched on their murderous career – Graham Young, for example, had spent seven years in a hospital for the criminally insane and was discharged as cured, despite his obsession with poison – while others had begun manifesting signs of unbalance, hearing voices and suffering hallucinations.

Included in this chapter are mass murderers, like Unruh, Whitman and Huberty. They belong to a distinct and fortunately rare class of killers who can appear to be ordinary, rational people up to the moment when the mind snaps and a fury of bloody slaughter is unleashed.

# Jane Toppan

IN COURT, Jane Toppan announced that it was her ambition 'to have killed more people – more helpless people – than any man or woman has ever killed.' She confessed to 31 murders but estimates of the number of victims who died at her hand range between 70 and 100. She poisoned them with a mixture of morphine and atropin, producing a set of symptoms which confused doctors who might have recognized a more conventional poison.

There was madness in her family: her father was committed to an asylum after being found in his tailor's shop trying to sew his eyelids together. Later her sister was to suffer a mental breakdown and was also committed. Jane was adopted at the age of five, after a spell in an orphanage, and grew up to be an attractive and popular girl. Then, in her twenties, she was jilted by the young man she expected to marry and her personality changed; she shut herself away and made two suicide attempts. Eventually she seemed to recover and enrolled as a student nurse at the Cambridge Hospital in Massachusetts, USA, in 1880. However, she was dismissed when two patients under her care died unexpectedly. Undaunted, she offered her services as a private nurse and over the next 20 years worked for many of the best families in the state. Most of her patients died but then, they were old and ill and no one suspected that their cheerful and caring nurse had hastened their end.

In 1899, she went to stay with her adoptive sister Mrs Brigham and her husband at their home in Lowell. Mrs Brigham had looked after Jane for years after their mother, Mrs Anne Toppan, died, but Jane had a grudge against her sister because she thought she had taken more than her share of their mother's estate. After a two-day illness

Mrs Brigham died, at the age of 61, the cause of death being certified as 'cerebral apoplexy'. Jane's plan was to stay and look after Mr Brigham herself but he was perfectly happy with his housekeeper, whom he might well have married later. The housekeeper fell ill and died four months later. After that Mr Brigham's married sister moved in but she, too, soon took to her bed and died. Perhaps Mr Brigham suspected that Jane's sorrow over the deaths was not all it might be, for he sent her away soon afterwards.

In 1901 Jane was nursing an old friend, Mattie Davies, who was suffering from kidney disease. When she died on 4 July, Jane had no difficulty convincing the doctor that it was death from natural causes and she put on a convincing show of grief at the funeral. The deceased's husband, Alden Davies, was so impressed with her that he asked her to stay on and look after him and his two married daughters, Mrs Harry Gordon and Mrs Minnie Gibbs. Mrs Gordon died first, on 29 July, Mr Davies a few days later, supposedly after suffering a stroke and Mrs Gibbs on 19 August. In her confession Jane was to write, 'I made it lively for the undertakers and grave-diggers that time – three graves in little over three weeks in one lot in the cemetery.' She went to the funerals and felt 'as jolly as could be'.

This time she had overreached herself. Once Mrs Gibbs' husband, a sea captain, returned from his latest voyage he demanded a post-mortem. When a lethal amount of morphine and atropin was found in the body the other members of the family were exhumed, with the same result. While investigations were under way, Jane managed to poison her adoptive sister Mrs Edna Bannister, and at the time of her arrest was nursing another patient in New Hampshire.

The true number of her victims was never known, as many of the families involved refused permission for exhumations and autopsies. She had remained undetected for so long because she was so cunning in her timing. With her sickly patients she would start by building them up so that the doctors thought they were on the way to recovery then, once the physicians stopped visiting regularly, she would begin feeding the poison to her patients, a little each day. With her friends and family members, she always chose a time when they were weakened through natural causes to begin administering her lethal mixture. Mrs Davies, for instance, had fainted after running for a train: Jane 'revived' her with water and an initial dose of morphia. Mr Davies had been prostrated by heat after a trip to Boston when she administered the poison, so the doctor easily accepted the possibility of a stroke.

'I fooled the stupid doctors and the ignorant relatives: I have been fooling them for years,' she wrote. 'Everybody trusted me. It was so easy. I felt strange when I watched them die. I was all excited and my blood seemed to sweep madly through my veins. It was the only pleasure I had.' Sometimes, in her confession, she claimed that some of her victims had lent her money that she could not pay back or stood in the way of marriage she hoped for, but mostly she killed for the sheer enjoyment of killing. 'They hadn't done anything to me and I gained nothing from their deaths except the excitement of watching them die. I couldn't resist doing it.'

She traced her terrible obsession back to her disappointment in love as a young woman: 'People say I have no heart, but I have. While I have been in prison a friend in Lowell sent me some forget-me-nots and I cried. They were the flowers that my first lover sent me when I was a schoolgirl, and a forget-me-not was engraved on the ring he gave me. He broke off the engagement and it seemed that my light-hearted nature changed after that. I still laughed and was jolly, but I learned how to hate, too.'

Leading experts examined Jane Toppan and decided that she was insane. 'She is suffering from a form of insanity that can never be cured,' said a psychiatrist at her trial, though Jane insisted that she understood the difference between right and wrong, which proved that she was sane. She was committed to Taunton State Asylum where at first she was quiet enough, but as the years went on she suffered from paranoia, imagining that all her food was poisoned, so that in the end she had to be force-fed. She died on 17 August 1938, at the age of 84.

# Albert Fish

ON 28 May 1928 a white-haired, mild-mannered man arrived at the basement apartment of Albert and Delia Budd in Manhattan, USA. He had come in answer to an advertisement that 18-year-old Edward Budd had placed in a New York newspaper, asking for a job in the country. The visitor was well-dressed and seemed to have plenty of money; Edward could hardly believe his luck when the old man, who introduced himself as Frank Howard, offered him a job on his farm on Long Island at a good wage. Moreover, when Edward asked if there might be a job for his friend Willie as well, Mr Howard agreed to take on both boys. He would return to collect them the following weekend, he told the family.

When he came back the next week he arrived early and the boys were not ready so he passed the time with the Budd's 10-year-old daughter Grace, who took to the kindly old man immediately. Mr Howard had a suggestion to make: his niece was giving a birthday party and Grace would love it – why didn't he take her along? Delia Budd hesitated but her husband thought it was a splendid idea, so Grace went off in her white confirmation dress, holding Mr Howard's hand. She was never seen alive again. The party was supposed to be at 137th Street and Columbus Avenue, an address that did not exist, and there was no farmer named Frank Howard on Long Island.

The headlines shrieked about the missing child while the police organized a widespread search and followed endless leads that led nowhere. The whereabouts of Grace, alive or dead, remained undiscovered. It was to be six years before the Budds heard of their daughter again. Then, on 11 November 1934, Grace Budd received a letter that left her – and the detectives who read it – appalled and sickened.

The writer reminded the Budds of the day he had called at their house and Grace had sat trustingly on his knee. He said that he had taken her to a deserted house in Westchester and while she was still picking flowers in the garden he had gone inside and taken off all his clothes, not wanting to get blood on them. When Grace came inside and saw him she tried to run away but he grabbed her. He gave a horrifying description of what happened next:

'First I stripped her naked. How she did kick and bite and scratch. I choked her to death, then cut her in small pieces so I could take my meat to my rooms . . . how sweet and tender her little ass was roasted in the oven. It took me nine days to eat her entire body. I did not fuck her though I could of had I wished. She died a virgin.'

Detective Will King of the Missing Persons Bureau, who had been deeply involved in the original investigation, was determined that this time the kidnapper would not escape. The envelope containing the letter bore the initials of a chauffeur's benevolent association and he spent a good deal of time investigating the members, with no result. He then questioned anyone who might have taken away any of the stationery for their own use and one of the chauffeurs admitted that he had left some of the envelopes at a previous address. This turned out to be a rooming house where one of the tenants fitted the description of Frank Howard. When the tenant returned to his room he was taken to the station for questioning.

His real name turned out to be Albert Fish and he admitted to killing Grace Budd. He had gone to the Budd's apartment intending to murder Edward, but when pretty little Grace had sat on his knee and smiled at him, he had decided to eat her. After he had strangled her he cut off her head, then cut her body in half and sliced it into pieces. He had cooked her flesh with onions, carrots and strips of

*Albert Fish*

bacon and for the whole nine days he was eating her he was in a high state of sexual excitement. He took the police to the Westchester house where he had committed the murder and they found the child's skeletal remains buried in the garden. Meanwhile, Fish had confessed to sexually assaulting several hundred children over the past 20 years and killing perhaps a dozen of them.

Fish was born in 1870 to a respectable Washington family but there was already a history of mental instability running through the past two generations and two relatives had died in institutions. His father died when he was five years old and he was sent to an orphanage, where discipline was rigorous and beatings commonplace. Fish, who was a persistent runaway and who wet his bed regularly up to the age of 11, came in for plenty of beatings and his leanings towards sadism and masochism began at this time, for he gained a sexual thrill from being flogged on his bare bottom, and from watching punishment administered to other boys.

At the age of 15 he was apprenticed as a painter and decorator and in 1898 he married a woman nine years younger than himself. They had six children before she ran off with another man and it was at that time that his children noticed his behaviour becoming strange and erratic. He heard voices, experienced hallucinations and became obsessed by sin, sacrifice and pain. Fish himself said that he committed his first murder, of a homosexual, in Wilmington, Delaware, in 1910. In 1917 he tortured and murdered a mentally retarded homosexual.

He felt that God had ordered him to castrate young boys and he abused both girls and boys 'in every state' of the USA, according to his own claims. He was always changing jobs and his work gave him access to basements, attics and other quiet spots suitable for abusing a child. He usually chose children from poor families, black children especially, as he said there was no great fuss if they disappeared or were hurt. He wore no clothes under his overalls, so that when he had persuaded a child to accompany him by coaxing him or her with gifts of sweets or money, he could undress in seconds to carry out his assault.

The police knew him as a minor offender; over the years he was arrested eight times for theft, passing dud cheques and violating probation. He was also arrested after sending obscene letters – one of his favourite hobbies – and sent to a psychiatric ward for observation, but released soon afterwards. The nearest he had come to being identified as a murderer was when a bus conductor identified him as the man he had seen with a tearful small boy who had since disappeared. Fish was taken in for questioning but released because no one could suspect such a mild, gentle man of indulging in violence.

If he enjoyed inflicting pain on his victims, Fish was just as eager to hurt and mutilate himself. He soaked balls of cotton wool in alcohol, then pushed them into his rectum and set fire to them. He regularly stuck needles into his groin and genital area, inserting some of them so deeply that they never came out – a prison X-ray was to reveal 29 needles, some of them eroded over time so that only fragments remained. When he tried to stick needles under his fingernails he could not stand the agony: 'If only pain were not so painful!' he exclaimed.

According to psychiatrist Dr Frederick Wertham, 'there was no known perversion which he did not practise and practise regularly'. The list included caprophagia – eating human excrement – which he had indulged in since the age of 12. Wertham maintained that Fish was insane, though Fish himself reasoned, 'I'm not insane! I'm just queer.' However, the prosecution was set on the death penalty, even bringing doctors to argue that caprophagia 'is a common sort of thing. We don't call people who do that mentally sick – socially they are perfectly all right.' It seems quite possible that the jury cared little whether he was legally sane or not and believed that he deserved the death penalty anyway.

Fish, sentenced to die in the electric chair, said that it would be 'the supreme thrill of my life'. Dr Wertham did his best to obtain a reprieve, insisting that executing a man so mentally sick was like burning witches. 'This man is not only incurable but unpunishable,' he said. 'In his own distorted mind he is looking forward to the electric chair as the final experience of true pain.'

Albert Fish had his final experience at Sing Sing on 16 January 1936.

# Howard Unruh

HOWARD UNRUH was a quiet, reclusive Bible student who went ber-serk in a small American town on 6 September 1949 and gunned down 13 people in 12 minutes. He was never brought to trial but was committed to a mental institution and he expressed no remorse for his actions. 'I'd have killed a thousand if I'd had bullets enough,' he said simply.

He had an unremarkable childhood in Camden, New Jersey, and wanted to become a pharmacist. However, World War II intervened and he enlisted in the army, soon showing great proficiency with a rifle. He fought in Italy and France and distinguished himself in combat but he never mixed socially with the other soldiers, preferring to divide his spare time between reading the Bible and cleaning his rifle with loving care. Every day he made a careful entry in his diary and one day a roommate, overcome with curiosity, took a peep, only to find that Unruh had recorded the details of every German he had killed: the date, the circumstances and exactly how his enemy had looked at the moment of death.

When he was demobbed in 1945 he enrolled at Temple University but he soon dropped out and took a succession of jobs, unable to settle to anything. He became silent and withdrawn, scarcely speaking to his parents and spending most of his time practising marksmanship in the shooting gallery he had set up in the basement. He began keeping a diary again, listing all his fancied grievances against his neighbours, with notes about planned times for retaliation. There were plenty of entries about the Cohens next door, who had rebuked him for taking a short cut to his door across their yard.

He built a high fence all round the yard of his father's house to shut out the world but on 25 September his hatred of his neighbours came to a head when he found that someone had taken away the gate, leaving the yard exposed to passers-by. Perhaps he lay seething with fury in his locked room all night and rose next morning determined to exact vengeance on all and sundry. Whatever the case, in the morning he emerged with a powerful German Luger, a second pistol and a pocketful of spare clips.

He walked down River Avenue and into John Pilarchi's little shoe shop, a few yards from his home. Without saying a word he shot the cobbler dead, with a single bullet through the head. He walked out with the gun still in his hand and turned into the barber's shop next door, where Clark Hoover was cutting the hair of six-year-old Orris Smith. Unruh shot first Hoover then the child, leaving Mrs Smith hysterical as she cradled her dead son in her arms. Her screams followed him down the road on his way to the drugstore owned by his principal enemy, Maurice Cohen.

In the doorway of Cohen's store he met James Hutton, an insurance agent who had been on good terms with the Unruh family for years. He fired and Hutton fell to the pavement, dying instantly. Inside the store, Maurice Cohen screamed at his family to hide; his wife Rose shut herself in a cupboard while 12-year-old Charlie, followed by his father, scrambled through the window on to the roof. Unruh reached the top of the stairs just in time to see the cupboard door closing. He fired three shots and the door fell open as Mrs Cohen's body collapsed on to the floor. Leaning out of the window, he fired twice into Cohen's retreating back then, when the storekeeper fell to the street below, he fired a third shot into his head. Hearing a noise from the next room, he threw open the door and, finding Cohen's elderly mother trying to phone for help, he shot her too. Only young Charlie managed to reach safety and escape the carnage.

As Unruh walked out into River Avenue again, he saw a stranger who had stopped to try to help the insurance agent and immediately shot him dead at point blank range. He strolled on down the street

*Police move in and overpower Harold Unruh*

with no sign of hurry, as panic raged on all sides with people screaming and yelling, running for cover and barricading themselves into shops, frantically phoning for the police. Unruh was unmoved and even when café owner Fred Engel shot at him, hitting him in the leg, he did not pause. Among those who died in the next few moments were a three-year-old boy who was gazing out of his window and two women and a young boy whose car had stopped at a red traffic light. He missed the driver of a bakery van but wounded a lorry driver who was just climbing into his cab. He tried to shoot his way into the grocery store but the lock held and he passed on.

Unruh next walked into a house where Mrs Madeline Harris had forgotten to lock the door and found her hiding in the kitchen with her two sons. Seventeen-year-old Armond threw himself at the gunman, whose shots went awry, one wounding the boy in the leg, the other hitting his mother in the shoulder. The younger boy was left unhurt, one of the luckiest participants in the morning's horrific drama.

At last Unruh had run out of ammunition and headed home to reload, but by now the police were arriving and he was pinned down in his house by a ring of police marksmen. In the gun battle that followed Unruh rained bullets from the upstairs window. Amazingly enough, a reporter from the local newspaper rang the house and found the phone answered by Unruh himself. Asked how many people he had killed, Unruh replied: 'I haven't counted. It looks like a pretty good score, though.'

When tear-gas canisters came flying through the windows Unruh was forced to surrender, walking out with his hands up under the aim of over 50 police guns. Under questioning, his only explanation for his actions was that people were picking on him and he had to get his own back. Experts judged him to be a schizophrenic with violent paranoid tendencies. Unruh himself insisted, 'I'm no psycho. I have a good mind.'

# SERIAL KILLERS

# Hans van Zon

IT COULD be argued that many serial killers are unbalanced whether or not they are legally judged insane, and a good example is the Dutch killer Hans van Zon, who lived in his own world of fantasy and had no apparent motive for most of his crimes.

He was born in Utrecht in 1942 and brought up by his mother with a completely unfounded idea of his own importance. He was quiet and introverted, only playing with children younger than himself, and was deferential towards adults. He did poorly in school and later was unable to keep a job because of his light fingers. At 16 he took off for Amsterdam, where he lived on his wits and enjoyed a number of sexual liaisons with both men and women. The real world scarcely impinged on him as he played the roles of private detective, wealthy entrepreneur, film star, fashion designer or ace pilot in his head.

In July 1964 he committed his first murder. He had been on a date with a young woman called Elly Hager-Segov and at the end of the evening he pretended that he had missed his last train home and was invited to spend the night in her apartment. They went to bed together, but when she would not let him have sex with her for a second time he was overcome with a sudden urge to kill her. He strangled her until she lost consciousness, then cut her throat with a breadknife.

He confessed to murdering homosexual film director Claude Berkely in 1965. This may have been another facet of his fantasy life, for he later withdrew the confession, saying that he had only seen the murder in a psychic vision. Soon afterwards he married an Italian chambermaid, Caroline Gigli, and lived off her income while he pursued affairs with other women. In 1967 she complained to the police

268

that he was trying to kill her and, as he was already on probation for another offence, he spent several weeks in custody.

However, it was not his wife that he murdered later the same year but his mistress, Coby van der Voort. He gave her what he said was an aphrodisiac but was really a powerful barbiturate, then while she was drugged he battered her with a lead pipe and stabbed her with a breadknife. He stripped her body and tried, unsuccessfully, to have intercourse with the corpse.

In a drunken moment he bragged about the murder in front of an ex-convict known as Oude Nol who proceeded to half-persuade, half-blackmail him into a rash of further crimes, which gave him the chance to put his favoured lead piping to good use. Oude Nol may have instigated the robberies but van Zon certainly went overboard with his methods. In May 1967 he battered 80-year-old Jan Donse to death in his firework shop and robbed the till, dividing the takings with Oude Nol. Two months later he smashed the skull of Reyer de Bruin, a farmer, and cut his throat into the bargain.

His last victim was an elderly widow, once a girlfriend of Oude Nol, but this time van Zon's murderous touch deserted him – he did not hit Mrs Woortmeyer hard enough to kill her. When she came round she raised the alarm and later identified him as the man who had attacked and robbed her.

Once in custody, van Zon did his best to put the blame on Oude Nol and he too was arrested. Oude Nol was sent to prison for seven years while van Zon received a sentence of life imprisonment. It was recommended that he should serve no less than 20 years, so he had plenty of opportunity to retreat into his beloved world of fantasy.

# Lucian Staniak

THE KILLER known as 'Red Spider' stalked the blonde young women of Poland for three years between 1964 and 1967, raping and murdering them in a twisted scheme for revenge. Most of the murders took place on public holidays, when victims would be least on their guard, and the bodies were horribly mutilated, often completely disembowelled.

The murderer taunted the police in a series of letters, sometimes giving directions to the latest body, and sent strange messages to the newspapers, all written in red ink, in the thin, spidery writing that earned him his nickname. The first letter read: 'There is no happiness without tears, no life without death. Beware! I am going to make you weep.'

The Spider struck for the first time at Olsztyn, raping and mutilating a 17-year-old girl on the anniversary of Polish liberation from Nazi occupation. The killer wrote to the police with a sinister threat: 'I picked a juicy flower in Olsztyn and I shall do it again somewhere else, for there is no holiday without a funeral.'

A letter to the police described the whereabouts of the next body, a 16-year-old who had caught the killer's attention when she led a student parade. The girl's remains lay in a factory basement, with a spike hammered through the genitals. Next the killer used a screwdriver to mutilate the sex organs of a young hotel receptionist murdered on All Saints Day and wrote to the newspapers saying: 'Only tears of sorrow can wash away the stain of shame: only the pangs of suffering can cancel out the fires of lust.'

On May Day 1966 a 17-year-old was raped and killed, her body left in the toolshed behind her home, the entrails removed and piled beside it. Then on Christmas Eve the body of 17-year-old Janina

Kozielska was found on a train; she had been raped and mutilated. The killer wrote to the press stating proudly: 'I have done it again.' Janina's sister Aniela had been killed two years before, so enquiries concentrated on anyone who had known them both. This included members of the Art Lovers' Club in Krakow, to which both girls belonged.

One of the members of the club was 26-year-old Lucian Staniak and as soon as detectives saw his paintings, with huge blood-red splashes and pictures of disembowelled women, they decided that they had found a likely suspect. When they arrested him on 1 February 1967 he was only too willing to confess: he was just on his way home from his latest killing, he said. He had murdered Bozena Raczkiewicz at a railway station because he was disappointed at the level of publicity his crimes were receiving at the time.

Staniak's life had been changed when his parents and sister were killed in a car accident and the driver responsible, a serviceman's wife, had escaped conviction, so he was determined to revenge himself on any young blonde woman who bore a passing resemblance to her. He admitted to 20 murders and was tried for six of them. Judged insane, he was committed to an asylum.

# Charles Whitman

IN MARCH 1966 Charles Whitman, a 25-year-old student of architectural engineering at the University of Texas, USA, went to see the campus psychiatrist. His mother had recently left his father, a brutal and domineering man who had frequently beaten her and his children. Mrs Whitman had moved to Austin, Texas, to be near her son and his wife and Mr Whitman was always involving Charles in his marital difficulties, trying to persuade him to act as a go-between. Young Whitman, who loved his mother and hated his father, was full of anger and hostility, which sometimes erupted into violence, resulting in him assaulting his wife Kathleen. He confided this to the psychiatrist but decided not to return for a second visit. He could work things out alone, he said. Four months later Charles Whitman was standing on top of the university observation tower, firing indiscriminately at the people below.

There was nothing in Whitman's past record to indicate that he was a mass murderer in the making: as a youngster he had been an Eagle Scout and an altar boy, he was no trouble in school, he served in the Marines and was now attending university on a Marine scholarship.

Yet, on the night of 31 July, he began writing a 'to whom it may concern' note. 'I am prepared to die,' it read. 'After my death I wish an autopsy on me to be performed to see if there is any mental disorder.' He then went to his mother's apartment and stabbed her to death. In the early hours of the following morning he returned home and stabbed, then shot, his wife, a high-school science teacher. He then finished his letter, noting first: '12.00 am – Mother already dead, 3 o'clock, both dead.' He then said that he loved both his mother and his wife and had no idea why he had killed them and went on to rail against his father. He concluded with: 'Life is not worth living.'

He then began collecting together his weapons, including several high-powered rifles and hundreds of rounds of ammunition. He packed them into a box along with a clock, binoculars, nylon rope, a transistor radio, a thermos of coffee and toilet paper. He loaded the box on to a three-wheeler trolley he had hired, pushed it to the observation tower and took it up in the lift.

On the twenty-seventh floor he met the 51-year-old receptionist Edna Townsley, who was there to monitor anyone who went up to the observation deck. He smashed her skull with his gun butt, then dragged her body behind the desk. Just afterwards a young couple, Don Walden and Cheryl Batts, came down from the deck and greeted Whitman pleasantly. They must have been the luckiest people in Austin that day, for Whitman returned their greeting and let them walk out unharmed.

The next people to arrive at the twenty-seventh floor were 19-year-old Mark Gabour and his family. As Mark opened the reception-room door he was killed with a shotgun blast. His aunt, following behind him, was also killed and his mother was wounded. The husbands of the two women, bringing up the rear, quickly dragged the bodies into another room and locked themselves in. Whitman barricaded the reception-room door and took his box out to the observation deck.

At 11.48 he started to fire from the tower, the highest point in Austin. It was a splendid vantage point for a sharpshooter and he fired on men, women and children alike. At first no one could believe what was happening and even as bodies dropped to the ground, those who were still standing were too shocked to run for cover and made perfect targets. Claire Wilson, eight months pregnant, took a bullet in the stomach which killed her baby. As 19-year-old Thomas Eckman tried to help her, he was shot dead. A law student was standing with a policeman, Billy Speed, behind some pillars when a bullet ricocheted and killed the officer.

Police rained bullets on the tower but had little hope of hitting Whitman. An armoured car toured the area, trying to pick up the wounded, while a light plane circled the tower carrying a sharpshooter who attempted to take out the murderer. The plane was driven off by Whitman's bullets.

Eventually a group of policemen led by officer Romero Martinez managed to get into the tower along underground conduits. They took the elevator to the twenty-seventh floor, keeping in constant touch with colleagues outside by walkie-talkie, so that the latter could give warning if the gunman left his vantage point on the tower. They eased their way into the reception room, pushing the furniture barricade out of the way a centimetre at a time, then finally burst out on to the deck, riddling Whitman with bullets. Martinez then waved a green flag to tell the policemen waiting below that they had succeeded. An hour and a half after Whitman entered the tower, his blood-soaked body was carried out.

A postmortem revealed a malignant tumour the size of a walnut in Charles Whitman's brain. At first it seemed as though this might be the cause of his sudden rages and his final mad act, but eventually doctors decided that the location of the tumour made this unlikely.

The tower still stands dominating the town of Austin. After the massacre on that hot August day it attracted many sensation-seekers and also a number of suicides. As a result, it was closed to the public. No other gunman will even use its height to terrorize the town.

# Graham Young

WHEN Graham Young answered an advertisement for a storeman at John Hadland Ltd, a firm specializing in specialist optical and photographic instruments based in a Hertfordshire village in England, he stated on his application form that he had 'previously studied chemistry, organic and inorganic, pharmacology and toxicology over the past ten years'. At the time Young was on a government training course at Slough, Berkshire, but the managing director of the firm was curious about his past work record. Young said that he had suffered a nervous breakdown after his mother's death and had needed mental treatment but that he was now perfectly well. Hadland's managing director, Godfrey Foster, said that he would require a reference from Young's psychiatrist. When the report came from Dr Edgar Unwin it read: 'This man has suffered a deep-going personality disorder which necessitated hospitalization throughout his adolescence . . . He has, however, made an extremely full recovery and is now entirely fit for discharge, his sole disability now being the need to catch up on his lost time.' The doctor went on to say that Young was of above-average intelligence and 'would fit in well and not draw attention to himself in any community'.

The letter did not mention that Young had spent nine years at the Broadmoor hospital for the criminally insane and that he had been committed there after poisoning his father, sister and a schoolfriend.

Young, born in 1947, was always a bit of a loner who became fascinated by chemistry at an early age, experimenting with explosives and studying books on poison. He admired Hitler and thought the persecution of the Jews a good thing. His heroes were merciless poisoners like William Palmer, George Chapman and Edward

Pritchard. His family did not take any of it seriously; they thought he was just 'daft' and would soon grow out of it.

By the age of 14, Young had acquired a wide knowledge of poisons and their effects. In 1961 his stepmother, who had brought him up since infancy, began suffering stomach cramps. Soon afterwards Fred Young, a 44-year-old engineer, experienced the same symptoms as his wife. So did Chris Williams, a schoolfriend of Young's who had recently beaten him in a fight. They assumed there was a 'bug' going round the neighbourhood but over the months that followed Molly Young grew weaker and weaker, losing weight fast, and in April 1962 she died in convulsions. In the meantime, Young's sister Winifred had also suffered a violent illness, eventually diagnosed as belladonna poisoning. Fred Young's symptoms returned with increased intensity after his wife's death and he was taken into hospital, where it was found that he had been poisoned with antimony and had narrowly escaped death.

A science master at Young's school, who knew of the boy's obsession, heard him talking about the family illnesses and went through his desk, finding phials of poison, notes on amounts to administer and sinister drawings of bodies writhing in pain. He alerted the police, who search Young's room, finding stacks of books on poisons and poisoners and an array of poisons that had been obtained with false prescriptions.

At his trial in July 1962, Young pleaded guilty to poisoning his father and sister and also Chris Williams. He was not charged with murdering his stepmother as she had been cremated and the evidence lost, but he told the police that he had been dosing her with antimony for 12 months. Judge Melford Stevenson sent him to Broadmoor, saying that he should not be released for 15 years and then only with the authority of the Home Secretary. 'Such people are always dangerous and are adept at concealing their mad compulsion which may never be wholly cured,' he said. If his words had been heeded, the tragedy that followed would have been avoided.

After several years of treatment Young's doctors at Broadmoor were convinced that his obsession with poisons was a thing of the past and informed the Home Office that their patient had undergone 'profound changes'. On 4 February 1971 he was released with Home Office agreement, though only shortly beforehand he had told one of the nurses: 'When I get out I'm going to kill one person for every year I've spent in this place.'

On 10 May, Young went to work at Hadland's, where his workmates were friendly and helpful, particularly the head storeman, 59-year-old Bob Egle, and 61-year-old Fred Biggs, who was in charge of stocks and distribution. Both frequently gave him cigarettes and lent him money when he was hard up and in return he regularly fetched their tea from the trolley for them.

Then a peculiar illness began to hit the staff at Hadland's. About 20 members of staff were affected by what they called the 'Bovington Bug' – after the village where the factory was situated – suffering stomach pains, sickness and numbness in the limbs. Some mentioned that their tea tasted bitter and blamed water contamination, others thought chemicals used in the factory must be responsible.

Bob Egle had a bad stomach upset in early June and took a week's holiday, returning fit and well. A day later he was ill in bed again and this time numbness spread throughout his body. By 7 July he was dead and Graham Young represented the firm at the funeral. Colleagues noticed that Young was always talking about the dead man; they assumed he had been deeply attached to him.

Early in September Fred Biggs became violently ill, made a partial recovery, then had a relapse and was admitted to hospital, where doctors were mystified. When he died on 19 November, Young remarked to his workmates: 'Poor old Fred. I wonder what went wrong? He shouldn't have died. I was very fond of old Fred.' In the meantime other employees had suffered badly: David Tilson, a clerk, fell ill after sharing a tea break with Young and was admitted to hospital with pains throughout his body and dramatic hair loss. Jethro

Batt, who had worked late with Young one night and drunk coffee with him, fell ill with excruciating pain, suffered hallucinations and went completely bald.

Panic was mounting at the factory and the management called a meeting of the entire workforce, where the firm's medical expert could reassure them that there was no water contamination or poisoning from chemicals. He was surprised when one employee, Graham Young, asked a number of searching medical questions and even referred to the possibility of thallium poisoning. The medical officer took Young on one side afterwards and the storeman could not resist boasting about his knowledge of poisons.

The police were contacted, Young's background was checked and as soon as it was revealed that he was a convicted poisoner the police arrived to question him. When he was found to have a phial of thallium in his pocket and an ample supply of both thallium and antimony in his bedsitter he was arrested on suspicion of murder. During questioning he boasted of killing his stepmother as a teenager, getting away with it because she was cremated, and also outlined at length the effects of poisoning by thallium, which is tasteless and odourless and causes gradual paralysis of the nervous system. When he was charged with the murder of Fred Biggs he said simply: 'The charade is over.'

Young's diary was found and turned out to be a chilling record of a poisoner's exploits. He referred to his workmates by the initial of their Christian name and about Jethro Batt he wrote: 'I feel rather ashamed of my action in harming J . . . the nearest to a friend that I have at Hadland's.'

Thirty-nine-year-old Diane Smart had got on the wrong side of him one day and he wrote: 'Di irritated me intensely yesterday, so I packed her off home with an attack of illness.' Fred Biggs' decline was recorded in great detail, first: 'I have administered a fatal dose of the special compound to F. and anticipate a report on his progress on Monday 1 November. I gave him three separate doses.' Later he wrote, 'Brain disease would render him a husk. It is better that he should die . . . F. is responding to treatment. He is being obstinately difficult.'

In June 1972 he was put on trial for the murder of Bob Egle and Fred Biggs, the attempted murder of David Tilson and Jethro Batt, who both suffered long-term effects, and the malicious poisoning of several other colleagues. He pleaded not guilty and gave every appearance of thoroughly enjoying the trial, making the most of his days in the full spotlight of public attention. He asked prison officials regularly if Madame Tussauds had requested his details in order to make an effigy.

The diary was a vital piece of evidence, though Young maintained that it was a work of fiction, just a set of notes for a novel he was writing, based on the strange events at the factory. However, the jury needed little more than an hour to find him guilty and he was sentenced to life imprisonment. He served his sentence at Parkhurst, where in August 1990 he was found dead in his cell after a heart attack.

There was never any suggestion that Young had a motive for his poisonings beyond indulging his scientific curiosity and enjoyment. Psychiatrists who examined him as a teenager concluded that he had no animosity towards the relatives he poisoned; in fact, he was on good terms with them and felt no grievances towards them. They were simply 'the nearest people to hand for his purpose'. His sister Winifred, in her book *Obsessive Poisoner*, wrote that he craved attention and publicity. Shortly before his arrest he told her that he was lonely and depressed, referring to himself as 'your friendly neighbourhood Frankenstein'. When she tried to encourage him to go out more and make friends, he said: 'Nothing like that can help me . . . you see, there's a terrible coldness inside me.' Perhaps he was simply incapable of normal human feelings towards anyone. 'He killed as though conducting experiments on rats,' wrote Winifred.

# Carroll Edward Cole

FROM his earliest childhood, Carroll Cole's mother planted the seeds of hatred deep within him and throughout his troubled adult years he looked for ways of revenging himself for those early experiences, killing women he regarded as promiscuous because it was the nearest he could come to killing her.

He was only five years old when his mother started taking him along when she met her lovers, using various painful means to make him promise not to tell his father. She would ask the women of the neighbourhood round for coffee parties where young Cole was forced to serve them, dressed in skirts and frilly blouses, which made the guests scream with laughter. Word got round among his schoolmates, who made his life a misery, making fun of his Christian name and forcing him to sit with the girls. Mockery sent him wild: once he retaliated by crushing another boy's hand while they were playing on some road-mending machinery, another time he managed to drown a nine-year-old tormentor, but it was regarded as an accident resulting from natural horseplay.

As he grew to adulthood his impulses became darker and more dangerous: he was haunted by daydreams about raping and strangling women. At this point he was still fighting to keep himself under control and he begged doctors for psychiatric treatment. The result was that he spent three years in mental hospitals, where he was considered 'anti-social' but no danger to society. He proved the doctors wrong in 1966 when he tried to strangle an 11-year-old girl.

Four years later he was in Nevada, USA, when the murderous urge came over him again and he once more appealed for psychiatric help. This time doctors refused to take him seriously and were anxious to get rid of him as soon as possible. His case notes read: 'Condition on release: same as on admittance. Treatment: express bus ticket to San Diego, California.'

It was a disastrous decision that led to the death of up to three dozen women, for it was at this point that Cole tipped over the edge. He would pick up girls in bars or on the street and the very fact that they were willing to have sex with him on first meeting branded them in his sick mind as 'loose women' who 'deserved all they got'. In 1971 in San Diego he strangled Essie Buck, and though the police knew that he had had contact with her they had no proof to enable them to bring charges. He killed again in 1975 in Casper, Wyoming, and then, on a week-long drunken binge in Oklahoma in 1976, he carved up the body of a victim in the bath and fried a couple of steaks of human flesh for supper. In 1977 he strangled a Las Vegas prostitute and in 1979 Bonnie O'Neill was killed in the street in San Diego; Cole then stripped her and had sex with the dead body.

He had married an alcoholic prostitute, a combination that could only feed his growing compulsion, and he threatened to kill her a number of times before carrying out his threat, afterwards wrapping her body in a blanket and hiding it in a cupboard. He was found by police trying to dig a grave, but he was so obviously drunk and his wife's alcoholism had been so advanced that her death was accepted as accidental. There must have been something about Cole that made it impossible for police or doctors to admit that he was capable of doing anyone serious harm.

In November 1980, Cole was really busy: Dorothy King took him home to her apartment and he strangled her there, then the next night he met Wanda Roberts in a bar and proceeded to strangle her in the parking lot. He then went back to Dorothy King's apartment, where she still lay undiscovered, and had sex with the corpse. Even though Cole had been seen drinking with Wanda Roberts shortly before her death, the police failed to find him. The third November victim was Sally Thompson, strangled in her own apartment, but she put up enough of a struggle to alert the neighbours, who called the police to report the strange thuds and thumps. The police arrived to find Cole standing over the body but they were still not wholly convinced that he was the murderer until, once in custody, he began confessing to a series of homicides, some of which had been written off as accidents. Once he started talking he seemed unable to stop and admitted to 35 murders, even apologizing for not being able to provide all the details because he had been too drunk to remember.

At his trial in 1981 he pleaded guilty to the three Texas murders and was given three life sentences, two of them to be served consecutively. He was then extradited to Nevada to stand trial for two murders committed in that state. He pleaded guilty again, requesting a non-jury trial because he felt that judges would be more likely to use the ultimate sanction and sentence him to death. Sure enough, they imposed the death penalty and Cole thanked them sincerely.

There were a number of organizations eager to take up Cole's cause but he steadfastly refused to appeal against his sentence, apparently welcoming the thought of death. His life was ended by lethal injection on 6 December 1985.

# David Berkowitz

ON A HOT night in July 1976 two girls, 18-year-old medical technician Donna Lauria and 19-year-old student nurse Jody Valenti, were sitting talking in a car outside Donna's New York home when a young man walked over to them. He pulled a gun out of a brown paper bag and fired five shots. Donna, who was just opening the car door, was hit in the neck and killed and Jody was hit in the thigh.

Three months later 18-year-old student Rosemary Keenan and her boyfriend Carl Denaro were parked in a secluded spot when a gunman fired through the back window of their red Volkswagen. Fortunately for Carl Denaro the path of the bullet was deflected by the glass; instead of penetrating his brain it took a piece out of the back of his skull and he recovered after surgery.

The two incidents took place in different parts of the city and there was no reason to connect them. Then, in November, 18-year-old Joanne Lomino was sitting on her porch chatting with her schoolfriend Donna De Masi shortly after midnight when a man walked up to them. He began to ask directions but stopped in the middle of a sentence, produced a gun and fired. Both girls were wounded: Donna recovered in a few weeks but a bullet had hit Joanne in the spine, leaving her paralysed for life.

Bullets from the same .44 revolver had been used in all three shootings and detectives realized that they had a random killer on their hands, someone who would shoot at complete strangers for no other purpose than the enjoyment of maiming and murdering. He seemed to choose girls with long dark hair and the theory was that Carl Denaro had been targeted by mistake – he had shoulder-length hair and was sitting in the passenger seat, so the gunman might well have mistaken him for a woman in the dark.

In 1977 the attacks continued. Panic spread through the city until young women and courting couples were reluctant to venture out after dark, for fear that a homicidal maniac was watching them from the shadows. On 30 January 26-year-old Christine Freund and her boy-friend John Diel were kissing goodnight in their car after an evening at the cinema when a bullet shattered the windscreen and ploughed into Christine's head. She died a few hours later in hospital. On 8 March an Armenian student, Virginia Voskerichian, was on her way home at 7.30 pm when a young man about to pass her on the footpath aimed a revolver at her. Virginia tried to shield herself with the books she was carrying but the bullet went straight through them into her mouth, shattering her teeth and killing her instantly.

At the next shooting the killer left the perplexed detectives a letter. This time he had claimed two victims: 18-year-old Valentina Suriana and 20-year-old Alexander Esau, killed as they embraced in the front seats of a parked car. When the police reached the scene they found a letter lying in the road, a few metres from the bodies of the dead lovers. It was addressed to Captain Joseph Borelli of the New York Police, the officer in charge of the investigation, and ran: 'I am deeply hurt by your calling me a woman-hater. I am not. But I am a monster. I am the Son of Sam . . . I love to hunt. Prowling the streets looking for fair game – tasty meat.'

Soon afterwards 'Son of Sam' sent another letter to journalist Jimmy Breslin, who had been covering the story. This letter was as rambling and incoherent as the first, apparently the babblings of a madman, but it hinted at further killings and fuelled the growing hysteria in New York.

In the summer there were more attacks: on 26 June Salvatore Lupo and his girlfriend Judy Placido escaped without lasting injury when they were wounded by bullets which shattered the car windscreen, on 31 July Stacy Moskowitz was killed by a shot in the head and her boyfriend Robert Violante was blinded for life after they had parked their car near a playground. After each murder the police switchboards were flooded with calls from members of the public who thought they had seen something suspicious, and all had to be checked out as a matter of routine. After the last shooting, the police were contacted by 49-year-old widow Mrs Cacilia Davis, who had been returning home in the early hours of the morning, at around the time of the murder. A couple of blocks from the playground she had seen two traffic officers fixing a ticket to the windscreen of a yellow car illegally parked near a fire hydrant. Then, only moments after the officers had left, she saw a young man walk up to the car, screw up the ticket then jump into the car and pull away so fast that the tyres screeched.

Police enquiries revealed that only four tickets had been issued in that area on the morning in question and only one of the four cars fitted Mrs Davis's description. It was registered to David Berkowitz at 35 Pine Street, Yonkers. When the police arrived at the address they found the car parked outside and in the back a duffle bag with a rifle butt sticking out of it. When the glove compartment was searched they discovered a letter addressed to one of the officers heading the murder hunt; it was written in the distinctive style of 'Son of Sam'.

Six hours later a pudgy young man with a round face and short dark hair came out of the apartment block and climbed into the car. The police moved in, trained their guns on him and asked who he was. He beamed at them and said: 'I'm Sam!' At first the officers took him to be retarded; even when two guns were pressed against his head he was still grinning. Detective John Falotico remembered: 'He had that stupid smile on his face, like it was a kid's game.' At the time of his arrest his apartment walls were covered with strange messages like 'I kill for my Master' and 'In this hole lives the wicked king'.

David Berkowitz was a loner, spoilt and shy as a boy, who grew up resentful and frustrated because girls never showed any interest in him. He was an illegitimate child, born of an affair between his mother and a married man, and was given up for adoption at birth. His adoptive parents were a Jewish couple, Nathan and Pearl Berkowitz, who had been unable to have children of their own. As David turned 14 Pearl died, and when Nathan Berkowitz remarried in 1971 his adopted son was hurt and angry. He joined the army to get away from home and further alienated himself from the family by becoming a Baptist. In 1974 he returned to New York but by then his father had decided to move to Florida. Nat Berkowitz realized from his son's letters, which grew strange and gloomy, that he had psychiatric problems. A month before Donna Lauria's murder he wrote to his father: 'Dad, the world is getting darker now, I can feel it more and more . . . The girls call me ugly and they bother me the most.'

Several of Berkowitz's neighbours knew him as 'a nutter' and had reported his activities to the police on more than one occasion. Sam Carr had received odd letters complaining about his labrador dog, Harvey, and shortly afterwards Harvey had been shot, though not fatally. The German shepherd dog belonging to another neighbour was shot through the window and killed, after a string of anonymous telephone calls. Craig Glassman, who occupied the apartment below Berkowitz, received letters accusing him of being part of a black magic group run by Sam Carr. All were convinced that the perpetrator of these incidents was Berkowitz but without proof the police could take no action.

After his arrest, Berkowitz happily confessed to the Son of Sam killings. He claimed that since 1975 he had been hearing voices telling him to kill and the commands were transmitted through Sam Carr's dog, who was possessed by demons. He had tried to kill Harvey but the demons had protected the dog and after that the voices had been louder and more clamorous.

His first attempts at murder had been made with a knife. On Christmas Eve 1975 he followed a woman as she left a supermarket and stabbed her in the back. Instead of falling down she turned and tried to grab hold of him, so he ran away. On the same night he tried a

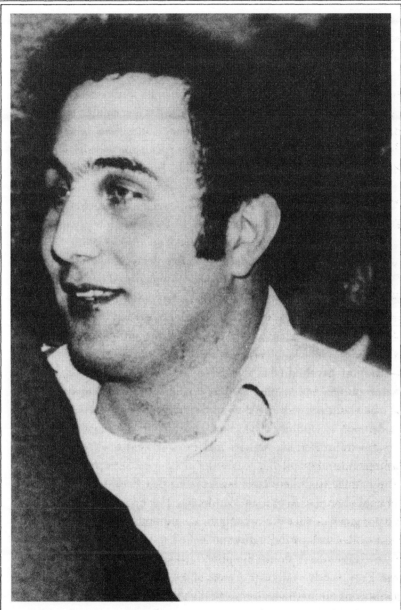

*David Berkowitz, 'Son of Sam'*

second time, stabbing 15-year-old Michelle Forman in the head and back outside her apartment building. She fell to the ground screaming and, as Berkowitz made off, she dragged herself into the building before losing consciousness. She was discharged from hospital after a week.

After that, Berkowitz obtained a gun and a few months later he was using it on the streets. After his first successful killing, he would drive around the New York streets looking for promising victims. Of his first murder, that of Donna Lauria, he said: 'I never thought I could kill her. I couldn't believe it. I just fired the gun, you know, at the car.' He liked to return to the scene of the murders. One night, after shooting a courting couple, he drove on a few blocks to catch a glimpse of the apartment block were Donna had lived, instead of getting away as soon as possible. After the fourth shooting, he remembered: 'I imagine I didn't care much any more: I had finally convinced myself that it was good to do it . . . and that the public wanted me to do it.' He told police that after a murder he felt 'flushed with power' and it was his habit to celebrate by going to a café to eat his favourite meal, hamburger followed by chocolate icecream.

Several psychiatrists considered that Berkowitz was a paranoid schizophrenic but another, Dr David Abrahamson, was convinced that it was all an act, that the story of the 'voices' was invented to provide a defence of insanity. The court considered him capable of taking responsibility for his actions and he was sentenced to 365 years' imprisonment.

Since the trial there have been claims that Berkowitz was only one of a number of 'Son of Sam' murderers. The eye-witness descriptions of the gunman varied markedly in height and looks and none of the police sketches of the murderer looked much like Berkowitz. Some investigators have drawn attention to the strange events surrounding the Carr family: Carr's two sons, John and Michael, both died in suspicious circumstances after Berkowitz was arrested. John Carr was found shot to death with a rifle in his girlfriend's apartment; at the time it looked like suicide but later it was judged to be murder. Michael Carr died in a car crash and was shown to have a high level of alcohol in his blood, though he was known as a non-drinker. These strange events led some people to believe that Berkowitz was only one member of a killer cult whose other members have never been brought to justice.

# Herbert Mullin

'SATAN gets into people and makes them do things they don't want to,' said Herbert Mullin after he had murdered eight people. Voices inside his head convinced him that he was the saviour of the world, that it was up to him to save the people of California from flood, fire and earthquake by regular killings.

Mullin was brought up in a devoutly religious Roman Catholic household. He always seemed a well-balanced boy, doing well at school and shaping up as a promising athlete, even voted 'most likely to succeed' by his classmates. By the age of 17 he was engaged and a happy future seemed assured, but it all began to fall apart when his best friend Dean Richardson was killed in a road accident in 1965. He turned his bedroom into a shrine for his dead friend and spent hours brooding in front of his picture. He began worrying that he might be homosexual and when he became eligible for conscription to military service he announced that he was a conscientious objector. His girlfriend, deciding that he was no longer the boy she had loved, broke off the engagement.

His family saw him becoming stranger and stranger, developing odd religious ideas and cutting himself off from the real world. They were sure that he needed psychiatric help and persuaded him to go into a mental hospital, but he refused to cooperate with the staff and was discharged after six weeks with no improvement in his condition. He became addicted to hallucinogenic drugs and began obeying voices which commanded him to stand on his head, shave off his hair or stub out cigarettes on his body. It was soon obvious that he was suffering from paranoid schizophrenia and over the next three years he alternated between spells of treatment in various institutions, trouble with the police and lying low in cheap San Francisco hotels. He was going downhill all the time and by 1972 his voices were telling him that he must kill.

In October he was driving along a quiet road through the Santa Cruz mountains when he saw an old tramp, Lawrence White. He stopped the car, got out and opened the bonnet. When 'old Whitey' drew level, Mullin invited him to have a look at the cause of his breakdown. As the tramp bent to peer into the engine, Mullin hit him a mighty blow with a baseball bat. He drove off, leaving the body lying by the roadside.

Eleven days later he gave a lift to Mary Guilfoyle, a student at the university in Santa Cruz, then drove her to a deserted spot and stabbed her. He cut open the body and ripped out her internal organs, scattering them as a meal for birds of prey. It was four months before her skeleton was found. A few days afterwards Mullin's Catholic upbringing reasserted itself temporarily and he went to confession in St Mary's Church. However, immediately afterwards he regretted what he had said and, afraid that the priest might betray him, he stabbed Father Henri Tomei to death.

At this time, Mullin's voices underwent a subtle change and he now heard people asking him to kill them. He bought a gun and no one who came in contact with him was safe. In his disturbed mind he blamed the man who had first introduced him to drugs, Jim Gianera, for all his problems, convinced that he had deliberately set out to scramble his head. He went looking for Gianera at an old address where the new tenant, 29-year-old Kathy Francis, gave him another address in Santa Cruz. He found Gianera there, shot him and stabbed his wife as she bent over his body. His voices still active, Mullin went back to Kathy Francis' home, and, finding her sharing a bed with her two small sons, he shot all three of them.

Twelve days later he was on the prowl again in Cowell State Park, where he found four teenage boys camping in a tent. He chatted to them for a few moments, then pulled a gun and shot all four of them dead.

On 13 February 1973, less than a week after the multiple murder, Mullin was driving towards his parents' home when his head was once more filled with voices, demanding another victim. He stopped and gunned down an elderly man called Fred Perez, who was tidying up his garden. A neighbour heard the shot and, looking out of the window, saw Perez fall and managed to note the number on the licence plate as Mullin's van drove off. A patrol car spotted him a few minutes later and Mullin was taken into custody.

He confessed to 13 murders, insisting that he had prevented thousands of deaths that would have followed the natural disasters that his actions had averted. He was tried in Santa Cruz in July 1973, when his defence was insanity – reasonable enough, considering the diagnosis of paranoid schizophrenia. However, it was decided that he was sane by legal standards and he was charged with ten of the 13 killings. He was convicted on two counts of first-degree murder and eight counts of second-degree murder and sentenced to life imprisonment.

# James Ruppert

ON THE evening of Easter Sunday, 1975, James Ruppert rang the police in Hamilton, Ohio, to tell them that his entire family, 11 people in all, had been shot. When officers arrived they found six bodies in the kitchen and four more in the living room: all had been shot at close range, all but one in the head, so that they had died instantly. Ruppert admitted that he was the murderer and was arrested and held for trial.

Ruppert, who was 41, was a deeply paranoid personality. He had always felt himself persecuted by his mother and his brother Leonard – with it seems, good reason. The family was always very poor, but after his father died of tuberculosis, leaving a woman and two teenage boys to work the small, subsistence-level farm, things became even worse. James was undersized and suffered from asthma, while his brother was bigger and stronger and always his mother's favourite; Charity Ruppert constantly praised Leonard and held him up as an example while denigrating everything James tried to do and putting him down at every opportunity. She encouraged Leonard to ill-treat his younger brother and did nothing to intervene when the former tied the latter up and locked him in a cupboard, or whipped him with the garden hose. By the time he was 16 James felt so miserable and worthless that he attempted suicide, trying to hang himself with the sheets from his bed.

He failed to graduate from college and was unable to keep a job, so in 1975 he was still living with his mother and Leonard, who now had a wife and eight children and a well-paid job. His paranoia was growing, for he believed that his family were making false reports about him to the police and the FBI and that Leonard was damaging his car, breaking off the wipers, loosening the bumper or punching holes in the exhaust. It was probably the last straw when, just before Easter, his mother told him that if he did not start contributing to the household expenses he would have to leave. He saw that as the final rejection, the proof that the family was out to get him, so he concluded that he had to get them first.

The night before the shootings he had been out drinking; he returned home in the early hours, then slept half the morning. When he came downstairs he carried a rifle and three handguns but this was not particularly unusual as his hobby was guns and marksmanship and he often spent part of the weekend target-shooting. As he appeared, Leonard made a disastrous remark: 'How's your car going?' he asked. James Ruppert exploded and began shooting. In the kitchen he killed his mother, Leonard and his wife Alma, 13-year-old Carol, 11-year-old David and 9-year-old Teresa. In the living room he killed the other children – John, Ann, Thomas, Michael and Leonard, their ages ranging from 4 to 15. Except for Alma, who tried to make a grab for the gun, they were all so shocked that they had no chance to resist.

The trial revolved round Ruppert's sanity, the prosecution maintaining that he had known exactly what he was doing and that he knew full well that if he was found insane he could inherit a healthy sum from his family (which would not be possible if he was found guilty and sane) and would be free to enjoy his inheritance after a spell in a mental hospital. The final verdict was that he was guilty of murdering his mother and brother but that the first two killings had tipped the balance of his mind and he had no longer been responsible for his actions. He was given two life sentences, to run consecutively.

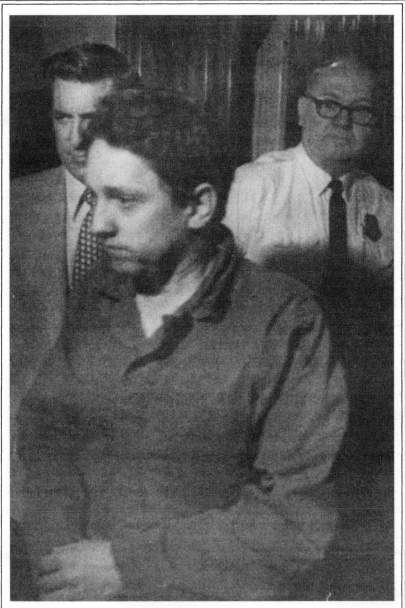

*James Ruppert*

# Edmund Kemper

AS A BOY, Edmund Kemper had a crush on his schoolteacher. When his sister teased him about wanting to kiss his teacher he said, quite seriously, 'If I kissed her I'd have to kill her first.' It turned out to be a tragically prophetic remark.

Edmund's parents separated when he was seven. His mother set high standards for him, using a sarcastic tongue to whip him into line, and he grew up timid and resentful. He took out his anger on the household cats: one was buried alive and the other hacked to pieces. He kept the remains in his cupboard to gloat over until his mother discovered them. His favourite game was 'executioners', where his sister strapped him into an 'electric chair' and pretended to throw the switch while he writhed in well-simulated agony.

His mother thought him a 'real weirdo' and sent him off to live with his father, who passed him on to his grandparents. When he was 14, in August 1963, he shot his grandmother in the head with a rifle, then took the kitchen knife and stabbed her over and over again. As his grandfather returned home he shot him before he even reached the door. He then phoned his mother to tell her what he had done and when the police arrived he said off-handedly: 'I just wondered how it would feel to shoot Grandma.'

Kemper spent the next five years in a psychiatric hospital, and by the time he was discharged into the care of his mother he had grown into a 2.06 m (6 ft 9 in), 149 kg (21½ stone) giant. He quarrelled frequently and violently with his mother and afterwards would go out driving round the town of Santa Cruz, USA. On 7 May 1972 he picked up two student hitchhikers, Anita Luchese and Mary Ann Pesce. He held them at gunpoint, drove them to a quiet spot then stabbed them over and over again. Later he smuggled the bodies into his bedroom while his mother was at work, using them for sexual acts, then dissecting them with a large hunting knife he called 'the General'. Eventually he distributed the pieces in the Santa Cruz mountains.

In September he gave a lift to 15-year-old Arko Koo. He suffocated her by pressing his huge hands over her nose and mouth, then had sex with the dead body before cutting it into pieces. The following day he had an interview with his psychiatrists, who found that he was adjusting satisfactorily to the outside world and were satisfied with his progress.

By this time the newspapers were calling him the 'Co-ed Killer' and in January 1973 he struck again, picking up Cindy Schall as she hitchhiked to college, forcing her into the boot of his car and then shooting her. He took the body home and hid it in his bedroom cupboard overnight. His mother suspected nothing and after she had left for work in the morning he took the body to bed and performed sex acts before cutting it to pieces in the bath. He then stowed the remains in plastic bags and threw them into the sea from the cliffs at Carmel.

A month later Kemper gave a lift to 23-year-old Rosalind Thorpe, then stopped again for 21-year-old Alice Lui. He shot both of them, then stacked them in the boot. When he got home his mother was already there, so he sat and ate dinner as usual. Later, after she had gone to bed, he went out and decapitated both bodies where they lay. He carried Alice Lui indoors and had sex with the corpse, then chopped off her hands for good measure. He disposed of the bodies in a quiet canyon, where they were discovered ten days later.

Easter was a time of unbearable tension for Kemper. His hated mother was around all the time, nagging at him as usual, and making it more difficult for him to relieve his tension by bringing home another victim. On Easter Sunday he walked into her bedroom while she was still sleeping and smashed her skull with a mallet. He cut off her head and sliced out the larynx, which he threw into the waste-disposal machine, to demonstrate that she would never be able to nag him again. The larynx caught in the machinery and flew out again, an event which caused him to tell the police: 'Even when she was dead, she was still bitching at me. I couldn't get her to shut up.'

His lust for killing was still unsatisfied so, with his mother's body still in the house, he telephoned a friend of hers, Sally Hallett, and invited her for tea. As she walked through the door he hit her over the head with a brick then strangled her and cut off her head. He had sex with the body then left it in his bed overnight while he slept in his mother's room.

In the morning he drove off in Mrs Hallett's car with no destination in mind. When he was stopped by the police he thought they were about to arrest him but instead they gave him a speeding ticket and, not noticing the gun lying on the passenger seat, let him go on his way. Three days later he reached the town of Pueblo in Colorado and, finding that he had apparently escaped pursuit, he rang the local police and confessed to being the 'Co-ed Killer'. At first they brushed him off, assuming that it was just a crank call, but he persisted, ringing over and over again until they were forced to take notice. When he was asked why he had not given himself up in Santa Cruz, he said he thought the police there, being familiar with his crimes, might beat him up in the course of arrest and he was 'terrified of violence'.

He seemed happy and relieved to tell the whole story: how he had kept teeth, hair and portions of skin from each victim as mementoes and had buried the head of one of the girls in the back garden, facing the house so that he could imagine her looking at him. 'These girls are dead because of the way that mother raised her son,' he said simply.

Though obviously unbalanced, Kemper was judged legally sane and convicted on eight charges of murder. He asked to be executed or, preferably, tortured to death, but instead he was sentenced to life imprisonment without possibility of parole.

# Ronald De Feo

THE PATRONS of Henry's bar on Long Island, USA, were enjoying a quiet drink in the early evening of 13 November 1974 when Ronald 'Butch' De Feo appeared in the doorway, gasping that he needed help: someone had shot his father and mother. Earlier in the day De Feo had told his friends that he could not get into the house where he lived with his parents and four younger siblings; he did not have his key and, though the two family cars were in the drive, no one answered his knock.

Now five friends drove the short distance to the De Feo house with Butch. A few minutes after their arrival, the local police department received a frantic call about a houseful of bodies. When officers arrived they found Mr and Mrs Ronald De Feo lying side by side, face down, on their bed. They had both been shot twice in the back by a killer who had stood in the doorway of their bedroom; they had both been trying to get up from the prone position at the time of the shooting. Across the corridor the gunman had stood between the beds of 11-year-old Mark and 9-year-old John and shot each boy in the back at close range. In the next room lay 13-year-old Alison; it seemed that she had woken and sat up, only to be shot in the face. On the floor above were two more bedrooms; one, belonging to Butch, was empty but the other contained the body of 18-year-old Dawn De Feo. All five members of the family had been shot in the early hours of the morning. There had been no resistance and no attempt at flight; all five bodies lay on their own beds.

Butch De Feo had an instant suspect for the police, a hitman named Louis Falini, who had once been a friend of his father's. Butch had quarrelled with Falini, who had threatened to get even with the whole family. At first it seemed a possible explanation but when detectives learned that Butch owned several guns, including a .35 calibre rifle – the type used in the shooting – and had been enquiring about buying a silencer a few weeks before, they changed the focus of their enquiries. Eventually De Feo admitted that he alone was the killer.

The story that emerged of Butch De Feo's relationship with his family was one of anger and hatred. His father was a violent man who knocked his wife about and often laid into his eldest son too, once knocking out his front teeth with a chair. He grew up with no respect for his mother and utter disgust for his noisy sisters and two younger brothers whose careless, dirty habits nauseated him.

Materially, young De Feo had all he wanted – a boat, a car, plenty of cash – but by the age of 18 he was filling some gap in his life with drugs, soon turning from speed to heroin because it calmed him instead of exciting him. He spent a good deal of time in bars and quite often the evening ended in a fight. Several times he had threatened friends with guns, only half seriously, and once he had levelled a shotgun at his father, who had knocked his mother to the floor and was standing over her menacingly. He actually pulled the trigger but the gun failed to fire. De Feo must have felt the tide of violence rising within him, because a few weeks before the killings he went to stay with a girlfriend to get away from the family, fearing that he might injure them. His father did not take him seriously and persuaded him to move back into the family home.

On the evening of 12 November, De Feo had been watching a war film on television and had fallen asleep. When he woke in the early hours of the morning he went to his room, loaded his rifle, then walked into his parents bedroom and shot them. Next he killed Alison, then his young brothers. He paused to reload the rifle, then went up to the next floor. Dawn, who had been disturbed by the noise, came out of her bedroom to see who was on the stairs. De Feo told her that everything was all right and she turned and went back into her room. De Feo followed behind and shot her. Afterwards he went from room to room collecting up the used cartridges, which he put into a pillow-case, along with his bloody clothing. On his way to work he dropped the pillowcase into a sewer and threw the rifle into the river.

At the trial, defence and prosecution lawyers argued over whether or not De Feo was legally responsible for his actions at the time of the murders. The defence maintained that De Feo was suffering from paranoid delusions: his anger and hostility had reached such a pitch that on the night of 12 November he believed that if he did not kill his family, they would kill him. The defence psychiatrist pointed out that in De Feo's account of the killings the young man had claimed that he had never heard the sound of the rifle firing and that this was an important indication of his strange mental state. The state psy-chiatrist, on the other hand, found no evidence of insanity and summed him up as aggressive, anti-social and self-obsessed. Prose-cution lawyers argued that De Feo had mentioned that all the time he was shooting, the family dog, Shaggy, was barking hysterically out in the yard. If he could hear the dog, they reasoned, then obviously he could hear the shots and saying that he could not was simply part of a pretence of insanity.

The jury found him guilty and he was given six life sentences, to be served concurrently. The judge recommended that he should not be considered for parole.

The story of the murders did not end with Ronald De Feo's convic-tion. A year later the Lutz family moved into the De Feo house, which was on the market at a bargain price because of its history. The few weeks they lived there were filled with terror; there were supernatural manifestations, levitations, strange and overpowering smells. One night they panicked and fled, leaving all their possessions behind, and later a book based on their experiences was published, entitled *The Amityville Horror.* The address of the De Feo house was 112 Ocean Avenue, Amityville.

# Henry Lee Lucas

HENRY LEE LUCAS confessed to several hundred murders during the 18 months following his arrest in Texas, USA, in June 1983. Later he was to change his story more then once. Some of the confessions were obviously false and a major newspaper series claimed that the whole thing was a gigantic hoax, but the law enforcement agencies still believe that he was responsible for an enormous number of killings. From various states he collected a death sentence, six life sentences and several other long prison terms.

Lucas had the sort of childhood that might leave anyone unbalanced and he grew up hating the world. His family lived in a primitive cabin in the backwoods of Virginia, where his parents ran an illegal whisky still. His alcoholic father had lost both legs to a freight train as he lay drunk on the railway line and pulled himself around the floor as best he could. His mother, Viola, part Cherokee Indian, seems to have been a complete sadist. She beat him unmercifully, belabouring his head so that later X-rays were to reveal brain damage, and once left him lying semi-conscious for three days after stunning him with a wooden bar. She sent him to school dressed as a girl with his long hair curled into ringlets so that the other children would find him an object of ridicule, and gave him so little to eat that he searched through neighbours' rubbish bins for discarded food. When she was earning a little extra as the local prostitute, she forced both her young son and her husband to watch her activities. One night when Lucas senior could bear it no longer, he dragged himself out into the snow and lay there all night. He contracted pneumonia and died a week later. Lucas was not exaggerating when he said later: 'I was brought up like a dog. No human being should have to be put through what I was.'

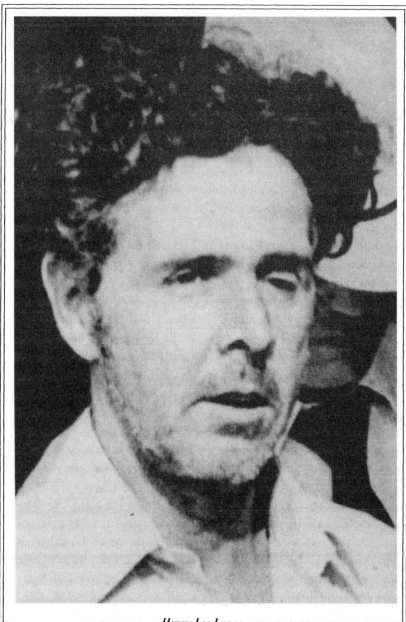

*Henry Lee Lucas*

Lucas claimed to have committed his first murder at the age of 15, when he strangled a girl who refused his advances. After that he left home and embarked on a career of petty crime, eventually being imprisoned for six years after a series of burglaries. Soon after his release, he stabbed his mother to death in a fight and afterwards boasted of having sex with her corpse. He was committed to a psychiatric hospital, where he was diagnosed as a psychopath and sexual deviant; when he was paroled in 1970 he told the doctors, 'I'm not ready to go.' He asked them to keep him inside for he was certain that he would kill again, but they paroled him anyway and within hours of his release he apparently murdered a young woman a few blocks from the hospital.

He then apparently embarked on a murder spree that lasted for 13 years across a number of states, though his favourite venue was the 800 km (500 mile) interstate highway between Laredo and Gainesville in Texas. Scores of bodies were found here over the years, killed in a variety of ways – shot, strangled, bludgeoned – sexually assaulted and sometimes dismembered. Lucas eventually laid claim to most of them and police nicknamed the road the 'Henry Lee Lucas Memorial Highway'. He met up with another serial killer, Ottis Toole, and each recognized a kindred spirit. Over the next few years they often travelled together, raping, killing and dismembering. Lucas preferred to have sex with his victims after death: 'I like peace and quiet,' he explained. Toole was an arsonist who often liked to barbecue and eat his prey, though Lucas claimed that he never joined in that part of the proceedings. 'I don't like barbecue sauce,' was his reason.

Toole's teenage niece Becky and nephew Frank travelled with them and Frank was to be driven into a mental hospital in 1983 by memories of the deeds he had witnessed. When Toole went his own way in 1982 Lucas and Becky settled together in Stoneburg, Texas, where they earned their keep by doing odd jobs for 80-year-old Kate Rich. Both Becky and Mrs Rich disappeared at around the same time. Becky had quarrelled with Lucas and tried to hit him, whereupon he stabbed her to death then chopped her body into small pieces and distributed them in various parts of the desert. He pretended that Becky had gone off with a lorry driver but when Kate Rich also went missing, the police became suspicious and Lucas was forced to flee. When he was finally taken into custody he admitted that he had stabbed Mrs Rich and burned her body in the church store.

Lucas was first arrested for illegal possession of a handgun, but on his fourth night in custody, on 14 June 1983, he called a prison officer to his cell and told him: 'I've done some bad things.' This was the beginning of a confession that amazed law officers and caused a nationwide sensation. In October more than 80 detectives from 20 states gathered in Louisiana to view 48 hours of tapes in which Lucas recounted his long lists of crimes, with names, dates and details. Officers came from all over the States to interview him and he revisited the scenes of many crimes in the company of detectives.

Perhaps the police, anxious to close the file on troublesome murder enquiries, were sometimes a little too eager to believe that Lucas had the answer, but on many occasions he recounted details that had never been publicized and would be known only to the killer; he was able to lead the police to the exact location of many murders without any guidance. However, only Lucas can ever know how many killings he perpetrated, either alone or in company with Toole. He is currently appealing against conviction, saying that he was never a serial killer and only made up the stories because he enjoyed being in the limelight following his arrest.

# James Huberty

'I'M GOING hunting humans,' James Huberty told his wife as he left their apartment on the afternoon of 18 July 1984. He was dressed in khaki camouflage trousers and a black T-shirt and carried with him a Uzi machine gun, a 9.9 Browning automatic and a shotgun. Over his shoulder he had slung a bag filled with ammunition. He was about to turn the McDonald's restaurant in the Southern border town of San Ysidro, USA, into a slaughterhouse and become one of the worst mass murderers in American history.

Huberty was an angry man and it was an anger that he carried with him constantly, lashing out at the slightest opportunity. He came from a broken home, growing up mainly under the care of his grandmother, and he was always a loner. When his father remarried in 1971, Huberty hated his stepmother and from then on became estranged from his father. However, he married and was able to provide his family with a comfortable three-storey house in a good area of Massillon, Ohio, the town where he had grown up. Then he lost his job as a welder, failed to find another, and things began to fall apart. He was forced to sell the house and move to San Ysidro, where he worked as a security guard.

The Hubertys had never been liked by their neighbours. Back in Massillon they had been reported to the police several times for their anti-social behaviour and both had been arrested as a result of angry confrontations. In their new home they made no friends and Huberty was known for his bad temper and the way he was always shouting at children – his own and other people's. Once his daughter had to take refuge with a neighbour because her father had been hitting her. No one will ever know what finally tipped Huberty over the edge, but when he once more lost his job, his behaviour became even more strange and he began hearing voices.

What is known is that he walked into a branch of McDonald's a few metres from the Mexican border, loaded down with weapons. As he started firing, one customer said that he yelled: 'I killed thousands in Vietnam and I want to kill more.' Another reported him as saying: 'I'm going to kill you all.' He fired indiscriminately, mowing down men, women and children, even including a six-month-old baby. One survivor, Mrs Griselda Diaz, could scarcely believe what she was seeing: 'He just came in and started shooting at everyone. I dived on the floor with my boy and we crawled behind a counter.'

Huberty fired round after round at the customers, and occasionally sprayed passers-by outside with bullets. When one weapon was empty he used another, disregarding the screams of the living and the moans of the dying. When all his weapons were empty, he calmly reloaded and circled the restaurant, firing at those who had taken cover the first time and finishing off some of the wounded.

The police had been called and a team of sharpshooters was positioned in the post office across the street. Some of those wounded in the street managed to crawl into the office for safety. The police delayed firing because there were reports that the gunman was holding a dozen or more hostages, but as the killing continued the order was given to shoot to kill. Three minutes later Huberty was dead, killed by a marksman from the post-office roof. He had killed 20 people and wounded 30 more.

There was an attempt on the part of Mrs Huberty to sue McDonald's, claiming that chemicals used in their food had caused her husband's mental breakdown but, of course, it came to nothing. The restaurant, where the walls and floor had run with blood, was pulled down.

# Chapter Seven

# UNLIKELY KILLERS

# Introduction

THE STEREOTYPE of the serial killer is that of a wild-eyed psychopath, inadequate or unbalanced in some way, a loner who cuts himself off from his fellow beings and finds it impossible to hold a normal place in society. There are killers like that, their manner and habits marking them out, but there are also those who appear as smiling and cooperative colleagues, helpful neighbours or desirable dinner partners.

They can amass quite a collection of victims before they come under suspicion because no one suspects the attractive, buxom widow so adept at making her men happy and comfortable, or the merry, chatty little woman whose only aim in life is to find the ideal man. Ted Bundy, who is credited with battering and violating some 40 women, was one of the least likely killers of all time: well-educated and good-looking, the all-American boy who could attract all the girls he wanted, he still felt the compulsion to kill, using his superior intelligence to lure girls to their deaths and to evade capture. Almost as surprising are the health professionals who devote their lives to the care of the sick, earn a caring, compassionate reputation and then make a habit of killing their patients.

# Belle Gunness

THE TOWNSFOLK of La Porte, Indiana, USA, woke on the morning of 28 April 1908 to find that the farm belonging to Belle Gunness had caught fire in the night and was now nothing but a charred ruin. Everyone said it was a tragedy: the hardworking widow and her three children had been burned to death in their beds. No one knew her very well as she had kept herself to herself, but she had been a pleasant enough neighbour with a ready smile for everyone and they admired the way she had built up the neglected farm from nothing. It was now one of the best-kept properties in the area, the fence always freshly painted, the yard neat and tidy.

They could hardly believe the revelations that followed an investigation into the fire, for Belle's business had been not farming but murder. She had lured one man after another to her home with the promise of marriage and a comfortable life, then killed them for their money. All their bodies were buried on her carefully tended property.

When she arrived in La Porte, Belle already had an interesting past. She was born in Norway but emigrated to the United States in 1883 and married a Swede, Mads Sorenson, who worked as a security guard. After two years Sorenson died, and though doctors thought he had suffered a heart attack his family was suspicious about the cause of death. There was talk of an exhumation, but nothing came of it. Later Belle's house burned down and she now had two sets of insurance money which was invested in a bakery, which also burned down. This time the insurance company was unwilling to pay out, but they could prove nothing.

All the same Belle decided to move on, settling on the farm at La Porte. She married Peter Gunness, a well-liked local widower who died soon afterwards: according to Belle he had been sitting under a shelf on which was a heavy sausage grinder when the shelf collapsed and the grinder fell and split his skull. Once again Belle collected the insurance money, and when one of her children told playmates that her mother had hit her stepfather with a cleaver it was written off as childish prattle.

Belle continued to run the farm with the help of various hired men, one of them Ray Lamphere, who became her lover and was completely under her spell. By now she had thought up a new scheme for making money and she began inserting adverts in newspapers circulating in the Scandinavian communities of the US:

> 'Rich, good-looking widow, owner of a large farm, wishes to contact a gentleman of wealth with cultured tastes. Object: matrimony.'

Other adverts added 'Triflers need not apply' or 'No replies by letter will be considered unless the sender is willing to follow an answer with a personal visit'. There was no shortage of applicants and Belle was able to pick and choose, setting up a correspondence with likely prospects so that she could find those with a tidy little nest-egg and the minimum of close relatives to interfere with their plans or make a fuss if they disappeared from view.

A succession of men came to visit Belle at her farm and were delighted by what they saw: a smiling blonde with huge blue eyes and an honest peasant face. To be sure she was overweight – 93 kg (14 stone) – but she exuded a strongly sexual aura and after a good meal and a pleasant chat she always made them welcome in her bed. Their stay was usually short but they never returned home again.

Andrew Hegelein, a bachelor from South Dakota, had been exchanging letters with the sympathetic-sounding widow for several months and had been assured 'my heart beats in wild rapture for you'. He arrived in January 1908 and was seen being driven to the farm in Belle's pony and trap. Soon afterwards Belle deposited $3000 in her

*Belle Gunness*

bank account. For some reason, Lamphere was particularly jealous of Hegelein – perhaps Belle had a soft spot for him and he thought she might take him as a husband – and after a quarrel with Belle, he left the farm. He often boasted to his drinking partners that he 'had something' on Belle, but he was not the most reliable man in town and no one paid much attention.

As the farmhouse caught fire on the night of 27 April, Lamphere was seen running from the blaze by a neighbour's son who was hiding in the bushes. Lamphere told him to get out or he would kill him. When the remains of the three Gunness children, together with a headless body assumed to be Belle's, were found in the farmhouse ruins, Lamphere was arrested and charged with murder.

The local sheriff needed proof that the dead woman really was Belle Gunness so his men continued to dig and sift through the debris. While they were still searching, Axel Hegelein arrived to make enquiries about his missing brother. Though he had corresponded with Belle and she had assured him that his brother had left the farm in perfect health, he was far from satisfied. On a hunch he asked the diggers to turn over part of the yard and they discovered first Andrew's torso, then his head and limbs, all separately wrapped in sacking. They went on to dig up the chicken pens, finding more bodies – among them Jenny Olsen, Belle's adopted daughter, who was supposed to have left for Los Angeles at the age of 16.

The bodies of ten men were recovered, most of them cut into pieces and badly decomposed, but Tonnes Peter Lien of Minnesota and John Moo from Wisconsin were both identified by their watches and Olaf Lindboe by his teeth. Newspapers all over America carried the story and friends and relatives came hundreds of kilometres in the hope of finding out about their missing men, who had all travelled to Indiana in the expectation of marrying a rich widow, most of them carrying several thousand dollars with them.

There were doubts, too, about the identification of the woman's body burned inside the farmhouse. The head was never found and the body seemed to belong to a much smaller woman. Moreover, considering the large sums of money Belle must have obtained over the years, her bank balance was remarkably low, leading to rumours that Belle had not died in the fire after all but had made off with her ill-gotten gains. She had been seen driving an unknown woman to the farm the day before and it seemed quite possible that she had killed the woman, decapitated her to prevent identification and then made her escape, leaving behind her dead children and arranging for Lamphere to set fire to the farm.

The search for clues continued and eventually a local miner known as Klondike Louis, sifting through the ashes, found a section of bridgework made of gold and porcelain and anchored to a tooth. Dr Ira P. Norton, the La Porte dentist, identified this as dental work he had done for Belle Gunness which would only disintegrate in a 'blowpipe flame'.

However, there were still enough doubts about Belle's whereabouts to enable Lamphere to escape a murder charge, though he was convicted of arson. He died of tuberculosis in 1909 and after his death the prison chaplain revealed that he had made a confession, admitting that he had known of Belle's murderous trade for several years and that during that time she had disposed of two or three men each month. He had seen her chloroform one of them and kill another with a hatchet and had occasionally helped her to dispose of a body. On the day of the fire Belle had brought a woman from Illinois to the farm, promising a job as a housekeeper but killing her instead. She disposed of the head in the swamp, covered it with quicklime and dressed the body in her own clothes. The children had been chloroformed and Belle had left before Lamphere set the fire.

There were several supposed sightings of Belle Gunness but even if she was still alive she was never found. No one will ever know whether or not Lamphere was speaking the truth, but Belle will live for ever in the verse that runs:

'Belle Gunness lived in In-di-an;
She always, always had a man,
Ten at least went in her door –
And were never, never seen no more. . . .

There's red upon the Hoosier moon
For Belle was strong and full of doom
And think of all them Norska men
Who'll never see St Paul again.'

# Nannie Doss

NANNIE DOSS of Oklahoma, USA, was one of life's romantics. She immersed herself in the stories of *True Romance* magazine, day-dreaming about the perfect man who would come along and sweep her off her feet so that they could live happily ever after. By 1954 she was on her fifth marriage and she still had not found the elusive 'Mr Right', but it had not soured her sunny disposition. She was fat and jolly, with a smile and a friendly word for everyone; it was impossible not to like her.

However, her girlish giggle and ingratiating manner hid another, darker side to her character, for she had already murdered ten people and was about to kill another. Her favourite method was to make a tasty dish of stewed prunes, mix in a liberal amount of arsenic – and serve it, of course, with a smile.

She was only 15 when she married George Frazer, and when she found that marriage failed to live up to her romantic dreams she looked elsewhere. Frazer was an easy-going man who took her back after several indiscretions but eventually he walked out. Nannie began looking for Mr Right all over again but found three children too much of an encumbrance. Two of them developed a mysterious stomach complaint and conveniently died before she married Frank Harrelson in 1947.

Harrelson did not come up to standard as the perfect husband any more than did George Frazer, but now that Nannie had discovered she could get away with murder she did not waste much time on him. She served him a delicious dish of stewed prunes, he developed violent stomach pains and vomiting and died soon afterwards. They had been married for less than a year, but Nannie already had her next husband in view. Arlie Lanning seems to have measured up to her high standards for a while for this third marriage lasted for five years, but in 1952 he too died from 'food poisoning'.

Like many multiple poisoners, Nannie seems to have been carried away by her own success and between husbands she disposed of several relatives for no apparent reason, including her mother and two sisters. It says a good deal for Nannie's winning personality and apparent devotion that no one suspected that anything was amiss. Doctors signed death certificates without a second thought, no post-mortems were suggested and everyone sympathized with poor Nannie over each new loss. Husband number four, Richard Morton, died within a year, leaving her $1500-worth of insurance.

Perhaps by now Nannie had reached the stage where she would have murdered any man she married once the initial excitement had worn off, but with her fifth husband her luck ran out. In 1954 she married 58-year-old Samuel Doss and within a few months he suffered a violent gastric upset. However, unlike the other husbands, Doss had a conscientious and careful doctor who sent him off to hospital immediately. There he quickly recovered and was discharged into Nannie's tender care. Nannie thoughtfully prepared his favourite dish, stewed prunes, to celebrate his homecoming. Later that day he suffered a relapse and died in hospital the following day.

Doss's physician was unlike those who had been fooled by Nannie's loving concern in the past and he refused to sign the death certificate, saying that he regarded the circumstances of her husband's death as suspicious and would require a postmortem. This showed that Samuel Doss had consumed enough arsenic to kill several men and Nannie was taken in for questioning. She remained cheerful and cooperative, chattering endlessly about her happy life with Samuel until the police interrogators were exhausted. It took days of questioning before she finally admitted to killing her husband.

Publicity about the case led to information pouring in from all sides about the deaths of previous husbands and close family members. Eventually ten bodies were exhumed and all showed signs of arsenical poisoning.

When she went on trial in 1964 Nannie Doss confessed to all the killings but resented it deeply when the prosecuting counsel accused her of murdering for monetary gain. Her only reason had been the pursuit of her romantic dream. 'I killed them because I was looking for the perfect mate', she told the court. She never volunteered any convincing reason for killing her mother, her sister and others unconnected with her love life. She was sentenced to life imprisonment but died of leukaemia the following year.

# Wayne Williams

BY THE LATE spring of 1981, the number of 'Atlanta Child Murders' had risen to 26. Over the past two years black children had disappeared one after another in the American city and it was sometimes months before their bodies were found, hidden in undergrowth or dumped in the river. Death was usually due to strangulation and police believed that the killer normally approached his victims from behind, locking his arm around their necks and choking them to death.

The first victims were two black teenagers, Edward Smith and Alfred Evans, whose bodies were found in July 1979. Their deaths passed as unremarkable and when a third youth, Milton Harvey, disappeared in September there was no reason to connect the two incidents. In October nine-year-old Yusef Bell, the son of an ex-civil rights leader, went on an errand for a neighbour and failed to return home. After ten days his body was found stuffed into the crawl space of an abandoned school building but he had been strangled only about five days before. This time there was a great deal of media interest, as his mother, Camille Bell, was well-known for her civil rights work. Also, the decomposed body of Milton Harvey had recently been found and people were becoming uneasy.

A year after the first murders a total of seven black children had been murdered and three more were missing. Many parents were convinced that a white killer was stalking their children on a macabre mission of assassination, but the police thought this unlikely: most of the children had been snatched in black neighbourhoods where a white person would be noticeable immediately. Some of those concerned, led by Camille Bell, called a press conference to complain of police inaction: if their children had come from white middle-class neighbourhoods, they argued, far more resources would have been devoted to the case.

As the killings continued, more manpower was drafted in to swell the special police task force. There was a rumour that the killer himself might be a policeman, who would find it easy to approach trusting youngsters. The sum of $100,000 was raised by local people as a reward for information leading to the arrest of the killer. As the hunt intensified, a grisly pattern began to emerge: all the children were aged between seven and 14, all but two were boys and except for one girl, whose murder was thought by some officers to be unrelated to the rest, they had not been sexually assaulted.

Feelings among the townsfolk were running so high that 35 FBI officers were sent to Atlanta to assist the local police chief, who was the target of almost universal criticism. The hunt for the killer became one of the biggest police operations ever mounted in the United States. Face-to-face interviews were conducted with over 20,000 citizens and a further 150,000 were questioned by telephone. Police talked to tens of thousands of children, reasoning that the killer must have been unsuccessful in some of his attempted abductions and that the children involved might be able to provide some valuable clues.

On 22 May 1981 there came a dramatic breakthrough in the investigation. Police on a routine patrol near the South Drive Bridge over the Chattahooch River heard a splash and identified the nearest vehicle as a station wagon. They radioed ahead and a patrol car stopped the vehicle as it left the bridge. The driver was a 23-year-old black man named Wayne Williams and after checking his documents the police allowed him to go on his way. Two days later the body of Nathaniel Cater, aged 27, was fished out of the river. If the same killer was again responsible, then he had varied his pattern by selecting an adult victim. Forensic tests showed that dog hairs found in the rear of Wayne Williams' car matched those on the body of Nathaniel Cater and he was questioned further.

All those who knew Williams were astonished to learn that he was a suspect. He was 23, the only child of two elderly schoolteachers, and lived with his parents in a modest single-storey house in west Atlanta. He had been a gifted child who spent his spare time studying the stars through his telescope and by the age of 14 he had set up his own radio station, selling advertising time and giving interviews to magazines and on television. When he left school he became fascinated by police work and would tune his shortwave radio to police frequencies so that he could arrive first on the scene, taking photographs that he sold to the highest bidder. The only time he had been in trouble was when he was arrested for impersonating a police officer. Now he was pursuing a new career as a music promoter and was inviting young men to audition for possible inclusion in pop groups.

On 3 June Williams was given a 12-hour grilling by the police and the next day he called a press conference to announce his innocence. The police, he said, considered him the prime suspect: 'One cop told me "You killed Nathaniel Cater. It's just a matter of time before we get you." He insisted, 'I never killed anybody and I never threw anything from the bridge.'

In January 1982 Williams was put on trial, charged with the murder of Nathaniel Cater and of Jimmy Payne, who had been seen in his company before being found in the river. The prosecution case was weak: no link could be proved between Williams and either of the dead men. There was no motive, though the prosecution argued that he was 'a frustrated man driven by a desire to purify the black race by murdering poor young blacks'. It was suggested that he had contacted potential victims through his musical scouting work. The trial took a remarkable turn when the judge acceded to a plea from the prosecution to allow them to introduce evidence linking Williams with the death of ten other victims. District Attorney Anthony Joseph Drolet said: 'He has not been formally charged with the killings but the cases will reveal a pattern and bend of mind.'

Forensic evidence showed that the hairs found in Williams' car and

*Wayne Williams* (centre), *being escorted from Fulton County Gaol en route to court*

home were similar to those found on all ten bodies. A 15-year-old boy said that he had been fondled by Williams and had later seen him with Lubie Geter, who disappeared from a shopping mall in January 1981 and whose body was found a month later. Another teenager testified that Williams had offered him money for oral sex.

When Williams gave evidence he denied everything. He had not stopped his car on the bridge; he had not thrown Cater's body into the river and doubted if he would have had the strength to lift it; he was not and never had been a homosexual. 'I never met any of the victims,' he told the court. 'I feel just as sorry for them as anybody else in the world. I am 23 years old and I could have been one of the people killed out there.' When cross-examined he accused the prosecutor of being a fool and described the two FBI men who had questioned him as 'goons'.

The jury, consisting of eight blacks and four whites, found him guilty and he was sentenced to two consecutive life terms. He was led away with tears streaming down his face, still protesting his innocence.

Since the conviction, there has been much argument over the Williams case and the quality of the evidence. There have been suggestions that evidence linking the Ku-Klux-Klan with the Atlanta deaths was suppressed at the time of the trial and further developments in the case are quite possible.

# Ted Bundy

TED BUNDY was just about as far from the popular idea of a homicidal maniac as it is possible to be. To all outward appearances he was the all-American boy: good-looking, well-educated, self-assured and ambitious, successful with girls and with an old-fashioned courtesy that appealed to their parents. But beneath the easy charm lay the raging sex drive, the immaturity and the suppressed resentment that turned him into one of America's most notorious serial killers. His victims may have numbered as many as 40 and they were raped, strangled and beaten to death.

The bloody trail of murders that was to follow Bundy for four years began in Seattle with the disappearance of six attractive and strikingly similar young women. In January 1974, 21-year-old Lynda Ann Healy, a psychology student, vanished from her apartment, leaving blood-stained sheets on the bed and a bloody nightdress hanging tidily in the wardrobe. It was not the first attack on girls in the area: a week before Sharon Clarke had been found battered into unconsciousness with a metal bar wrenched from the bed frame rammed into her vagina, though she had not been raped.

In the two months following Lynda Healy's disappearance 19-year-old Donna Manson vanished on her way to a concert and Susan Rancourt, a biology student, never arrived at the cinema, where she was due to meet a friend. Roberta Parkes, Brenda Ball and Georgann Hawkins all disappeared during May and June. Their abductor was choosing his victims with care: all the girls were intelligent and attractive, all in the same age group, all with long dark hair parted in the middle.

July was sunny and hot and Lake Sammamish State Park, outside

324

Seattle, was crowded with young people who had come to picnic and enjoy water sports. On 14 July 23-year-old Janice Ott was lying by the lake when a young man with his arm in a sling sat down beside her and began chatting. Those nearby heard him introduce himself as 'Ted' and noticed that after a while she got up and strolled off with him. She was never seen again. The same afternoon Denise Naslund left her friends to visit the lavatory and never returned. Enquiries showed that the man called Ted had approached two other girls, asking them to help him put his sailboat on to his car because he could only use one arm. One had refused but another had gone with him to his small Volkswagen, only to become suspicious and return to the beach when there was no sign of a sailboat.

Newspapers printed descriptions and artists' sketches of Ted, with the result that over 3000 calls were received, all naming possible suspects. One of them was from Ted Bundy's girlfriend, Meg Anders, who was worried about his strange sexual behaviour and had noticed that he was never with her on the days the girls disappeared. Police gave Bundy a routine screening but the respectable law student, active in law-and-order politics, was never considered a serious suspect.

In September a group of forestry students found a shallow grave containing human bones in a wood a few kilometres from Lake Sammamish. They were the remains of Janice Ott and Denise Naslund. Three months later the remains of four more missing girls were found 16 km (10 miles) away.

As autumn progressed the girls of Seattle began to relax; no more murders were reported and it seemed that the terror was over. At the same time, a wave of killings was beginning in Salt Lake City, Utah, where Ted Bundy had enrolled as a student. Nancy Wilcox disappeared on 2 October after accepting a lift in a Volkswagen; on 18 October Melissa Smith, daughter of a police chief, vanished while hitchhiking home from a restaurant; on 31 October Laura Aime failed to arrive at a Halloween party. The bodies of Melissa and Laura were later found: they had both been raped and beaten.

In November, 17-year-old Carol DaRonch was walking through a shopping mall when a young man approached her, identified himself as a police officer and told her that someone had been seen trying to break into her car in the parking lot. He accompanied her to her car, which proved to be still locked with none of her property missing. He then asked her to go with him to the station and, though his battered Volkswagen did not look much like a police car, she agreed. It was only when she realized that the supposed officer was driving the opposite way from the station that Carol panicked. There was a scuffle, with her captor threatening her with an iron bar and trying to snap handcuffs on her wrists, but she managed to escape, screaming for help. That same evening 17-year-old Debbie Kent was abducted from a high-school car park.

Over the winter the scene of action moved to the ski resorts of Colorado, where five more girls went missing, but the police made no further strides in identifying the killer until August 1975, when a highway patrolman noticed a Volkswagen shoot down the street when the driver saw a police car. When he stopped the Volkswagen and looked inside he found a stocking mask, an iron bar and a pair of handcuffs. At first the driver, Ted Bundy, was suspected as a burglar but detectives soon made the link between the items in Bundy's car and the abduction of Carol DaRonch. Her testimony was sufficient to convict him of attempted kidnapping, but by this time graver charges were on the horizon. A search of his flat had produced brochures and maps of the Colorado ski resorts, as well as credit card receipts that showed that he had been in several of the areas where girls had disappeared, only to be found violated and murdered. Bundy was sent to Colorado to face murder charges.

He escaped for the first time by jumping through the window of a courthouse but was rearrested a week later. A few months later he broke out of Garfield County Gaol by unscrewing a metal plate around

*Ted Bundy*

the light fitting, crawling along the roof space and dropping down into a room in the gaoler's house. A few days later a student calling himself Chris Hagen took a room on the outskirts of Florida State University in Tallahassee and no one connected the quiet, polite young man with escapee Ted Bundy.

On the night of 15 January 1978 a student returning to the Chi Omega sorority residence saw a man with dark clothes, cap and some sort of wooden club hurrying out of the door. As she went inside one of the sorority members, Karen Chandler, staggered from her room, blood streaming from her head. Inside, her roommate, Kathy Kleiner, was sitting on the bed holding her bloodsoaked head. Worse was to come. In another room Margaret Bowman lay dead; she had been strangled with a stocking, pulled round her neck with such ferocity that it looked as though she had been decapitated. A fourth victim, Lisa Levy, was already dying when she was found; the killer had been in such a frenzy that he had sunk his teeth into her buttocks and almost bitten off one of her nipples.

An hour and a half later, in a house six blocks away, a young woman heard cries and moans and sounds of rhythmic thumping from the next room, occupied by Cheryl Thomas. She dialled Cheryl's phone number and as the telephone rang next door she heard the sound of running feet and a door banging. When the police arrived they found Cheryl badly beaten but still alive. The weapon, a length of board, lay on the floor where the attacker had dropped it: he had been rhythmically beating Cheryl over the head while masturbating with his other hand.

On 9 February 12-year-old Kimberly Leach disappeared from a school yard and her body was found two months later in an abandoned cabin. She was Bundy's youngest victim and was also to be his last. In the early hours of the morning on 15 February a patrolman pulled over a car he believed to be stolen, and when the driver tried to run for it he was overpowered and arrested.

Bundy denied everything. When his defence lawyers wanted him to enter into a plea-bargain, pleading guilty to three murders in return for a guarantee that he would avoid the death penalty, he sacked them and decided to represent himself. The sensational trial that followed was broadcast to the nation on television and attracted newsmen from all over the world. Much of the evidence against Bundy was circumstantial but the young woman who had seen the killer leaving the Chi Omega sorority house was able to identify him. Even more damaging was the forensic evidence which proved that the bite marks on Lisa Levy's body had been made by Ted Bundy's teeth. He was found guilty on the two Chi Omega murders in July 1979 and sentenced to die in the electric chair. When he was asked if he had anything to say, he answered: 'I find it somewhat absurd to ask for mercy for something I did not do.' Later a third conviction and death sentence were obtained in the case of Kimberly Leach.

His current girlfriend, Carol Boone, remained convinced of his innocence and married him in a hurried ceremony in a Florida court just before he was given the third death sentence. 'Ted is not vicious or a savage mass murderer,' she insisted. 'The charges were the result of snowballing hysteria on the part of law enforcement people looking for a fall guy on whom they could pin all their unsolved crimes.'

To many people who watched his courtroom battles, it seemed incredible that this could be the same man who ravaged and battered women in frenzied sprees of violence and his personality remains a mystery. He was born to an unmarried mother and brought up believing that she was his sister; his grandparents treated him as their own son. His mother later married John Bundy, an ex-navy man who worked as a cook, and though young Ted was never close to his stepfather there was never any sign of hostility. To his mother he was 'the best son in the world,' who never forgot her on Mother's Day, however busy he might be. However, he was a lifelong liar and thief – he distinguished himself as a skier, but stole most of his equipment – and had an overpowering sex drive which no 'normal' behaviour with his girlfriends could satisfy. He was embittered by a failed relationship with a girl he yearned to impress: Stephanie Brooks, beautiful, clever and from a rich family, was taken in for a while by Bundy's undoubted charm and they became engaged, but she eventually jilted him because of his emotional immaturity. He was devastated, and some family members believed that he never recovered from the rejection. It was perhaps a deep resentment against women, allied to his overwhelming sexual urges for complete control over them, that led him to commit rape and murder.

# Donald Harvey

WHEN John Powell died in hospital in Cincinnati, USA, after lying in a coma for eight months following a motorcycle accident, a routine postmortem was carried out. The pathologist was amazed when he detected the telltale odour of bitter almonds which indicated the presence of cyanide. Once he had decided that the patient had been murdered, dozens of members of the hospital staff, as well as Powell's friends and relatives, came under suspicion.

Among those interviewed by the murder squad was nurse's aide Donald Harvey, a good-looking, smiling 35-year-old. Everyone at the hospital spoke well of him: he was always cheerful, always willing to help out. But when enquiries were made into his background, detectives unearthed facts that made them wonder if the real Donald Harvey might be rather different. It appeared that while in his previous job, as a mortuary attendant in the Cincinnati Veterans' Administration Medical Center, he had been suspected of stealing tissue samples from the morgue. Then, in July 1985, he was stopped by security guards when leaving work and found to be carrying a revolver as well as hypodermic needles, surgical scissors and gloves and anatomy textbooks. No charges were brought and he was allowed to resign.

Under rigorous questioning, Harvey admitted to poisoning John Powell by administering cyanide through a gastric tube. While he awaited trial a local television station reported on 23 other mysterious deaths in the hospital which had all taken place since Harvey joined the staff. Harvey's trial, scheduled for July 1987, was postponed until January 1988 to allow further investigations to take place. Complicated legal negotiations began behind the scenes to strike a deal: if Harvey gave details of all the crimes he had committed, pleaded guilty and agreed never to appeal his sentence, he could avoid the death penalty. As Harvey began his confession, it was soon obvious that the death toll was higher then anyone had imagined.

Harvey grew up in Kentucky, in a farmhouse surrounded by tobacco fields. His family were ordinary, hardworking people who went to church regularly and got on well with their neighbours. There seemed no reason why young Donald should grow up with major hang-ups; he was remembered as a winning child, well-liked by everyone. At the age of 19 he joined the Air Force and, stationed near San Francisco, he became involved in the gay community. A year later he was honourably discharged from the service and made a suicide attempt, followed by psychiatric treatment. He then took jobs in various hospitals, joining the staff of the Drake Memorial Hospital in Cincinnati in February 1986.

Most of the murders of patients that followed were accomplished by injecting cyanide into gastric tubes or with arsenic added to orange juice. Occasionally Harvey used petroleum distillate – a substance normally used to clean tubes – and once he tried to kill by injecting the victim with HIV-infected blood, but this was unsuccessful and he had to resort to cyanide after all. 'I got another one today,' he would tell colleagues each time a patient died on the ward and they would smile with him, never dreaming that there was any meaning behind the cheery young man's jokes.

Detectives listening to Harvey as he reeled off his list of victims were chilled by the matter-of-fact way that he talked about murder, as though he was discussing what to have for lunch. He claimed that he had killed the hospital patients because he felt sorry for them.

He made the same claim over some of those he killed, or attempted to kill, outside the hospital. In 1983 he poisoned Helen Metzger, an elderly woman in the flat above that occupied by Harvey and his homosexual lover Carl Hoeweler. She had been ailing for some time and Harvey often called in with shopping or an extra treat; this time it was a piece of pie, its whipped topping full of arsenic. Harvey was one

332

of the pallbearers at her funeral. When his lover's father went into hospital, he used a visit as an opportunity to sprinkle arsenic on the old man's pudding. He also fed Mrs Hoeweler arsenic over a long period but she survived his ministrations. There were other murders too, where there could be no suggestion of 'mercy killings'. Various neighbours were murdered after minor disputes and Harvey even gave arsenic to his lover after a quarrel, relenting later and nursing him back to health.

At his trial, the prosecutor argued; 'He's no mercy killer and he's not insane. He killed because he *liked* killing.' A psychiatric expert pointed out that the motive, like that of many serial killers, was power: 'Donald Harvey could kill these people – watch them die – and they couldn't do a thing.' When Harvey appeared in court a huge board listed the names of 28 victims and the dates of their death. He pleaded guilty to 24 murders and four attempted murders and received a life sentence on each count, the first three to be served consecutively.

This was only the beginning: in Kentucky Harvey pleaded guilty to eight counts of murder and one of manslaughter, then back in Ohio he pleaded guilty to three more murders, collecting in all 11 more life sentences and various other terms ranging from 7 to 25 years.

# SERIAL KILLERS

# Jeffrey Feltner

NURSE'S aide Jeffrey Feltner spent four months in a Florida gaol in 1988 for filing false reports and making harassing phone calls. The police were glad to see the case closed; it had already taken up far too much of their time since Feltner had made the first phone call, hinting that several patients at a Putnam County nursing home had been murdered.

He had begun by ringing a local television station pretending that a man he met in a bar had bragged about killing five nursing-home patients, but refusing to give a name. On the same day he called a crisis intervention centre, announcing himself as 'Jeff' and saying that he had already killed five patients at the nursing home and had planned to kill a sixth, only to have his attempt foiled at the last moment, after he had used a chair to climb in through the window of a sleeping female patient. He had been about to carry out his purpose when he heard a knock at the door and hastily retreated the way he had come. The police decided that the calls needed investigation, especially as the second caller had named all the patients he claimed to have killed.

Detectives who visited the nursing home discovered that there was a Jeff on the staff – Jeffrey Feltner – and the deaths mentioned had all taken place since his arrival. However, the idea that Feltner might be a murderer seemed laughable: he was a small, slight young man of 26, gentle and kindly, with a real feeling for the patients in his charge. He had been given the job on the recommendation of a relative who had worked at the home for years and no one had any criticisms of him. Moreover, there was no reason to suspect foul play in any of the deaths; all the patients had been old and ill and their demise had been

334

no surprise. When investigations were made into 'Jeff's' claim that he had just attempted another murder, a chair was found outside the window in question, but detectives were able to demonstrate that no one had stood on the chair and there was no sign that the window had been opened.

In due course Jeffrey Feltner admitted to making both phone calls but said that he had made up the murder story in order to draw public attention to the inferior standards of care provided for patients in nursing homes. The police took the view that he was more concerned with drawing attention to himself.

The authorities considered the matter closed with Feltner's gaol sentence but they were mistaken. The following year various agencies received phone calls – one of them purporting to come from Jeffrey Feltner's homosexual lover – saying that Feltner had killed two patients at nursing homes in Volusia County, as well as those already reported to the police in Putnam County.

Once again, Jeffrey Feltner admitted making the calls, for the same reasons as before. Detectives recommended that he should obtain psychiatric help and he committed himself to a mental-health treatment centre as a voluntary patient.

This time the police were not prepared to close the case so easily and under intensive questioning, Feltner confessed to seven murders. His method had been suffocation in every case: he would wait until the patients were asleep, then climb on top of them so that they could not move. Wearing surgical gloves to give him a better grip, he would place one hand over their mouths, then pinch their noses with the other. Within five minutes, they were dead. His only motive, he said, had been the relief of suffering: his chosen victims had been ill and in pain and this was the only way he could help them. He felt guilty about what he was doing but it was worth it to see the look of pain leaving their faces.

Proving a case against Feltner was not easy, as four of the seven patients he had named had been cremated, but the authorities in

Putnam County decided to exhume the body of one of the remaining three patients: Sarah Abrams, aged 75, who died on 10 February 1988. Of all the patients on the list, her death had been the greatest surprise and her family were anxious to help with an investigation. Examination of the body showed that she had been asphyxiated.

Feltner was charged with first-degree murder but his lawyers announced that he was planning to plead not guilty: 'He seems to have some kind of mental disorder that drives him to compulsive confessions to acts he has not committed' they announced. On the morning of the arraignment, Feltner was found lying in his cell with blood oozing from his slashed wrists. Doctors who treated him decided that the cuts were superficial and that his attempt at suicide had not been serious. Back in prison he lay curled up on his bunk, refusing to speak and taking nothing to eat or drink for five days.

He was examined by a psychiatrist and a clinical psychologist and both decided that he was unfit to stand trial, but at a competency hearing the judge preferred to accept the word of prison officers who considered that Feltner's depressed state was not abnormal among prisoners. He declared that Feltner had proved his own competence by his alert demeanour throughout the hearing.

As the trial approached Feltner was still announcing that he intended to plead not guilty but at the last moment his lawyers arranged a plea-bargain.

Feltner pleaded guilty to the first-degree murder of Sarah Abrams in return for an agreement that the prosecution would not request the death penalty. He would also plead guilty to the second-degree murder of 88-year-old Doris Moriarty at a Volusia County nursing home on 11 July 1989. He was given a life sentence, which in Florida meant a minimum 25 years, for the murder of Sarah Abrams and 17 years to run concurrently for the killing of Doris Moriarty.

Even after the conviction, Feltner's family and friends refused to believe that he was guilty. They always maintained that he had invented the story to highlight the poor care given to elderly patients in nursing homes. Two years before he had been diagnosed as an AIDS sufferer and they believed he wanted to achieve something useful in the time he had left, something that his family would be able to remember with pride.

# Chapter Eight

# UNSOLVED CASES AND ACQUITTALS

# Introduction

SERIAL killers rarely go uncaught – after a few killings their success leads them to become careless, or else their compulsions become so uncontrollable that normal caution deserts them. In some cases the killer, who in his saner moments realizes the enormous horror of his crimes, takes chances subconsciously, almost hoping to be caught. When, as sometimes happens, a series of killings ends with no apparent reason the police assume that the murderer has died or perhaps been committed to an asylum. That he has reformed is probably the least likely solution.

This section features stories of killers who were never caught, and who are known by the names which they either gave themselves or which the press bestowed on them – such as Jack the Ripper, the Mad Butcher of Kingsbury Run, the Zodiac killer and Bible John. There are two stories where people were accused but found not guilty – those of Dr John Bodkin Adams and the nurses charged with the mysterious deaths at Ann Arbor Hospital – and the case of Jack the Stripper, where the police believe they know the culprit and think he cheated them by committing suicide just before they would have caught him. Perhaps the most fascinating of all is the mystery of Birdhurst Rise, where somebody got away with three killings, and many people think they know who.

# Jack the Ripper

JACK THE RIPPER is Britain's best-known criminal. The terror he created in the country in 1886 was such that part of his name has been adapted for numerous more recent killers – the Yorkshire Ripper, Jack the Stripper, even the Rostov Ripper.

The original Ripper's first victim is taken to be Mary Ann Nichols, who was killed in Buck's Row, Whitechapel, on 31 August 1888. A prostitute living in a slum in London's notorious East End, she had been strangled, her throat had been cut and her stomach slashed. 'No murder was ever more ferociously or brutally done', said a report.

In this poverty-stricken area of London, with its alleys, gaslights, drinking dens and crime, it was not uncommon for prostitutes to be killed, violently or otherwise, and indeed the vicious stabbing of Martha Turner on 7 August in Commercial Street, Stepney, is sometimes thought to be the Ripper's first murder. Not much notice was taken at first of these two killings.

It was different, however, on 8 September, when the body of 'Dark Annie' Chapman, with her entrails hanging out, was discovered in Hanbury Street, Whitechapel. A fresh touch was that coins and brass rings had been laid round her feet as if in sacrifice. *The Lancet* reported: 'The intestines had been lifted out of the body and placed on the shoulder of the corpse', and the coroner declared that 'an unskilled person could not have done this'.

The newspapers were now wild with the story of the latest horrible murder, and there was speculation that perhaps a surgeon was responsible. Reference to this speculation was made in a letter the Ripper sent to 'the Boss' of the Central News Agency on 27 September, in which he said he wanted to be getting to work again right away

*A hawker discovers the body of Elizabeth Stride* (contemporary engraving)

and promised he would send the police a human ear. He signed the letter 'Jack the Ripper', with the added: 'Don't mind me giving the trade name'. He also asked that the letter be kept back until he 'do a bit more work', and this came immediately.

On 30 September Elizabeth Stride, known as 'Long Liz', was found in Berners Street. Her throat had been cut and an attempt had indeed been made to remove an ear. Her killer had been disturbed. Less than an hour later the Ripper had reached Mitre Square, in the Houndsditch area of London, and killed Catherine Eddowes. Despite the short time he had – the local policeman patrolled the square every 15 minutes – he slashed her from ribs to pubic area and removed an ear and a kidney. He washed his hands in a communal sink, and chalked a message on a wall: 'The Juwes are not the men who will be blamed for nothing.' The Police Commissioner, Sir Charles Warren, who was under pressure to resign over the affair, had the message rubbed out before it could be photographed apparently because he feared a wave of anti-semitic attacks.

The Ripper wrote again to Central News, apologizing for not having time to get the ears for the police. He also sent half a kidney in a box to George Lusk, Chairman of the Whitechapel Vigilance Committee, saying he had fried and eaten the other half and 'it was very nice'.

On 9 November the Ripper performed his most spectacular murder. Mary Kelly's body was found in her room in Miller's Court off Dorset Street. This time the Ripper had obviously had all the time he wanted. The head had been removed and the legs skinned. The intestines were hung round a picture frame and one hand was in the empty stomach. The heart was on the pillow.

This brutal murder caused a sensation. Even Queen Victoria voiced her opinions and Sir Charles Warren finally resigned. However, it was the last of the Ripper murders. A lawyer, Montague John Druitt, who drowned himself in the Thames in December, was claimed by Scotland Yard to be the murderer. Yet there was no evidence, and over the years there have been numerous other theories. The most striking is that the Ripper was Queen Victoria's grandson, the Duke of Clarence, who died in the flu epidemic of 1892. Another is that he was James Stephen, a homosexual friend of Clarence and man-about-town, who also died in 1892. Sir William Gull, Queen Victoria's physician and also connected with Clarence, is another whose name is put forward. Over a hundred years after the crimes, there is still no definitive solution.

# The Mad Axeman of New Orleans

ON 25 May 1918, brothers Jake and Andrew Maggio, a cobbler and a barber who lived with another brother, Joe, and his wife at their grocery store in New Orleans, heard groans from their brother's bedroom. Investigating, they found Mrs Maggio in a pool of blood, her head almost off her body, and Joe groaning on the bed with his throat cut. While awaiting the police they discovered that an intruder had entered the house by chiselling·a panel from the back door. In the yard was a bloodstained axe and razor.

The New Orleans police, who seem to have been singularly incompetent, arrested the two brothers for murder. But two streets away, a message had been chalked on a pavement: 'Mrs Maggio is going to sit up tonight, just like Mrs Toney.' It was recalled that seven years earlier three other Italian grocers and their wives had been similarly attacked: their names were Cruti, Rosetti and Schiambra, and Schiambra's Christian name was Tony. Was his wife Mrs Toney? The Maggio brothers were released while New Orleans, and particularly Italian grocers, wondered if there was to be another spate of murders.

Five weeks later, on 28 June, a baker went round the back of the grocery store of Louis Besumer. Most people lived in wooden-framed buildings with back yards, and the baker was horrified to see a panel chiselled from the back door. He knocked, and Louis Besumer, his head pouring blood from an axe wound, opened it. Inside, Mrs Harriet Lowe, who lived with him as his wife, was similarly injured. Besumer was Polish rather than Italian, but many locals thought he was German, and therefore probably a spy. When Mrs Lowe died, apparently saying Besumer was the axeman, he was arrested for murder.

On 5 August, however, the day Besumer was charged, the axeman struck again: Edward Schneider arrived home to find his pregnant wife covered with blood. She was able to tell police she had been attacked by a man with an axe. She recovered, a week later giving birth to a girl, and this time the police showed unusual restraint in not arresting the husband.

It was only another five days until the next attack. Two nieces of Joseph Romano, a barber, heard noises from their uncle's room. They crept to the door, and saw a man holding an axe by their uncle's bed. They screamed and he vanished. Two days later Romano died. The method of entry had been the usual one through a panel of the door, and the axe was found in the yard.

By now panic reigned in New Orleans, especially among Italians; many claimed sightings of the axeman, and there were numerous reports of panels chiselled from doors. However, there were no more attacks until March. Then a grocer, Iorlando Jordano, heard screams from over the road where a rival grocer, Charles Cortimiglia, lived. He dashed across, and found Cortimiglia on the floor, with blood pouring from wounds. His wife Rosie, with her head spurting blood, was sitting on the floor holding their dead and bloody two-year-old daughter. The back door had the familiar missing panel, and the bloody axe was outside. Mrs Cortimiglia was two days in shock – then she accused 69-year-old Iorlando Jordano and his son Frank of the crime. Despite the heated assertions of husband Charles, who recovered, that the Jordanos were not involved, the two men were arrested.

The axeman then sent a letter to the *Times-Picayune*, the local paper, saying that he would attack next on 19 March, St Joseph's Night, and that he would avoid any houses with a jazz band in full swing, as he liked jazz. Students invited him through a newspaper advertisement to join their party, and it is reported that New Orleans that night was noisy with music. There was even a tune composed: 'The Mysterious Axeman's Jazz, or Don't Scare Me Papa'.

It was not so funny for Louis Besumer, who stood trial in April. The evidence against him, however, was weak to non-existent, and he was acquitted. In May, however, the Jordanos were convicted solely on Mrs Cortimiglia's assertion – all the other evidence, including that of her husband, was against conviction. The young Jordano was sentenced to hang, his father to life imprisonment.

On 10 August 1919 an Italian grocer, Frank Genusa, opened his door to find his friend, neighbour and fellow grocer Steve Boca outside, blood pouring from a head wound. He had been attacked by the axeman. Naturally the police arrested Genusa, but released him on Boca's insistence.

On 2 September a man heard scratching at his back door and, after shouting a warning, fired a revolver through it. Chisel marks were found on the door. Next day a 19-year-old girl was badly injured by an axe attack. She eventually recovered, but could not remember the attack.

Mike Pepitone, another grocer, was attacked on 27 October. His wife, who slept in a separate room, heard noises and saw the axeman disappearing. Her husband was dead, attacked so violently that blood had stained the wall and ceiling.

There were now no attacks for over a year, but the *Times-Picayune* had another exclusive when, in December 1920, Mrs Cortimiglia burst into the office and confessed that it was untrue that the Jordanos, whom she disliked, had attacked her husband. In the past year she had been ravaged by smallpox, her husband had left her and she believed God was punishing her for her sins. The Jordanos were released.

The incompetent New Orleans police heard of the last act in the mystery of the axeman when their counterparts in Los Angeles told them that, on 2 December 1920, a man from New Orleans named Joseph Mumfre had been shot dead in the street by a veiled woman dressed heavily in black who had stepped from a doorway and emptied a revolver into him. The mystery woman was caught and, after lengthy questioning said she was Mrs Pepitone, and that Mumfre was the axeman she had seen running from her husband's bedroom when he committed his last murder. She had followed him to Los Angeles to exact revenge. The New Orleans police checked Mumfre's record. He was a criminal who had been in and out of prison and the axe murders tallied neatly with his periods of freedom. Mrs Pepitone was sentenced to ten years but served only three. Had she solved the identity of the axeman?

# The Mystery of Birdhurst Rise

ON 23 April 1928 59-year-old Edmund Duff set out from his house at 16 South Park Hill Road, Croydon, for a fishing holiday with an old friend in Fordingbridge, Hampshire. When he returned a week later, he was feeling ill. The family doctor, Dr Robert Elwell, could find little wrong with him, but during the night and following morning he got worse and late that night he died. Elwell and his partner Dr Binning, who had also been present at the death, could not issue a death certificate and an inquest was held. Duff's wife Grace, much younger than him at 41, told of a flask of whisky he had taken with him on his holiday and then finished when he got home, although the flask was never produced. Dr Bronte, the pathologist who carried out a postmortem, said there was no poison in the body, and the verdict was death from natural causes.

Mrs Grace Duff took her three children to live a few streets away at 59 Birdhurst Rise, to be nearer to her widowed mother Mrs Violet Sidney and sister Vera Sidney, who lived at number 29. Mrs Duff's brother Tom and his wife and family also lived nearby, at 6 South Park Hill Road. They were a close-knit family, always in each other's homes.

On 11 February 1929 Vera Sidney became ill. This was attributed to some soup made up by Kate Noakes, the servant, from vegetables and a powdered base, as Mrs Noakes and Bingo the cat, who also took a little, were also ill. Vera, usually the only one in the house who took soup, recovered a little and, on 13 February, was well enough to have lunch with the family and an aunt, Mrs Greenwell, who was visiting from Newcastle. Vera was not pleased to see some fresh soup of the same kind as before, but drank some, only to find that she was immediately very ill again with sickness and diarrhoea. So was Mrs Greenwell, who had also sampled the soup.

Next day Vera was considerably worse, and Dr Elwell was called. A specialist was summoned but, at just past midnight on 15 February, Vera died. Mrs Greenwell lay ill in her London hotel for days before recovering. Dr Elwell issued a death certificate stating natural causes and Vera was buried near her brother-in-law.

Vera's mother, Violet, took the death badly. Dr Elwell gave her a tonic called Metatone, and her other children, Grace and Tom, were always calling round. On 5 March Violet felt very ill near the end of lunch and announced she had been poisoned. Dr Binning and Dr Elwell called, and another specialist was sent for, but at 7.30 pm Violet Sidney died. Again there had to be a postmortem, and Violet's major organs were sent away for analysis. The CID were called in and a number of bottles, including Violet's medicine bottle, were removed. After Violet's burial arsenic was discovered in her medicine bottle and organs, and on 22 March 1929, in the middle of the night in a futile attempt to avoid publicity, the bodies of Violet and Vera Sidney were exhumed from Queen's Road Cemetery, Croydon.

While separate inquests were proceeding on Vera and Violet, Edmund Duff's body was exhumed on 18 May 1929 and a second inquest on him opened in July. All three inquests overlapped, and the same principal witnesses were at each. It was now announced that Edmund Duff had also died of acute arsenic poisoning. Dr Bronte was strongly suspected of having mixed up Edmund Duff's organs with those of another person when performing his original autopsy, although he denied this. The verdicts reached in the inquests on Vera Sidney and Edmund Duff were 'murder by poison administered by person or persons unknown'. In Violet's case the verdict was much the same, although the jury would not rule out the possibility that she had poisoned herself.

Who was the triple killer? There were only two serious possibilities: Grace Duff or her brother Tom Sidney, despite an anonymous letter to the coroner which claimed that Tom's wife was guilty. Grace benefited financially by all three deaths and Tom by two of them, although not by a great amount. After the inquests, Tom, who was by profession an entertainer, took his family to New Orleans, where he eventually became an antique dealer. Grace moved to the south coast and opened a boarding house. Despite their previous closeness, they did not see each other again. At the inquests, Grace made the better impression: quiet, considerate, apparently grieving. Tom was more irritable, and had exchanges with a coroner, particularly at the suggestion in the latter's summing-up that Tom had not always taken the proceedings seriously and, as opposed to Grace, was not the most truthful witness. The maidservant made the point that Tom was hanging about strangely at the times of his mother's and sister's poisonings, while the detective-inspector reported that Tom had claimed he was indoors with flu at one of the crucial times. On the other hand, there were those who thought Grace's calm and dignity were part of an act.

Detective-Inspector Fred Hedges wanted to charge Grace, partly in view of Tom's suggestion that there was something between her and Dr Elwell, but the Director of Public Prosecutions thought the evidence too thin. Tom also alleged that Grace was behind the anonymous letter, a copy of which Grace said she had herself received but destroyed. An interesting fact to emerge later was that the Duffs had had a paying guest from 1924, a Miss Anna Kelvey, but that soon after they moved to South Park Hill Road she had died of a stroke aged 76. On her deathbed she was alleged (by Tom) to have said: 'Mrs Duff, you are a wicked woman.' There was much speculation during the inquests that her body would be exhumed too, but police suspicions about it were left at that.

In the 1960s Richard Whittington-Egan interviewed many of the principals, including the doctors and main suspects, for his book *The Riddle of Birdhurst Rise*. He pointed the finger of suspicion at Grace Duff and the book could not be published until after her death in 1973.

# The Mad Butcher of Kingsbury Run

KINGSBURY RUN is an old creek running through Cleveland, Ohio, which now carries several railway lines. The waste ground either side of the lines was popular in the 1930s as camping ground for tramps, and a dangerous play area for children.

On 23 September 1935 children found two headless and castrated male bodies. The missing parts were found nearby. Decapitation was the cause of death, and only one victim was identified – Edward Andrassy, 29, a bisexual with numerous convictions. A reddish tinge on the other body, as if it had been treated with a chemical, recalled half of a woman's torso found a year before at Euclid Beach, a few kilometres to the east, with similar staining.

On 26 January 1936 a Cleveland butcher, told by a customer that there was some meat behind his shop, found a basket which contained parts of a woman's body. The remaining parts were discovered two weeks later behind a nearby empty house, but the head was never found. The body was identified as that of Florence Polillo, a prostitute.

During the rest of 1936 further heads and bodies – usually unidentifiable – were found in Kingsbury Run or nearby, and when the total of victims reached seven, a special 'torso squad' of detectives was formed to find the killer. However, over the course of 1937 and 1938, when numerous other body parts were discovered in the region, the squad had no success at all.

Then, in 1939, a letter addressed to the Cleveland chief of police was received from Los Angeles. This purported to come from the killer, a man who was going to 'astound the medical profession' after

*Frank Dolezal, at the time of his confession to the Kingsbury Run murders*

his experiments on his 'laboratory guinea pigs'. He promised that Cleveland could 'rest easy now' as he proposed to carry on his work in Los Angeles, and pinpointed where a head was buried on Century Boulevard in the latter city. However, no heads were found in Los Angeles.

In 1939 a private detective helping the Cleveland police discovered that Florence Polillo and one or two other Kingsbury Run victims had all used a particular tavern. Police arrested another customer, Frank Dolezal, and extracted a confession from him. But Dolezal hanged himself in his cell (or perhaps was murdered) and he is not seriously considered to have been a killer.

In May 1940 three male corpses were discovered in abandoned rail trucks outside Pittsburgh. All were decapitated, and bore the mark of the Kingsbury Butcher. They had met their deaths between three and six months earlier, possibly when the trucks were in Youngstown, Ohio. One victim was identified as a homosexual ex-convict.

A possible final victim of the killer was discovered over ten years later. On 23 July 1950 a headless, castrated male body was found in a timber yard a few kilometres from the Kingsbury Run. The head was found and identified four days later, and the coroner pointed out the resemblance of the crime to the torso murders.

It is unknown how many victims the Kingsbury Run Butcher claimed. Between 1925 and 1939 there were several decapitations near New Castle, Pennsylvania, near the railway line which runs to Cleveland; none of the victims were identified and no murderer was found. However, the Butcher killed at least 16 times, and eight of his heads were never traced.

# The Moonlight Murderer

TEXARKANA, a small town right on the border of Texas and Arkansas, hit the headlines of the American newspapers in May 1946 as the story broke of a serial killer who murdered when the moon was full. The 'Moonlight Murderer' spread terror among the townsfolk.

The killer's first attack occurred on 23 February 1946. A couple were parked by the side of a lonely road just outside the town when a tall man wearing a mask approached their car. Jimmy Hollis, aged 24, was ordered from the car at the point of a gun and clubbed to the ground. The man now turned his attention to 19-year-old Mary Lacey and inflicted such serious sexual assaults on her, using the barrel of his gun, that she asked him to kill her to end her ordeal. Instead the man clubbed her to the ground and began assaulting her companion, not bothering when the girl stumbled off to seek help. On this occasion both victims were allowed to live.

The next couple were not so lucky. On 23 March 29-year-old Richard Griffin and 17-year-old Polly Ann Moore parked their car on another lonely road in Texarkana. Both were found next morning in the car, shot dead through the back of the head. Blood found 6 m (20 ft) away from the car suggested that they had been killed there and their fully clothed bodies taken to the car, where the girl's body was sprawled on the back seat, the man's stuffed between the dashboard and the front seat. Immediately locals linked the crime to the one before, and the papers added to the horror by reporting, wrongly, that the sexual assaults of the first attack had been repeated and, indeed, exceeded in the second.

Exactly three weeks later two youngsters who had been last seen entering Spring Lake Park following a local dance were killed. The body of 17-year-old Paul Martin was found the following morning,

14 April, beside a road leading out of Texarkana. He had been shot four times. The body of his friend, 15-year-old Betty Jo Booker, was found 1.6 km (1 mile) away a few hours later; she had been shot in the heart, and also in the face. There was more colourful reporting about the 'Moonlight Murderer' and locals firmly believed that there was at large a sex-fiend whose lust for torture and killing was prompted by the sight of a full moon. The Texas Rangers patrolled the lovers' lanes and detectives were planted as decoys to try to attract the killer. Needless to say, several innocent people were challenged and, in some cases, subjected to violence by over-zealous citizens by mistake.

Three weeks later, perhaps in order to foil all this attention, the killer changed his style. On 4 May, 36-year-old Virgil Starks was reading the paper after supper in his farmhouse 17 km (10 miles) outside Texarkana when he was shot through the window. His wife, entering the room at the noise, was hit by two shots before managing to get out and summon help. While she was away the killer roamed through the house, leaving footprints from the blood of his victim. Tracker dogs were brought and a flashlight was found outside, but the killer had escaped by car.

With every adult man in Texarkana a suspect in a highly charged atmosphere, there was particular excitement when a man's body was found two days later on the railway line to the north of Texarkana, towards the town of Hope. He was Earl McSpadden, and the coroner found that he had been stabbed before his body was placed on the line to be run over by the 5.30 am train. It is possible that McSpadden was the last victim of the Moonlight Murderer, the killing designed to look like a suicide in the hope that the manhunt would be called off on the assumption that he had been the murderer. Some reporters did indeed claim the killer had committed suicide, ignoring the stab wounds.

It is true that the murders stopped. There have been claims since that the killer's identity has been discovered, or at least suspected, but there have been no charges or convincing evidence. The case remains a mystery.

# Dr John Bodkin Adams

IN 1956 Fleet Street editors felt that they were on the edge of one of the greatest criminal stories of all time. It seemed that in the respectable seaside resort of Eastbourne a prosperous doctor had been collecting large legacies from wealthy widows whom he had been easing into the next world. The *Daily Mail* suggested that the wills of more than 400 of the doctor's patients were being examined, and anticipated a sensational murder trial.

The doctor in question fitted the role perfectly. Dr John Bodkin Adams was only 1.65 m (5 ft 5in) tall yet weighed 114 kg (18 stone); he was bald, and his fleshy round face supported round spectacles. He was either an old buffoon or, as the *Mail* suggested, a sinister maniac.

Bodkin Adams at times seemed to be his own worst enemy, and helped precipitate rumours into something more serious by his own impetuous and odd notes to coroners. When energetic, 49-year-old 'Bobbie' Hullett died soon after giving him a cheque for £1000 and leaving him a Rolls-Royce, such a note prompted the suspicious coroner to hold three postmortems in an effort to ensure the death was not foul play. The eventual verdict was suicide by means of an overdose of drugs. Twenty years before, a Mrs Whitton had left Adams £3000, at that time a huge sum, and made him her executor, a curious arrangement which led the family to challenge the will, without success. Soon afterwards the doctor received an anonymous note in his mail: 'Keep your fingers crossed and don't bump off any more wealthy widows.'

So many rumours had circulated in Eastbourne over 20 or more years that after Mrs Hullett's death Scotland Yard were asked to investigate, and Superintendent Hallam went to the town. It was

*Dr John Bodkin Adams*

quickly established that during these years Dr Adams had benefited from 132 wills of his patients to the tune of £45,000. Further, in many cases he had authorized the cremation of the bodies without declaring his interest – thus avoiding an obligatory postmortem. Witnesses were found to attest to a rapid decline of patients after they had made out a will – often with Dr Adams 'guiding their hands'. He was found not to keep a poisons register, as required by law. Superintendent Hallam's final dossier was a thick one. He reported that in his view Adams had killed 14 people in just the previous few years. Adams's case seemed a lost cause, and foreign newspapers, outside the reach of the British libel laws, freely described him as a 'Bluebeard'.

Adams was arrested on 18 December 1956 and charged with the murder in 1950 of Mrs Edith Morrell, who had left Adams a Rolls-Royce and her collection of silver. The crown was given permission to link the deaths of both Mr and Mrs Hullett in 1956 to show systematic poisoning. The prosecution at the committal proceedings explained the pattern: rich patient receives heavy drugging, leading to a fatal final dose; the patient is kept under the influence of the doctor who benefits under the will; his impatience and desire for money is not kept in check. In the event the prosecution decided to keep the Hullett case in reserve and proceed with the Morrell charge.

The trial opened at the Old Bailey on 18 March 1957, with the prosecution led by the Attorney General, the unpopular old Etonian Sir Reginald Manningham-Buller, who was widely known as Bullying-Manner. The basic prosecution case was simple. Mrs Morrell, who was 81, was half-paralysed and irritable, but not in pain. Four nurses attended her round the clock, with Adams always on call. He dosed her with huge amounts of morphia and heroin to make her an addict. He called her solicitor so that she could change her will, and she bequeathed him her Georgian silver. A little later he instructed the solicitor to prepare a codicil in which Mrs Morrell also left him her Rolls-Royce and jewellery, the codicil to be destroyed later if Mrs Morrell did not approve. The solicitor called on Mrs Morrell and she executed the codicil. Adams immediately increased the drugs alarmingly: in her last few days she was in a coma and given massive overdoses.

The prosecution's star witnesses were the nurses who, on Dr Adams's instructions, had helped to deliver the drugs. Nurse Helen Stronach described Mrs Morrell in those last days as 'rambling and semi-conscious'. She referred to injections given by herself and Dr Adams. The defence counsel, Geoffrey Lawrence, asked her in cross-examination if she had kept a written account of events at the time, as was the practice. Nurse Stronach agreed that everything had been entered in a book and signed. She agreed that the book would be absolutely accurate. Lawrence innocently put it to her that if only the records were available they would all know exactly what was given to Mrs Morrell. 'Yes, but you have our word for it,' was the reply.

Lawrence then produced the sort of stroke familiar to all viewers of the television series *Perry Mason*. He produced eight exercise books containing all the nurses' notes for the last months of Mrs Morrell's life; the police had missed them at Adams's home, where they had been behind a desk. Nurse Stronach now had to face her own notes which proved that her memory was utterly at fault regarding the injections. The patient, on a day when evidence had said she had been semi-conscious, had actually eaten a lunch of partridge, with a pudding and brandy to follow. The nurse was also forced to admit that her notes showed that on one occasion the patient had called her a nasty, common woman.

The other nurses fared no better than Nurse Stronach. In their discomfort they made the mistake of discussing their evidence amongst themselves on the train to Eastbourne one morning, contrary to the orders given to all witnesses, and an eavesdropper passed on remarks to Mr Lawrence. Thus Sister Helen Mason-Ellis was forced to admit that Nurse Stronach's testimony that Mrs Morrell's drugs were kept in a locked cupboard was a lie – they had been in an unlocked drawer. On the last evening of Mrs Morrell's life Dr Adams was alleged to have given her a huge injection of heroin, and to have left Nurse Randall a repeat injection which he instructed her to give later. The exercise books showed that no such injection was made. The trial lasted for 13 more days after the nurses' evidence, with points scored by both sides, but in reality the exercise books settled it. The judge pointed out that not all fraudulent rogues were murderers and it took the jury only 44 minutes to bring a verdict of not guilty. The prosecution saw no point in proceeding with its 'reserve' case on the Hullett deaths.

Later Adams pleaded guilty to 14 charges of professional misconduct and was fined £2400 and struck off the medical register. However, he continued his pleasant life in Eastbourne, retaining many of has friends, and in 1961 he was reinstated to the medical register. He won huge libel damages from newspapers who had rashly and too early presumed his guilt. He died in 1982, aged 83, whereupon some of the papers immediately returned to the attack with headlines such as, 'Did this man get away with murder?'

After Adams's death, the prosecution let it be known that they had plenty of evidence against him, and some think that his counsel's decision that he should not go into the witness box himself possibly saved him. He was certainly greedy, and he no doubt 'eased' the last hours of old people. In 1985 his judge, who by then was Lord Devlin, gave his opinion that Adams 'sold' an easy death to his clients.

# The Sign of the Zodiac

ON 20 December 1968 a woman driving past a lovers' lane near Vallejo, California, saw what appeared to be bodies near a parked estate car. She drove on and alerted police. The bodies turned out to be of 17-year-old David Faraday, shot in the head near the car, and his girlfriend Bettilou Jensen, shot in the back a few yards off, probably as she tried to run away. There was no sexual interference or robbery, and no other apparent motive for the killings.

On 5 July 1969 the Vallejo police received a call from a man with a gruff voice, who reported a double murder, describing a car in a car park 3 km (2 miles) from where the earlier murder took place. He ended by saying: 'I also killed those kids last year.' Police found 19-year-old Michael Mageau, seriously injured with gunshot wounds, and a 22-year-old waitress, Darlene Ferrin, who was dead. Mageau later told how a car pulled up beside them and a man got out, shone a blinding light at them and began shooting. Mageau provided a description as best he could.

Nearly four weeks later, on 1 August, three evening newspapers received letters from the killer threatening to go on a 'kill rampage' if the letters weren't published that day. Each paper was sent part of a coded message which the murderer said would reveal his identity when put together. The letter was signed with the symbol of the zodiac, a circle with a cross superimposed, so that each arm of the cross breaks the circle. The three papers – the *Vallejo Times-Herald* and two in San Francisco, the *Chronicle* and *Examiner* – printed the letters, and the fragments of code. When the code was cracked the message was found to read:

'I like killing people because it is more fun than killing wild game in the forest because man is the most dangerous animal of all to kill something gives one the most thrilling experience it is even better than getting your rock off with a girl the best part of it is when I die I will be reborn in paradise and all I have killed will become my slaves I will not give you my name because you will try to slow down or stop me collecting slaves for my afterlife.'

The message ended with a jumble of letters. Over a thousand readers offered leads, but all proved fruitless. Then, on 27 September, the gruff voice reported another killing. On the shore of Lake Berryessa police found another couple of students, both stabbed. Bryan Hartnell, aged 20, survived and told how a hooded figure had approached from the trees. On his chest was the zodiac sign. He had a pistol and a knife and said he was an escapee from the Deer Lodge state prison and needed money and their car. It sounded plausible and they allowed him to tie them up with clothesline. Then he said that he was going to have to stab them. He repeatedly stabbed Hartnell in the back, then turned to his companion, 22-year-old Cecilia Shepard, a strikingly beautiful blonde girl. He stabbed her in a frenzy, first in the back and then several times in the stomach, on which he carved a cross with his knife; Cecilia was to die two days later in hospital. Before he left, the killer wrote his sign with a black marker pen on the door of their white car, with the dates of his previous assaults. Hartnell gave police a description of what he could see of his assailant through the hood, but it was not much.

Two weeks later, on 11 October, Zodiac struck again. Two youths saw a taxi pull up in San Francisco and heard a shot. The passenger got out of the back, tore some cloth from the driver's cab, wiped the cab with it, and hurried off when he saw the youths. The driver was 29-year-old student Paul Stine, and he had been shot dead through the head; it was part of his shirt that had been ripped off. The youths were able to give the police the best description yet of Zodiac: 1.72 m (5 ft 8 in) tall, fortyish, with reddish-brown hair in a crew cut and thick horn-rimmed glasses.

Zodiac sent a piece of bloodstained shirt to the San Francisco *Chronicle* with a letter criticizing the inefficiency of the police and threatening to wipe out a school bus next. A few days later, however, he rang the police, offering to give himself up if he could have a famous lawyer and talk on a television show. Police arranged it and lawyer Melvin Belli stood by on the Jim Dunbar morning talk show, which drew a record audience. At 7.41 am a caller with a soft voice identified himself as the Zodiac killer. Those who had heard the gruff voice shook their heads. The caller, who asked to be addressed as 'Sam' rang back 15 times and spoke to Belli, who tried in vain to persuade him to give himself up. When they were off the air, 'Zodiac' arranged to meet Belli, but he failed to keep the appointment, where armed police were on hand. Experts are divided as to whether the caller really was Zodiac.

Just before Christmas, Belli received a letter asking for help from Zodiac (another piece of shirt was enclosed as proof of identity). The letter claimed eight victims and threatened a ninth, causing the San Francisco police urgently to search the files for the missing eighth victim.

There were no more 'official' Zodiac killings after this, but the Los Angeles *Times* received a letter in March 1971 intimating that the total had reached 17 and, amid several hoax letters, the San Francisco police received what seemed a genuine one in 1974 claiming the total was now 37. An officer using a computer and details of unsolved murders found this a possibility, but nothing has been heard of the Zodiac since. Police opinion is that he is dead or perhaps is in a mental institution.

# The Babysitter Murders

IT WAS snowing in Bloomfield Township, near Detroit, on the morning of 15 January 1976. Lying by a road was the naked body of Cynthia Cadieux, aged 16, who had disappeared in Roseville the previous day. She had been raped and killed by a blow from a blunt instrument. Her clothing was in a neat pile a few metres from the body, and tracks could be seen where the body had been dragged for some way along the pavement.

Four days later police were investigating an incident in nearby Birmingham, where John McAuliffe had been bound and robbed by an intruder in his house, when they discovered that 14-year-old Sheila Schrock had been raped and shot in her home two blocks away.

Three weeks passed and then 12-year-old Mark Stebbins disappeared in Ferndale. His body was found six days later, on 19 February, in the car park of an office building. He had been sexually assaulted and smothered. An odd point was that his body had been carefully cleaned and manicured before he was laid out in the snow as if in a coffin. It was estimated that the body had been there for a day and a half before discovery.

It was August before the killer made his next strike. A 13-year-old, Jane Allan, disappeared while hitchhiking in Royal Oak, on the outskirts of Detroit. Her body was found in Miamisburg, Ohio, three days later. Three days before Christmas 12-year-old Jill Robinson disappeared, also from Royal Oak. Her body was found on Boxing Day, near Troy, laid out neatly on a bank of snow by the side of a road. She was the victim of a shotgun, and her body had been scrubbed before she died. The similarity between the way that her body and that of Mark Stebbins had been laid out suggested a link in these two killings and awoke the citizens of Oakland County, Michigan, to the fact that a serial child-killer might be at work in their area.

This seemed to be confirmed on 21 January 1977. Kristine Mihelich, aged ten had disappeared in Berkley nearly three weeks previously, and her body was now discovered not far from where Cynthia Cadieux had been found almost exactly a year earlier. She had been suffocated and her body had been washed and laid out in the manner of the two previous victims.

At least three victims now seemed certainly to be linked, and there was a fourth on 23 March, when the body was found of 11-year-old Timothy King, who had disappeared on 11 March in Birmingham. Timothy's mother had pleaded on television for the return of her child, and said she would have his favourite chicken dinner waiting for him. Examination of his body showed that Timothy had indeed been given a chicken dinner by his killer before he had been suffocated. After he died he had been scrubbed and his clothing had been cleaned and pressed.

The care with which the killer treated his victims led the papers to call him the 'Babysitter'. Despite the striking similarities it is not certain that all the deaths were linked, since there were variations in the circumstances – the use of the shotgun, for example, and the fact that some were sexually assaulted and others not. After the discovery of the last body, an open letter to the killer from a psychiatrist inviting him to seek help was published in the newspapers. One caller phoned with the message, 'You'd better hope it doesn't snow any more', thus emphasizing another link between some of the crimes. Another caller who wrote and telephoned often claimed to be the roommate of the killer, a Vietnam veteran with a grudge against soft-living well-off Americans.

When the snow returned late in 1977 the frightened citizens of Oakland County were at their most vigilant, but the Babysitter did not strike again.

# The Ann Arbor Hospital Murders

IN THE summer of 1975 the administrators of Ann Arbor Veterans Administration Hospital in Michigan, USA, were forced to admit that there was a killer loose on the wards. On 15 August the FBI was called in to investigate the astonishing number of respiratory arrests occurring over the past few weeks, for no apparent reason. Since 1 July there had been 56, while the usual number for that period would have been between eight and ten.

The majority of the unexpected breathing failures occurred on the 3 pm to 11 pm shift and though most of them were in the intensive care unit, some patients suffering arrests had undergone only minor surgery and were otherwise regarded as fit and healthy. In the first four weeks of July there were 22 breathing failures, on 28 July alone there were three and after that the number went on rising steadily. On the nightmare night of 12 August there were eight respiratory arrests between 6 pm and 9 pm. Prompt intervention by nursing staff saved all but one patient, an elderly man who was recovering from an operation for a broken hip. Internal investigations indicated that the victims had been given a dose of the muscle relaxant Pavulon, a drug derived from the South American poison curare and normally used before surgery. As no needle marks were found on the patient's arms it seemed likely that it was being added to the intravenous drips.

The doctors still hesitated over calling in outside help but when one of the patients, a 49-year-old man who had suffered two respiratory arrests since undergoing open heart surgery, confided that a Filipino nurse called Filipina Narcissco had left the room immediately before one of his attacks, it was obvious that action must be taken and taken quickly.

The last two surprise respiratory arrests happened on the day the FBI arrived. A fortnight later one of the patients who had suffered three arrests died, probably from the delayed effects of his breathing problems. Two more of the victims died on 29 August. In all, the deaths of eight patients were probably caused by induced respiratory arrests. The hospital was closed to all but emergency admissions.

The FBI agents questioned every patient in the hospital and as a result of their enquiries two experienced Filipino nurses, 30-year-old Filipina Narcissco and 31-year-old Leonora Perez, came under suspicion. No one could suggest any reason why they should want to injure patients, but they had been on duty in the vicinity of victims shortly before the respiratory arrests took place. Both were transferred to non-nursing duties, Miss Narcissco at the same hospital and Mrs Perez to a Veterans Administration hospital in Detroit. Steps were also taken to make sure that Pavulon could only be obtained on an anaesthetist's authority.

Psychiatrists who worked on the case to compile a profile of the killer decided that he, or she, must have a grudge against the hospital or the medical profession in general and, perhaps, wanted to bring about such a lack of confidence in the hospital that it would be forced to close. There were fears at one time that this might happen, but once the doors were open again the excellent reputation of the hospital soon reasserted itself. Some psychiatrists favoured the theory that the killer might be a Vietnam veteran who was trying to draw attention to the plight of ex-soldiers who were poorly treated by their country; others thought it more likely to be a nurse with a hatred of men in general and her medical superiors in particular.

The long-running investigation turned up little in the way of hard evidence. In 1976 a former supervisor of the hospital committed suicide after writing a letter confessing responsibility for the deaths but she had been in a mental hospital for some time, suffering from acute depression and hallucinations as well as terminal cancer, and the confession was discounted because of her state of mind. At the end of the day, the prime suspects were still Miss Narcissco and Mrs Perez and they went on trial in March 1977 on eight charges including murder, poisoning and conspiracy.

The prosecution called a number of patients and relations to testify that they had seen one or other of the nurses in the patients' rooms at or near the time of the respiratory arrests and made much of the fact that from the moment the nurses had been transferred to other duties, not a single unexpected seizure had been reported. However, they could produce no evidence to link either woman with the unauthorized use of Pavulon and no witness who had seen either of them tampering with the intravenous lines.

Halfway through the trial the murder charge against Perez was dismissed on instructions from the judge and after 13 weeks of evidence Narcissco was found not guilty of murder, though both nurses were convicted of poisoning and conspiracy. Both were freed on bonds of $70,000 each while appeals were lodged and both were ordered to undergo psychiatric testing before sentence was decided. The convictions were set aside on appeal and a new trial was ordered; meanwhile the psychiatric testing showed that the behaviour patterns of both women were normal. A second trial took place in February 1978 and all charges were dismissed. The mystery of the Ann Arbor killings remains unsolved.

# Jack the Stripper

ON 2 February 1964 the body of a prostitute, Hannah Tailford, was found in the water by Hammersmith Reach on the Thames. She was naked except for her rolled-down stockings, and fabric from her briefs was stuffed in her mouth. An open verdict was recorded, although murder was the probability.

On 9 April the naked body of another prostitute, Irene Lockwood, was found only 270 m (300 yd) from the first, tangled among weeds by Dukes Meadow. Neither the clothes nor the handbags of either girl could be found, and the police faced the possibility that a cunning serial killer had begun work. They recalled the death of another prostitute, Gwynneth Rees, whose body was found by the Thames in November 1963, and wondered if her death could be linked with the other two.

There was little doubt that a serial killer was operating when the body of Helen Barthelemy, another prostitute, was found dumped on garden rubbish in an alley in Brentford on 24 April. She had been stripped and had had three teeth removed after her death. Tyre marks suggested she had been murdered elsewhere and her body brought to the alleyway. Three days later Kenneth Archibald, a caretaker at Holland Park Tennis Club who lived at Hammersmith, confessed in Notting Hill police station to the murder of Irene Lockwood. However, at his trial in June he withdrew his confession and was acquitted.

Meanwhile, in May, examination of Barthelemy's body proved fruitful. Traces of paint spray of various colours were found, suggesting that the body had been kept in the spray shop of a factory using many colours. Commander Hatherill, head of the CID, appealed for prostitutes to come forward in absolute secrecy to help the police

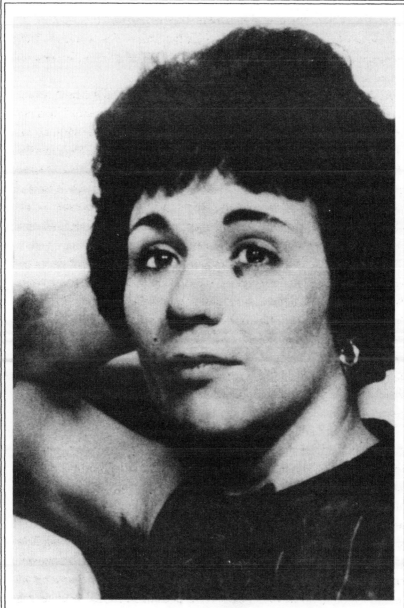

*Bridie O'Hara, the last victim of Jack the Stripper*

catch the killer. By now the papers had seized on the story of a maniac sex killer, and the name of 'Jack the Stripper' was coined. The response from prostitutes was good but, on 14 July, the killer struck again.

At 5.30 that morning painters working all night had heard a van door shut and seen a man standing by a van in a cul-de-sac. The man drove out of the cul-de-sac so fast he nearly collided with a car in Acton Lane whose incensed driver informed the police. Shortly afterwards the naked body of prostitute Mary Fleming was found sitting against a wall outside the garage door of the end house in the cul-de-sac. She had been missing for three days and the same paint was found on her body. Unfortunately, the irate car driver had not been able to take the number of the van.

On 25 November the naked body of prostitute Margaret McGowan was found hidden by rubble in a car park near Kensington High Street. It had been there a week and she had died much earlier than that. A tooth was missing, and the paint was present.

The final known victim of Jack the Stripper was Bridie O'Hara, whose bright red toenails were noticed by a man walking to work along Westfield Road, Acton, on 16 February 1965. Her naked body was lying on bracken behind a store shed, and was partly mummified, suggesting it had been kept where it might have dried out.

Detective Chief Superintendent John Du Rose, head of the Yard's murder squad, was now put in charge of the hunt, with a 300-strong special patrol group reporting to him. They were helped by 200 CID officers and 100 uniformed police. Various facts suggested a possible picture of the killer and his operation. All the murdered prostitutes were small, between 1.52 m (5 ft) and 1.6 m (5 ft 3 in) suggesting the killer might be a small man. They were picked up in the Notting Hill area, probably between 11 am and 1 pm. Most had had teeth removed and semen was found in the throat, suggesting that the killer had insisted on fellatio and after death had performed further acts of oral sex on the body after removing the teeth. The bodies were stripped and kept at a paint-spray shop before being dumped by van in the early morning near the Thames. The killer was probably a night-worker.

The biggest find the hours of police checking produced was a disused warehouse by a paint-spray shop on the Heron Factory Estate, Acton. Globules of paint exactly matched those on the bodies. Du Rose decided to frighten the killer by hinting to the press that the number of suspects was diminishing – he finally reduced it to three – and that an arrest was approaching.

Then suddenly the murders stopped, and gradually the police operation was wound down, public interest faded and there were rumours that the police knew the identity of Jack the Stripper.

Du Rose told the rest of the story on his retirement in 1970. In March 1965 an unmarried man committed suicide in South London, leaving a note saying he was 'unable to stand the strain any longer'. The man was a security guard on the Heron Factory Estate, and his hours fitted in with police theories about the Stripper. There was other circumstantial evidence to suggest the hunt had ended. Du Rose stated in 1970 that the man, whose identity was not revealed, was indeed the Stripper.

# Bible John

GLASGOW'S Barrowland dance hall was very popular in the late 1960s, particularly for its Thursday 'Over-25s' night, when the dating was necessarily more furtive since many patrons were without their spouses and used false names.

On such a Thursday, on 22 February 1968, 25-year-old Patricia Docker, separated and with a son, went out dancing and didn't return to her parents' home. Next morning her naked body was found outside a lock-up garage; she had been strangled. Her handbag was missing and her body was not identified until Friday evening. She had said she was going to the Majestic ballroom, and police enquiries therefore started in the wrong place. No one amoung the clientele who were eventually questioned at the Barrowland was prepared to say anything at all.

Over a year later, another mother from a single-parent family, 32-year-old Jemima McDonald – a regular at the Thursday night Barrowland dances – failed to return home from a Saturday night dance. She wasn't missed at first, and her sister, Mrs Margaret O'Brien, only became worried when she was still not home on Monday morning. On the Sunday Mrs O'Brien had heard children talking of a body where they played in derelict flats nearby – childish chatter which nobody had taken notice of. She decided to search, and found her sister's partly clothed body. Jemima had been strangled with her own tights.

Police linked the deaths of the two women because of the Barrowland connection, the strangling and, despite a huge search by corporation dustmen, the disappearance of their handbags. There was another link, which might be coincidence – both women were menstruating when they died.

This time police did better with clues, as Jemima had been seen with a man both outside the dance hall and later near her home. An artist's impression of a man was shown on Scottish television and published in the papers. He was aged 25–35, between 1.82 m (6 ft) and 1.88 m (6 ft 2 in), slim, neatly dressed, and with fair, reddish hair worn in a then unfashionable style for the Barrowland, neat and short. However, nothing came of the police enquiries, and, in October the police stopped their surveillance at the Barrowland – which, to the disgust of the management, had caused attendances to drop dramatically.

It was an unfortunate decision. On 30 October 29-year-old Helen Puttock went dancing there, as she often did, with her sister Jeannie Williams who lived nearby. Helen's husband, George, was happy to babysit, and he gave the two women the cab-fare home, as the buses would not be running. They met two other girlfriends as arranged, and had a few drinks before entering the dance hall around 10 pm. Jeannie soon met a man, John from Castlemilk, who was as good a dancer as herself, and they stayed together all evening. Helen also met a man called John, and the couples made a foursome for the night. Soon after 11.30 pm the dancing ended and the four went to a cab rank where Jeannie's partner, whom she suspected was married, left them to catch a bus. The two girls and John took a cab.

Jeannie sensed that John was not happy with her playing gooseberry, and he insisted she be dropped off first. It was the last she saw of her sister alive. Early next morning a neighbour found Helen's body at the back of a tenement block. She had been strangled with one of her stockings and her handbag was missing. While police were still trying to establish who she could be, George Puttock, who had seen the activity from his flat just up the road, arrived to tell them his wife hadn't come home. He had assumed she was at her sister's, but when he was shown the body he immediately identified it. There was one other fact to link this death with the others. Helen Puttock also was menstruating and, although she was fully clothed, her sanitary pad had been removed and tucked under her armpit. Was the killer a man who killed in rage at being denied sex because his intended partner was at the 'wrong time of the month'? Or was he a peculiar sexual deviate? Or was it just an odd coincidence?

Jeannie Williams was an observant woman with a good memory and she provided police with plenty of clues. John didn't drink. He was tall, about 1.78 m (5 ft 10 in), and aged between 25 and 35. His short, sandy, reddish hair was neatly cut and rounded at the back. He had a tooth missing, and one front tooth slightly overlapped the other. She helped in the drawing of an identikit picture.

John had been so polite, well-mannered and soft-spoken in the dance hall – even pulling out a chair for his partner to sit down – that he stood out from the usual clientele. In the taxi, however, his chivalry had vanished, and he was broody and aloof. He spoke of the 'adulterous' women at the dance halls, places which his father had told him were dens of iniquity. He said he prayed rather than drank at Hogmanay, and talked a lot about the Bible and its laws, and about the woman taken in adultery who was stoned. When these facts were publicized, the man immediately became tagged by the papers as 'Bible John'. When Jeannie saw the drawing of the Jemima McDonald suspect, she immediately recognized the likeness.

The police also had a clue in that a passenger had seen what was probably the killer on a night service bus at about 2 am, and had remembered where he alighted. But despite many calls from the public, hundreds of police visits to hairdressers and dentists and a half-hour BBC documentary on the case in 1970, 'Bible John' was never found.

# The Monster of Florence

EVERY summer tourists flock to Florence, one of the cultural centres of Italy and indeed the world. The countryside around also has its attractions, especially in the summer, and is popular with hikers, nature-lovers and courting couples. Since 1968 it has also gained a reputation as the territory of a sadistic killer, who seemed to settle into a routine which required the annual sacrifice of a loving couple to keep him happy.

On 21 August 1968 Barbara Locci and her lover Antonio lo Bianco were shot dead as they lay together on the front seats of their car, parked in a lovers' lane. The woman's six-year-old son was in the back of the car and seemed to have slept throughout, suggesting that the murderer used a silencer. Perhaps the killer noticed the boy for the first time after he had committed the crime, and crept away. The woman's husband was arrested, charged with murder, and convicted. Sentenced to 13 years' imprisonment in 1970, the poor man had to wait another four years before the murderer struck again and proved his innocence.

It was on 14 September 1974 when the second couple were killed, again in their parked car. Forensic tests showed the same .22-calibre Beretta pistol had been used as in the first killing; the distinctive copper-jacketed bullets were manufactured in Australia during the 1950s. The bodies were naked and the female victim, Carmela de Nuccio, had had her genitals removed by a scalpel.

There was another long break, and then the killer struck twice in 1981. On 6 June the female victim, Stefani Pettini, was stabbed more than 300 times and was violated with a stalk from a grape vine, and on 23 October Susanna Cambi had her genitals removed.

From 1981 the killer found victims each year to 1985, all within 32 km (20 miles) of Florence. His established method was to approach a couple in a car, always on a moonless night between the hours of 10 pm and midnight. The man was shot first and then the woman, on whose body he practised his sadism, mutilating the body with his scalpel. From 1984 this mutilation included the removal of the left breast, as well as the genitals. No fingerprints were ever found, and it was suspected that the killer used surgical rubber gloves. The killer probably made a mistake in 1983, when two homosexual West German men were shot while sleeping in a van. Perhaps the fact that one had long blond hair misled him.

The newspapers, who as usual needed a convenient label for the attacker, called him the 'Monster of Florence'. All the murders occurred in the holiday season from June to October, with the first two weeks in September being the favourite time.

On 8 September 1985 a French couple who were touring with a tent were murdered. The woman's body had suffered over 100 slashes, with the genitalia and left breast removed. This time one of the familiar cooper-jacketed bullets was found outside a nearby hospital. Coupling this fact with the killer's use of a scalpel and possibly surgical gloves, the police made a through investigation of the hospital staff. It provided no more results than anything else, and the police seemed to be mocked when an envelope was delivered to them. The address had been formed with letters cut from a newspaper to prevent discovery of the sender, and it contained a part of the genitalia of the murdered woman. However, this was the last of these distinctive killings.